A Semiotic Approach to the Theology of Inculturation

A Semiotic Approach to the Theology of Inculturation

Cyril Orji

FOREWORD BY
Dennis M. Doyle

◆PICKWICK *Publications* • Eugene, Oregon

A SEMIOTIC APPROACH TO THE THEOLOGY OF INCULTURATION

Copyright © 2015 Cyril Orji. All rights reserved. Except for brief quotations in critical publications or reviews, no part of this book may be reproduced in any manner without prior written permission from the publisher. Write: Permissions. Wipf and Stock Publishers, 199 W. 8th Ave., Suite 3, Eugene, OR 97401.

Pickwick Publications
An Imprint of Wipf and Stock Publishers
199 W. 8th Ave., Suite 3
Eugene, OR 97401

www.wipfandstock.com

ISBN 13: 978-1-4982-0074-5

Cataloguing-in-Publication Data

Orji, Cyril U.

    A semiotic approach to the theology of inculturation / Cyril Orji ; foreword by Dennis M. Doyle.

    xviii + 218 p. ; 23 cm. Includes bibliographical references and index(es).

    ISBN 13: 978-1-4982-0074-5

    1. Christianity and culture—Africa. 2. Theology, Doctrinal—Africa. 3. Semiotics—Religious aspects. I. Doyle, Dennis M. II. Title.

BR115.C8 O75 2015

Manufactured in the U.S.A.   03/19/2015

To my sister Margaret Orji and my brother Francis Orji

Contents

Foreword by Dennis M. Doyle | ix
Acknowledgments | xi
Introduction | xiii

1. The Problematic of African Theology of Inculturation | 1
2. Single Story Narratives and Resilience of African Independent Churches | 37
3. Metapragmatic Use of Language | 69
4. "Cultural Turn" and the Problematic of Inculturation | 102
5. Inculturation Reconsidered in Light of New Studies in Semiotics | 134
6. Ten Habits of Highly Effective Work in African Theology of Inculturation | 166

Bibliography | 199
Index | 211

Foreword

I REMEMBER HOW IMPRESSED and delighted I was when I read Cyril Orji's first book, *Ethnic and Religious Conflict in Africa*. Here was a young man writing about struggles in Africa while drawing accurately and constructively upon the thought of the Canadian Jesuit philosopher Bernard Lonergan. Now here he is back at it again, having thought through these issues even more deeply over the course of years. His focus now is on semiotics, particularly as it connects with cultural anthropology and as it can be applied to a theology of inculturation.

Lonergan is still a strong presence in this new book, *A Semiotic Approach to the Theology of Inculturation,* though he is accompanied by a range of other theorists. One of the many strengths of the work is that Orji explains several concepts associated with Lonergan by exploring similar concepts in thinkers such as the philosopher C.S. Pierce and the cultural anthropologist Clifford Geertz. Along the way he discusses in depth the thinking of Edward Sapir, Benjamin Lee Whorf, Susanne Langer, Judith Butler, and Jean-Marc Ela.

Africa remains a major presence in this new work, as Orji discusses African Traditional Religions (ATRs), the African Independent Churches (AICs), and Islam in Africa, noting the genuine challenges and opportunities they present to the non-native churches. Even more importantly, he carves out insights that a semiotic approach can yield concerning the tragic horrors in the recent histories of the Congo, Rwanda, Sudan, and Sierra Leone.

Orji, like the thinkers whom he emulates, is an integrator of ideas and methods. Few Western scholars can speak both as a Christian believer and as an academic researcher without switching hats in the process. Orji speaks in these two ways seamlessly with one voice as he weaves together into a coherent whole a range of elements that might otherwise seem disparate. For example, when I was a college student (way back in the last century) I myself studied Ogden and Richard's *The Meaning of Meaning,* the Sapir-Whorf

Foreword

hypothesis, and Susanne Langer's *Philosophy in a New Key*. Then in graduate school I became interested in the work of Clifford Geertz. I wrote my dissertation with a focus on Bernard Lonergan. Later I was introduced to the thought of C.S. Pierce. I found each part of this material to be fascinating in its own right, but I never thought through the interconnectedness of the various authors' approaches. Orji puts together the pieces of this puzzle. All of these thinkers focusing on the world as constructed through human meaning in a way that fights against various forms of reductionism. How is it that one can think through and implement practical solutions to concrete problems in the real world without becoming reductionist?

Semiotics serves as Orji's focal point for addressing this question. Semiotics informs a cultural anthropology that takes seriously the open-ended nature of the human quest, the reality and value of various types of diversity, and the inevitability of communicative interaction among different groups. It is no accident that the final chapter offers practical advice about the do's and don'ts of developing and applying a theology of inculturation. Orji passionately believes that, when it comes to human conflicts leading to atrocities, human beings can do better. If we are to understand ourselves as well as others, we must seek out together the higher viewpoints that are achievable by making use of our God-given capacities for making meaning. The universe in which we live may often seem puzzling, but ultimately it is coherent, and we have the tools to reach ever closer to grasping its coherence. Let us focus together on meaning, language, symbols, cultures, actions, and God.

—Dennis M. Doyle
Professor of Religious Studies
University of Dayton

Acknowledgments

THIS RESEARCH WAS YEARS in the making and many people contributed in various ways at every step of the way. Thanks to all those who made this project possible, especially Dr. Paul Benson and Dr. Sandra Yocum of the University of Dayton who supported my research initiatives with encouragement and summer grant. Thanks also to Mrs. Marva Gray and Mr. Sherman Gray for all their logistical support. Special thanks to Patrick Byrne, Fred and Sue Lawrence, and all the good people of the Lonergan Center at Boston College (particularly Kerry Cronin and Susan Legere) for the 2013 fellowship that helped towards completion of this project. My special thanks to Prof. Steven Caton of Harvard University, Cambridge, MA for his seminar ideas and for introducing me to cultural anthropologists whose thoughts enriched my work. I am also indebted to Prof. Mark Morelli of Loyola Marymount College, Los Angeles, for providing me the platform to test out these ideas at different Lonergan Conferences in Los Angeles.

Introduction

WHEN CATHOLIC THEOLOGY WAS still very much classicist Bernard Lonergan (1904–1984) made the case that the odyssey of the Christian gospel allows for transcultural communication and pluralism of expressions. He suggested correctly that the contemporary world is becoming increasingly diverse and that if the church is to remain relevant in contemporary society that the church needs to devise new methods of communicating the Christian message. He also suggested correctly that, since classical culture has become passé, meeting the needs of a world church that is increasingly becoming diverse means that Catholic theology, particularly its assumptions about culture, needs to be transposed and rethought in light of the new findings in anthropology and the social sciences. Only those who wrongly assume that the church is a pure spirit incorrectly assume that it does not exist in cultural forms.[1] Lonergan's forward-thinking program of how to transpose and communicate effectively the gospel message in different cultural situations is scattered throughout his works but specifically itemized in the last of his eight functional specialties he dubbed *communications*.[2] What Lonergan calls *communication* is more commonly referred to as inculturation—the call for shift in perspective arising from the growing sense on the part of the Christian churches of Latin America, Africa, and Asia "that the theologies being inherited from the older churches of the North Atlantic community did not fit well into these quite different cultural circumstances."[3] While theoretically inculturation has been embraced by the newly emerging churches of Latin America, Africa, and Asia and has indeed become the theology of a world cultural church, the practice of inculturation is still dogged by methodological problems and "conceptual logjams."[4] This study is a modest attempt to break through the method-

---

1. Arbuckle, *Culture, Inculturation, and Theologians*, 47.
2. See the last chapter of Lonergan, *Method in Theology*.
3. Schreiter, *Constructing Local Theologies*, 1.
4. See Arbuckle, *Culture, Inculturation, and Theologians*, xx.

ological problems and conceptual logjams that have hindered the practice of inculturation. Since "the thorniest methodological problem in inculturation is the confusion surrounding the meaning of culture,"[5] this study suggests that a semiotic approach to culture (along the lines delineated by C. S. Peirce and Clifford Geertz in anthropology and Lonergan in theology) provides the best meaningful way for conceptualizing and understanding the practice of inculturation, particularly African theology of inculturation. The semiotic system that Peirce, Geertz, and Lonergan provide is the much needed antidote to the naïve realism that conceives cultures or identities in classicist categories that are rigid, homogeneous, eternally fixed, inflexible, and stable.

The word *church*, as used in this book, is always in reference to the Christian church. In places where the word is not used in its generic sense to refer to Christianity in general it is used to refer specifically to the Roman Catholic communion. Context always determines which "church" is referenced. Reference to "Africa" is almost always to Africa south of the Sahara (sub-Saharan Africa), unless context dictates otherwise.

Although the ideas and research material for this book were years in the making, everything came to maturation and parturition during my fellowship year at the Lonergan Center at Boston College in 2013. Chapter 1 examines the Church's role in African public life and offers reasons to validate the suggestion that was made long ago that much of Africa is inconceivable without Christianity. Using the "shade-tree" theology of the Cameroonian theologian Jean-Marc Ela (1936–2008), the chapter shows why the history of Christianity in Africa is a mixed bag. To help realize the new praxis of meaning that the contemporary situation demands, the chapter concludes by putting Ela in dialogue with the semiotic work of the Russian literary critic and semiotician, Mikhail Bakhtin (1895–1975) in order to transcendentally ground Ela's key insight that the two foci of liberation and inculturation be held in dynamic tension. Bahktin's notion of polyphony, his umbrella term for different interacting voices in discourse, and his helpful suggestion that we move from a monoglossic situation to heteroglossic one provides a good theoretical model for the kind of theology of inculturation that can serve the world church.

Chapter 2 recognizes that a key problem in contemporary society is the breakdown of traditional identities and boundaries resulting from some postmodern attempts to define other people's identities in one single

5. Ibid.

INTRODUCTION

narrative. Taking seriously the insights of the American philosopher and gender theorist, Judith Butler (b. 1956) that we pay careful attention to the frames we use to describe the other because some frames may be loaded with violence and also that some frames we use are meant to preclude certain kinds of questions and justify a certain kind of position, the chapter attempts a critical assessment of the frames that have been used to depict the story of Africa. The chapter is more or less an attempt to recast the African story from a semiotic perspective and by so doing clarifying what makes Africa similar and different from others in the present global configuration. In writing this chapter I was encouraged by the narrative experience of Greenland, a tiny country of about fifty-six thousand people that voted to loosen its ties with Denmark in 2008 in spite of its limited resources. With great delight its premier commented that at long last Greenlanders could tell their own story to the world.[6] This chapter is guided by that kind of philosophical supposition and more. As for its implications for a theology of inculturation, the success of African Independent (or Initiated) Churches (AICs) is offered as a good example of the failure of metanarratives or grand narratives to provide an answer to how Christianity should and/or ought to be practiced in the continent.

Chapters 3 and 4 were the fruits of research I conducted at Harvard University during my fellowship year at Boston College in 2013. Chapter 3 examines what contributions theoretical linguists can make to the study of culture. Beginning with Edward Sapir (1884–1939) and his close ally Benjamin Whorf (1897–1941), to George Lakoff who rehabilitated the Sapir-Whorf hypothesis by showing how language is about meaning-making and how people are influenced by the metaphors they use in language, the chapter carefully examines contributions of the structuralist and interpretive traditions of anthropology, showing how their findings depict the language of a people as mediating their culture. The chapter also shows that language confers a distinctive identity on a people, gives them a sense of belonging, and avails them of resources for managing information and handling innovation. This provides us a matrix for developing a theory of culture that is consistent with semiotics. The chapter concludes by showing the implications of the metapragmatic ideas of theoretical linguists, particularly those deriving from Bakhtin-Volosinov that view discourse as poly-vocal and connect dialogicality with power, for a theology of inculturation.

---

6. Ibid., 64–65.

Introduction

Chapter 4 anticipates chapter 5 on many levels. The chapter lays the groundwork for the task of critical exigence (clarification of terms and concepts that have hitherto been confusedly used in the work of inculturation) of chapter 5 by attempting a cultural hermeneutic with a view to getting at the empirical meaning of culture. The principal focus of the chapter is the American cultural anthropologist Clifford Geertz (1926–2006), who was a major influence in the new "cultural turn." Geertz's findings are like an antidote to the foundationalist ahistorical and essentialist assumptions about human nature that have characterized the study of culture prior to the new "cultural turn." The chapter shows how Geertz's "thick description" regarding how signs are used in social context and his understanding of culture as a complex web of meanings and values which make a people's way of life worth living helps our quest to see how cultures have both their similarities and differences and how these similarities and differences help societies, nations, and states organize their ideas about politics and religion. As for a theology of inculturation, Geertz helps us realize that what is needed is a new way of thinking that is responsive to the particularities of a people's way of being human.

Chapter 5 denounces ideological stalemates by bringing together the semiotic ideas of C. S. Peirce (1839–1914) and Clifford Geertz and showing how their ideas converge with those of Bernard Lonergan in theology. Using their ideas as antidote to the counterpositions that developed out of the Anglo-American stream of thought, the chapter offers a clarification of the meaning of inculturation that is consistent with a semiotic approach. The chapter shows why such terms as adaptation, accommodation, interculturation, indigenization, contextualization, acculturation, etc., are inadequate and insufficient terms for the dynamic dialectical relationship that ought to exist between church, gospel, and culture. In suggesting that the complex matter of inculturation can best be sorted out semiotically, the chapter suggests that the science of semiotics is to the program of inculturation what Lonergan's functional specialty *systematics* is to theology—they seek increase in understanding regarding what church doctrines could possibly mean.

Chapter 6 was written at Boston College and was presented as a fellowship seminar paper to the fellows and graduate students at Boston College. Their critique and feedback was very valuable in getting the chapter to its finished form. The chapter captures the difficulties to be encountered in the practice of inculturation. One of the main difficulties being that classicism is so entrenched that it is easy to pass off some culturally derived principles as biblical and universally applicable even without knowing it. It is for this reason that the chapter argues that the church cannot do without inculturation because without it the church is unrecognizable and unsustainable. The chapter compares the task of inculturation to constructing a ship where half measures are not enough—one has to go all the way and implement a successful comprehensive strategy. To this end, the chapter offers ten habits (deriving from the semiotics of Peirce and Geertz and complemented by the theological insights of Lonergan) as an aid in the practice of inculturation. The ten habits are conceived as precepts or imperatives inherent in the notion of catholicity in that they suggest that catholicity is not identified with uniformity but with reconciled diversity.

1

The Problematic of African Theology of Inculturation

THE HISTORY OF CHRISTIANITY in Africa seems to mirror that of the continent itself in the sense that it is a very complex history. This "varied and long" history of Christianity in Africa defies all attempts at an easy explanation.[1] One thing that stands out, however, is that Christianity has massively impacted African social and political life, a reason for which Adrian Hastings suggested that much of Africa is inconceivable apart from Christianity.[2] This notwithstanding, Christianity is also a mixed bag on the socio-political spheres as well. The very Church that offers the citizenry a platform to express their discontent on myriads of political, economic, and even harsh cultural realities has, at times, seemed to reflect the same unjust political tendencies associated with the state machinery.[3] This ambiguity in the Church's role in African socio-political life, particularly in post-independence and post-missionary Africa (1950s–1980s) has resulted in two divergent trends of thought or ideas, each one producing a particular brand of African theology. The first trend is the theological reflections coming out of the social and political struggles of the peoples of South Africa. This reflection produced a black theology of liberation specific to the South African situation. It suggests that while *Christianity has played a positive role in dismantling of apartheid in South Africa and "in the second liberation of many African countries,"*[4] *it has also served as a tool of domination and division, in so far as the apartheid system was rooted (even if only in the view of the practitioners of apartheid) in Christian Scripture and tradition.* The sec-

1. Englund, "Rethinking African Christianities," 4.
2. Hastings, "Christianity in Africa," 208.
3. Ntarangwi, "African Christianity," 8.
4. Ibid., 2.

ond trend is the theological reflections coming out the other nation-states south of the Sahara as these countries seek political self-determination following colonialism. This theological reflection seeks "integration between the African pre-Christian religious experience and African Christian commitment in ways that would ensure the integrity of African Christian identity and selfhood."[5] The latter trend has been variously experimented using the neologism "inculturation."

The term inculturation was intended "conceptually both to safeguard the integrity of the Gospel and to encourage sensitivity to various cultural contexts."[6] At issue was the credibility of the Church in the wake of "the growing sense of disgrace of the colonial powers in their treatment of native peoples of various lands."[7] Among Protestants of post-World War II Europe, there was the general feeling that the faith of many European Christians "had proved to be more nominal than real and that European Christianity overall had failed in its obligations to transform culture as well as to oppose elements of culture that had become manifestly evil."[8] This sentiment provided the backdrop of H. Richard Niebuhr's helpful but nonetheless controversial work, *Christ and Culture* (1951) and Paul Tillich's now famed method of correlation, "by which human experience, understood with sensitivity to cultural diversity, poses questions to which Christianity must provide the orientation for an authentic response if it is to be existentially relevant."[9] Beyond safeguarding the integrity of the faith in the gospel encounter with local cultures, the Catholic Church was also concerned with how to re-evangelize those European cultures that were traditionally Christian but have since deviated from their Christian roots and become highly secularized and thus extended the term inculturation to John Paul II's program of "new evangelization."[10]

The program of "new evangelization" and inculturation resonated well with African bishops and theologians "who saw in it an ally against the consequences of cultural alienation and a guarantee of a genuinely African

---

5. Bediako, *Jesus and the Gospel in Africa*, 49.
6. Doyle, "The Concept of Inculturation in Roman Catholicism," 1.
7. Ibid., 2.
8. Ibid. See Niebuhr, *Christ and Culture*.
9. Doyle, "The Concept of Inculturation in Roman Catholicism," 2. See also Tillich, *Systematic Theology*; and Tillich, *A Theology of Culture*.
10. Doyle, "The Concept of Inculturation in Roman Catholicism," 1.

The Problematic of African Theology of Inculturation

Christianity."[11] Inculturation, in particular, became for Africans still reeling under the onslaught of colonialism an enterprise for which the Church must invest. The program to inculturate Christianity in Africa received, from an African Catholic Christian perspective, its first official authoritative backing at the 1969 meeting of the Symposium of Episcopal Conferences of Africa and Madagascar (SECAM), Kampala, Uganda. In attendance at the meeting was none other than Pope Paul VI himself who at the time was making a pastoral visit to Africa. The Pontiff declared in no uncertain terms to the African bishops and distinguished guests at the meeting: "You may, and you must have an African Christianity."[12] The Pope's declaration came in the wake of his 1967 Apostolic letter *Africae Terrarum* (The Land of Africa) in which he accentuated and paid tribute to the positive values in African Traditional Religions (ATRs) and invited Africans to devise new ways of becoming missionaries to themselves.[13] Even before the Pope's declaration that there must be an African Christianity some African theologians were already tapping into the new wave of optimism sweeping across the continent following political independence of many African countries and the religious optimism ushered in by the Second Vatican Council (1962–65). Among their many demands was that there be a recognition of African values and cultures in Christian liturgical services. Their argument was not only that the missionary experiment did not take African cultures into account, but also that terms like "accommodation," "adaptation," "contextualization," and "Africanization" need be embraced as a way of rediscovering what was lost during the missionary and colonial era. Pope Paul VI may have been aware of these demands prior to his *Africae Terrarum* (Land of Africa) and powerful speech to African bishops and theologians in Kampala. What Paul VI's declaration did, if anything, was give credence to a cry that was already gathering momentum—that there was a need to reconsider previous assumptions about African cultures and worldviews in light of the Gospel in other to arrive at an authentic African Christianity.

In the main, there are two parts of Paul VI's statement that galvanized theologians searching for an authentic African Christianity. The first was the admonition you may have an African Christianity and the second was the imperative you must have an African Christianity. The tension between

11. Shorter, *Toward a Theology of Inculturation*, xi.

12. See full text in Okure and Van Thiel, *32 Articles Evaluating Inculturation of Christianity in Africa*.

13. See Paul VI, *Africae Terrarum*.

A Semiotic Approach to the Theology of Inculturation

the desire to have an African Christianity and the obligation to realize it has dogged the African Church to this day. The first part, i.e., the admonition or desire to have an African Christianity, need not detain us here, in part because it does not demand thoroughness or rigor. In some sense, the demands of the first part have been attained by the different experiments that have gone under the garb of "adaptation," "localization," "contextualization," and "indigenization," etc. Our concern is rather on the second part, which is still far from being attained, i.e., the imperative "you must have an African Christianity." The search for an African (Catholic) Christianity is a laborious process demanding rigor. In spite of the fact that the center of gravity of the Christian faith has shifted southwards and millions of Africans have been baptized Catholic, many are still only nominally Christian because the faith has not been truly inculturated. Our contention here is that for the faith to be embedded in the lived lives of the African and be at home in the culture a semiotic approach to inculturation is desirable.

What is inculturation? How might one distinguish between inculturation and black theology? Is inculturation inherently different from black theology of liberation? Should black theology of liberation be limited only to the South African cultural milieu? As a concept, inculturation is related to, but not identical with liberation theology.[14] The connection between black theology of liberation and inculturation is not easy to navigate. There are those who see the two theologies as distinct and as having clearly designated boundaries. But a new empirical understanding of culture, particularly as uncovered by the science of semiotics, has necessitated a revision of previous views that see liberation and inculturation as mutually opposed. Thanks to the science of semiotics, there is now a move towards integration as many of the new studies of Christianity in Africa are now beginning to engage the intersection of ethnicity, identity, and development,[15] as well as the role played by individual Christians in the search for freedom and political self-determination in the new nation-states of Africa.[16] One of the leading voices in this area of integration is the Cameroonian theologian, Jean-Marc Ela (1936–2008), who insists that faith cannot be lived a temporally, but "must address the historical context in which repression and

---

14. Shorter, *Toward a Theology of Inculturation*, xi.

15. See Gifford, *African Christianity*; Ranger, *Evangelical Christianity and Democracy in Africa*; Longman, *Christianity and Genocide in Rwanda;* and Patterson, *The Church and Aids in Africa.*

16. Ntarangwi, "African Christianity, Politics, and Socioeconomic Realities," 2.

dehumanization sustain the powerful in their status and voices for reform are stilled."[17] To his ideas we turn next.

Setting the Context: Jean-Marc Ela of Cameroon

Jean-Marc Ela was born in 1936 in Ebolowa, a small town in South Cameroon. His parents were both devout Catholics. This was at a time when most of Africa was under colonial rule and France (and Great Britain) controlled most of West Africa. At the time of Ela's birth Cameroon was technically not a French colony, but what was known according to international law as a trust territory. France nevertheless, exerted a lot of influence in the area and extended its policy of assimilation on this trust territory.[18] Ela, very early on, felt called to the priesthood and after studying philosophy and theology at the seminary in Yaoundé was ordained to the priesthood in 1964. After his ordination he taught at the same seminary in Yaoundé, Cameroon. He also worked briefly with the pygmies of East Cameroon, but abandoned the ministry because of what he described as constant surveillance from government officials. He left for North Cameroon to work with an African priest, Baba Simon Mpecke, who at the time was working among an indigenous Cameroonian group of north Cameroon, the Kirdi people.[19] Baba Simon taught what Ela would later describe as a new self-consciousness. Baba Simon saw Christianity as a "Western" and "imported" product and wrestled with the idea of how to adapt the "imported" product to local customs and practices. Baba Simon's goal, as Ela describes it, "was to restore to the gospel in Africa its credibility and power of expression, quite apart from the theological discourse, which had developed in Europe."[20] Another thing that impressed Ela about Baba Simon was his austere lifestyle. Thus, when he took up apprenticeship with Baba Simon to work among the Kirdi of northern Cameroon, living austere lifestyle and making the Gospel relevant to the people was sine qua non for Ela who, throughout his ministry as a priest and theologian, had been grappling with how to make Christian

---

17. Hoekema, "Faith and Freedom in Post-Colonial African Politics," 39. See also Magesa, *Anatomy of Inculturation*.

18. Hetjke, "Thinking in the Scene of Disaster," 61.

19. See Hetjke "Baba Simon Mpecke of Cameroon, Mentor of Jean-Marc Ela"; and Baskouda, *Baba Simon, le Pere des Kirdis*.

20. Hetjke, "Thinking in the Scene of Disaster," 62.

theology address "the continuous pauperization of the common people by a ruthless and greedy ruling elite and their international collaborators."[21]

Ela worked under Baba Simon from 1971 to 1985 before interrupting this ministry for further studies in France. His sojourn in France led to two doctoral degrees, one in theology from the University of Strasbourg (1969) and the other in social and cultural anthroplogy from the Sorbonne in Paris (1978). Even while in France Ela never gave up on his love for the Kirdi people. It was no wonder that he wrote one of his dissertations on the traditional social structures and economic changes among the Kirdi or mountain people of north Cameroon. In the dissertation he espoused what he called *pedagogie du regard* (pedagoy of the look), a pedagogy that aimed to achieve three things: "to see all aspects of a society in a mutual relationship, to involve the population as a subject in social reforms and to enter upon a struggle with fate-thinking."[22]

Apart from the two doctoral degrees he earned in France, Ela was honored with an additional (honorary doctorate) by the Catholic University of Louvain in February 1999. He was described by the University as "one of the most prominent and critically committed thinkers" of Africa.[23] He was also singled out for his dedication to improving "the dialogue between the theological and sociological body of thought of the West and the portrayal of man and the community of values of Bantu Africa."[24] When he left France and returned to Cameroon, Ela continued with the ministry he had begun with the Kirdi people of north Cameroon. His continued work with these indigenous peasants helped him "see clearly both the glaring contradictions of the dominant presence of (Catholic) Christianity and the abject misery and marginalization of the peasants at the hand of the dominant political, economic, and ecclesiastical institutions."[25] These contradictions would become both the basis and point of departure of his theological reflections.

Ela's theological reflections somehow got him in trouble with the Cameroonian authorities. In 1984 when Cameroon was beset by an unsuccessful but bloody coup d'état that led to a protracted political unrest in the country Ela was among those identified by the military junta as the "bothersome" people to be eliminated for their liberation work and

21. Ngong, "The Theologian as Missionary," 5.
22. Hetjke, "Thinking in the Scene of Disaster," 63.
23. Ibid., 61
24. Ibid.
25. Katongole, *The Sacrifice of Africa*, 103.

conscience promoting activities.²⁶ The political unrest eventually claimed the lives of prominent clergy men and women, like Yves Lumey, the much beloved and respected bishop of Garoua in north Cameroon, and the Cameroonian Jesuit Engelbert Mveng who was Ela's partner in the struggle for social justice.²⁷ Ela was abroad visiting Louvain-la Neuve, Belgium, as guest lecturer when Mveng was murdered at his home on April 24, 1995. Angered by the death of his beloved friend, on his return from Belgium, Ela preached series of sermons that were critical of the government and the state of affairs in Cameroon.²⁸ Coincidentally, this was about the same time John Paul II was to make a visit to Cameroon to present the conclusions of the African synod of bishops to French-speaking Africa.²⁹ Ela depicted Cameroon as a country that had fallen into the hands of brigands, "supported by the North-Atlantic powers that wish to maintain control over Africa's resources."³⁰ Fearing that his life was more and more in danger, Ela left Cameroon for Canada on August 6, 1995 where he sought asylum. He taught sociology at the University of Quebec, Montreal and spent the rest of his life writing and publishing in Canada until his death in December 2008.

Ela's Shade-Tree Theology

Ela became famous as a theologian with the publications of *Ma Foi d'Africain* (*My Faith as an African*)³¹ and *Le Cri de l'homme* (translated as *African Cry*),³² a work in which he portrayed the "cry" of the African as a cry of pain. In these works Ela suggests that the damage done to the collective psyche of the African by centuries of slavery and colonization cannot easily be undone by a simple program of de-colonization.³³ His desire to effect the change that de-colonization failed to bring made Ela to brand his theology, not as an African theology,³⁴ but as a theology out of Africa. The difference between the two is subtle and easy to miss. In Ela's time it was very

26. Hetjke, "Thinking in the Scene of Disaster," 72.
27. Ibid., 76.
28. Ibid.
29. Ibid.
30. Ibid.
31. See Ela, *My Faith as an African*.
32. See Ela, *African Cry*.
33. Hetjke, "Thinking in the Scene of Disaster," 64.
34. For detailed discussion of the origin and meaning of African theology, see Bujo, *Africa Theology in Its Social Context*.

common for indigenous African clergy men coming out of the experience of colonialism to describe their theology as African theology—their way of distinguishing their theology from what was thought to be European theology taught by Western missionaries. But Ela takes a step further and distinguishes his theology both from the Western missionary practice and from his indigenous African clergy counterparts. His proper term for his theology is "shade-tree theology." In a 1999 interview on Flemish radio, Ela spoke eloquently about what distinguishes his theology from that of others:

> My theology under the tree developed during my period in North-Cameroon. I learnt a lot of things there that I had not learned at school. All day I was among the people in the mountains. I only studied or wrote at night. The gospel contains an enormous potential. On the terraces of the mountain slopes, where they had their small fields, we discussed together matters like the water supply, the soil, the millet. I still remember that the Book of the Prophet Isaiah suggested the subject of the suffering servant: "he had borne our suffering." During the very week I was reading that, people were forced to pull out their millet plants, in order to plant cotton instead. You cannot eat cotton. So this meant a heavy demand on their (way of) life. They had to pull out those plants, their food! It was like the thrust of a knife in one's heart. Talking under the tree, that meant not only talking in the shade, because of the heat, but for me, and gradually also for us: the realization of the tree of the Cross, of the suffering. Jesus assumes in his cry on the Cross the sufferings of all the African peoples, all the cries of distress of the world. Paul also speaks about the mystery of Cross. That is where the whole of creation groans.[35]

Emmanuel Katongole offers an insightful explanation as to why Ela's theological approach differs from that of many of his contemporaries. Other approaches begin with descriptions of reality and then proceed to see what insights or recommendations theology can throw upon the situation. But Ela sees the description of the situation as the theological reflection itself.[36] While working among the Kirdi, for example, Ela developed a habit of holding regular Bible study sessions with them. During one of those sessions he experienced an event that changed the entire process of his reflection and research. Ela had proposed for discussion for that day the topic "God," to which a young woman objected by retorting "God,

---

35. Hetjke, "Thinking in the Scene of Disaster," 64.
36. Katongole, *The Sacrifice of Africa*, 103.

The Problematic of African Theology of Inculturation

God, and after that what?" Ela realized there and then that for this young woman and others like her the question of God has to be reformulated and made relevant to their situation.[37] It also made him realize that the question of God has to address the significance of God in a situation of poverty, drought, war, famine, injustice, and oppression. The primary theological task in Africa, therefore, must address "anthropological poverty"—the kind of poverty that strikes at the very being, essence, and dignity of the human person.[38] It is the kind of poverty that destroys communities and renders people hopeless and useless. Thus, for Ela, the question of God has to be removed from the realm of the abstractly theological to practical human realm where the nitty-gritty of life is lived.[39] This is also why Ela brands his shade-tree theology as "a theology that, far from the libraries and offices, develops among brothers and sisters searching shoulder to shoulder with the unlettered peasants for the sense of the word of God in situations in which this word touches them."[40]

Ela harkens back to the problems besetting the African continent, pointing out that when one looks at the unprecedented high number of refugees and displaced persons in Africa it is difficult to escape the conclusion that Africa is a strangled continent and Kafkaesque. On human rights issues, Ela thinks Africa is like a concentration camp and a gulag—a place where the army swallows up a considerable part of the state budget while the head of state is surrounded by presidential guard that is armed to the teeth.[41] Living in Africa is, for him, a crucible worthy of a "cry." If Christianity is to be made intelligible in such a debilitating environment, there must be a hermeneutical key for unlocking these problems. Ela's hermeneutical key for addressing these problems is the "Cross" of Christ. The crucial question for him is: who is Jesus Christ to the African? Accepting an idea

---

37. Ngong, "The Theologian as Missionary," 10.

38. Ibid. See also Mveng, "Impoverishment and Liberation," 156.

39. Ela's dedication to the plight of the poor and oppressed has led David Ngong to suggest that Ela was one of the early African thinkers "to call for a new paradigm of mission which is not linked to the interest of the strong and powerful but rather is directed toward those who are marginalized: mission done in weakness and vulnerability." Ngong correctly points out, in what seems like a validation of Ela's pace setting work, that the paradigm of mission, which Ela envisioned, is what is practiced today by many of the African churches, particularly those of the Pentecostal/Charismatic persuasion. See Ngong, "The Theology as Missionary," 11.

40. Ela, *African Cry*, vi.

41. Hetjke, "Thinking in the Scene of Disaster," 65.

that was well formulated by Walter Kasper's,[42] i.e., that Christology is a conscientious elucidation of the proposition that Jesus is Lord,[43] Ela rejects any theological formulation that does not address the African in his or her concrete specific life situation. He makes a simple argument: that since "access to Jesus through the New Testament always involves a process of reading and interpreting from the perspective of the situation and problems with which the church is confronted in history, the version of Christianity received from the churches of the West cannot escape the risk of being reinterpreted in Africa."[44] His concern was that the theology he inherited from the West did not resonate with his cultural situation. He dismisses, for this reason, any Christological slogan (e.g., "Jesus is Lord" or "Jesus is Logos") that does not have analogue in traditional African worldview or that does not resonate with the African. To be clear, Ela is not opposed to the theological meanings behind Christological formulae like "Jesus is Logos." What he questions rather is why such formulae have to be imposed on non-Hellenistic cultures unfamiliar with Greek concepts, worldviews, and ways of life. Take the example of "Jesus is the Logos of God," this concept, as Ela sees it, was elaborated in the fourth century when Constantine embraced Christianity and used Christianity to justify his political ends. For Ela, therefore, the transformation of Christianity by Constantine from "religion of the people" (outlawed religion) to a "civil religion" (religion of the state) in effect makes Christianity a "mechanism of domination."[45] Ela therefore questions why non-Greco-Roman cultures must be forced to embrace Christological titles like "Lord" and "Master" when these were titles of Roman emperors and potentates that were taken over by the Constantine led Church and ascribed to Christ. "Given the conditions following the fourth century, in which the great dogmas were elaborated, taking an emperor's title and applying it to Christ was not innocent."[46] Not only is Ela adamant that we cannot repeat tradition as handed down in rote fashion, he also insists that from socio-cultural standpoint, the Roman titles that were applied to Jesus "do not correspond to traditional African concepts."[47] He insists that what the world church demands is both a pluralism in

---

42. See Kasper, *Jesus the Christ*, 15.
43. Ela, "The Memory of the African People and the Cross of Christ," 17.
44. Ibid., 18.
45. Ibid., 32.
46. Ibid.
47. Ibid., 19.

worldview and new theological and pastoral approaches that can meet the needs of African Christians. Ela suggests that any attempt to impose a theology exclusively meant for the Hellenistic world on the African amounts to nothing but foreign cultural monopoly. It is imperative for the African therefore, according to Ela, to liberate "the faith of the local churches from formulae that have the effect of obscuring Jesus from being recognized by other people."[48] To this end, Ela suggests a kind of (political) theology that fuses inculturation with liberation.

Ela the Inculturation Theologian?

The connection between liberation and inculturation, which is easy to miss, did not escape Ela. Among African theologians Ela was one of those who tried to hold the two threads in dynamic tension in his trademark "shade-tree theology"—a political theology that relates Christianity to socio-economic life of Africa. Ela's political theology can be likened to the political theology of the German Catholic Johann Baptist Metz (b. 1928) and that of the German reformed theologian Jurgen Moltmann (b. 1926). These two theologians incorporated insights from liberation theology in their works. There are some who describe Ela as a liberation theologian because of the parallels they see between his work and that of the Peruvian Catholic Liberation theologian Gustavo Gutiérrez (b. 1928). When the University of Louvain awarded him an honorary doctorate in 1999, for example, the University wrongly described him as a critically committed thinker of "liberation theology." [49] Emmanuel Katongole has been helpful in showing how misleading it is to refer to Ela's work exclusively as a work of liberation theology. One cannot deny that there are aspects of Ela's work that suggest such a designation because Ela does not only forcefully use the language of liberation, he also shares the uncompromising, total commitment to the plight of the poor that one sees in the work of liberation theologians.[50] Ela's indignant style of writing, including the employment of biblical theme of Exodus, his criticism of the capitalist market system, economic exploitation, and to some extent his use of Marxist analysis of history—features that have come to characterize liberation theology, as Katongole carefully points out, may indeed give the impression that Ela

48. Ibid., 20.
49. Hetjke, "Thinking in the Scene of Disaster," 61.
50. Katongole, *The Sacrifice of Africa*, 103.

is a liberation theologian in the South American liberation theology sense of the term.[51] But the themes of liberation in Ela's work should not be confused with liberation theology. As Katongole correctly points out, liberation theology does not have a monopoly of liberation themes. When Ela uses liberation themes it is only "with a view of a more demanding task, namely, rethinking the whole edifice of Christian faith in Africa."[52] Thus, when he reflects on the suffering of the African, it is in order to offer analyses of the mechanisms that produce them. And when he uses the incarnation of Jesus as a metaphor of God's liberation of the oppressed and as an analogue for contextualizing the Christian message (inculturation), it is as an attempt to show that in "approaching the major themes of the faith in the perspective of the Incarnation, we can scarcely afford to pass over in silence the human condition as assumed by Jesus of Nazareth."[53]

Although his primary goal is to hold the themes of liberation and inculturation creatively together, we cannot deny that Ela at times speaks as if he favors what has been conventionally conceived as "liberation" over "inculturation." There is evidence of this, for example, in a 1980 paper titled "From Assistance to Liberation" that Ela gave at the *Jeunesse Etudiante Chretienne* (Pan African Assembly of Catholic Students) in Dar-es-Salam, Tanzania. In the paper he proposed that what was needed in Africa was a theology of liberation, not the theology of inculturation that his peers were preoccupied with.[54] Critics interpreted this to mean that Ela is dismissive of theology of inculturation. But Ela's preference for "liberation" over the theology of inculturation of his peers should be understood in the context of Ela's overall approach to theology that we pointed out earlier, i.e., his desire to distance himself from the Western theology that he inherited and his desire to separate his theology from those of his peers whom he thought were accepting uncritically the theology they inherited from Western Christian missionaries. There is also the related fact that Ela's so called preference for liberation themes is also his own way of drawing attention to the "paternalism" that goes under the name of inculturation. His criticism of liturgical adaptations is a good case in point. Ela was dismissive of many of the liturgical adaptations approved by Christian missionaries, suggesting that what has been lumped under the name of inculturation was nothing

---

51. Ibid., 104.
52. Ibid.
53. Ela, *African Cry*, 135.
54. Hetjke, "Thinking in the Scene of Disaster," 67.

but "folkloristic" ritual, which does not serve the African interest. He also argued that what goes under the umbrella of inculturation is "an alibi for leaving other matters out of consideration."[55] His favorite example is liturgy in native music, which he thought was merely ritualistic. According to him, what liturgy in native music does to the psyche of African is simply make the African forget that they are oppressed.[56] For him, "drumming on the tom-tom and the rhythm of the balaphone in church cannot protect the rural population, which has already been crushed by the dictatorship of peanuts, cotton, and cocoa, against the food weapon with which they are threatened."[57] Thus, when Ela speaks forcefully about liberation (even if it seems like he is disparaging inculturation) it is in light of this concern that the problems with which the clergy were concerned were not the same as those of ordinary African men and women whose basic rights were flouted daily. "In many of our countries," he observed, "access to drinking water, a balanced diet, health and hygiene, education or self-determination are, more often than not, luxuries."[58] We should promote instead a theology that calls into question all unjust structures, colonial and neocolonial alike. Such a theology, in his view, must first be a sine qua non for learning "to pronounce God and Jesus using the words of our own soil and our own culture."[59] Lastly, Ela was also concerned by what he saw as an attempt by some of his peers to split theology of liberation from inculturation, two realities that are not opposed but should be placed in a relation of perichoresis.[60] Ela insists that the liberation of the oppressed must also be the sine qua non condition for any authentic inculturation of the Christian message.[61] He thinks that once liberation is split from inculturation then the argument in favor of Africanization of the Church becomes ambiguous.[62]

The challenge of "how to think about, understand and confess Jesus Christ in our cultures and our history fraught with tensions and conflicts

---

55. Ibid., 71.
56. Ibid., 67.
57. Ibid., 68.
58. Ela, "Christianity and Liberation in Africa," 137.
59. Hejtke, "Thinking in the Scene of Disaster," 67.
60. Bujo and Muya, *African Theology in the Twenty-First Century*, 212; cited in Katongole, *The Sacrifice of Africa*, 104.
61. Ela, *My Faith as an African*, xvi.
62. Hetjke, "Thinking in the Scene of Disaster," 67.

as they are," which Ela set out to address, is not an easy one.[63] Ela, as it were, was correct to insist that some kind of liberation is inevitably involved in any attempt to inculturate Christianity, at least in Africa. Rather than jettison him as favoring liberation over inculturation, the question should rather be: what does liberation mean for Ela? There are two ways of understanding Ela's use of the term liberation. The one is a socio-cultural understanding (freedom from colonial/postcolonial domination) and the other is theological (freedom from Western-style theology).

A. Socio-Cultural Locus of Liberation

Ela usually uses the term *liberation* to mean freedom from harsh political and economic realities. Liberation here is not only freedom from Western domination, but also from African elites who mismanage the resources of their nations. "Ela considers much of the so-called independent Africa to be in fact a neocolonial region. African governments seem to exist to serve the interests of the metropolises of the North in various ways while their own people languish in physical, intellectual and moral poverty."[64] Thus, liberation is Ela's way of calling for a new African world order. Independence for most sub-Saharan African countries came at a time of bitter ideological divide between the Marxist East (led by the Union of Soviet Socialist Republic) and the capitalist West (led by the United States and Great Britain). As one writer explains it, "each side sought to win the allegiance of Africans with advice, technical assistance, and development aid. Each party offered assurance that, when the ideological battles had all been fought and won, it would emerge victorious, delivering the poor and downtrodden from their suffering and ushering in a new era of peace and prosperity for all."[65] Faced

63. Ela and Brown, "First Colloquium of African and European Theologians," 58. This gathering, according to Ela and Brown, was the brain child of the Ecumenical Association of African Theologians (EAAT), supported by some representatives of the World Council of Churches (WCC). Ela and Brown estimated that about eighty participants from twenty-four countries in Africa, Europe, and America took part in the work of the conference. There were representatives from the Roman Catholic, Anglican, Oriental, Orthodox, and several branches of Protestantism. Among African participants there were representatives from the theological faculties of Abidjan, Port Harcourt, Kinshasa, Bangui, and Yaoundé. From Europe were representatives from universities in Leyden, Louvain, Lyon, Paris, Rome, and Berlin, as well as from missionary institutes in France, Germany, and the Netherlands.

64. Magesa, Review of *African Cry*, 255.

65. Hoekema, "Faith and Freedom in Post-Colonial African Politics," 28.

with the difficult decision of choosing between "the god of capitalism, free markets, and liberal democracy; or the god of socialism, mutual solidarity, and people's assemblies,"⁶⁶ some of the newly independent African leaders rejected the dichotomy presented by the East-West conflict and sought a new way forward in ideologies or philosophies that were deeply rooted in African cultural systems and symbols. In Tanzania, for example, Julius Nyerere (1922–99) formulated a model of African political and social organization he labelled *Ujamaa*- from the Swahili word "family." Nyerere insisted that the relations between African citizens must be guided not by the domination and suspicion that undergird the capitalist or socialist ideology, but by mutual trust and shared responsibility of all in a nation where there can be neither servant nor masters but fellow members of an extended political family.⁶⁷ In like manner, Ghanaian President Kwame Nkrumah (1909–72) developed a philosophy of African personalism similar to that of Nyerere, *Consciencism*.⁶⁸ In Zambia Kenneth Kaunda developed similar concept of African humanism (b. 1924),⁶⁹ while in Senegal Leopold Senghor (1906–2001) developed the concept of *Negritude*.⁷⁰

The political ideals developed by leaders, such as Nyerere, Nkrumah, and Senghor, served both as a myth and a method. As a myth, the ideals were rooted in African history and experience and served as a powerful motivator for political change. As a method, socialism in the African mode was a way of "governing the new states and advancing their welfare: it mandated certain economic and social policies intended to maintain a middle course between the fragmentation and alienation that that prevail under capitalism and the homogenization and repression that too often result when socialism is imposed by political fiat."⁷¹ But whether as a myth or

66. Ibid.
67. Ibid., 29.
68. See Nkrumah, *Consciencism*.
69. See Kaunda, *A Humanist in Africa*.

70. See Senghor, *The Foundations of "Africanite."* Ela dismisses *négritude* when translated as "Blackness." He thinks Blackness has been used to rationalize injustice and oppress the African. "If Blackness, had its way," he writes, "Africa would be transformed into one vast reserve for the ethnologist, where they could preserve the past and keep anything from changing . . . For all its vaunting cultural specificity, Blackness only promotes the values of the past, thus espousing a dead view of society, creating a mystique of vain expectation, and doing its best to check the revolt of the hungering masses feeding them soporifics." See *African Cry*, 124–25.

71. Hoekema, "Faith and Freedom in Post-Colonial African Politics," 32. In the 1990s South Africa will develop a similar vision of African socialism rooted in African history and experience called *Ubuntu*.

method, the different visions put forward by African leaders each had their own measures of success and failure. If the ideals were based on African history and experience as these leaders purportedly claimed, then why did they fail? While this is not the right place to address such complex issue, perhaps we should quickly point out some of the external and internal factors that contributed to their failure.

There were many factors on the external front. First, "the end of colonialism was by no means the end of Africa's vulnerability to exploitation or to its dependence on former colonial masters."[72] Second, before disengaging from their colonies the colonial leaders did not take serious steps to prepare their colonies for impending independence and self-government. What they did in most cases was that "they simply packed up for home and walked away without looking back."[73] Third, "demands from international banks and development organizations to enact 'structural reforms' led to spiraling poverty, diminished state capacity, and massive wealth transfers to domestic and international investors in many African nations."[74] Fourth, "because African export economies are heavily dependent on agricultural products and minerals, the collapse of world markets in many such commodities devastated national budgets across the continent."[75]

Many internal factors also played a role in crippling the political ideologies developed by postcolonial African leaders. First was the lack of authenticity. The ideal of brotherhood that was preached was reneged immediately as the leaders and their allies gained power. As one writer describes it, when these leaders "moved from the forests and the streets into the state house, they settled in all too quickly and granted themselves many of the benefits and prerogatives that their predecessors in the colonial regime had enjoyed, necessitating both high taxes and regular 'contributions' from those who stood to gain from their official acts."[76] Second, while corruption and nepotism were regular features of colonial life, "the newly independent African office- holders raised them to a high art. Where high government offices had been reserved for Europeans under colonial rule, under self-rule they were often effectively closed to all but the president's

72. Ibid., 34.
73. Ibid.
74. Ibid.
75. Ibid.
76. Ibid.

cousins and cronies."[77] Third, where under colonial rule African leaders advocated free and open election, when these same leaders came to office they rethought their position when faced with the prospect of leaving office and in most cases silenced all oppositions and indefinitely extended their terms.[78] Fourth, "freedom of the press was rare, and fragile, and many a journalist paid for his or her contribution to open political debate by spending time in detention, or worse."[79] Finally, when policies were enacted "too often they were implemented by government decree, with insufficient consideration of how they would be received or of their prospects of success."[80] A good case in point was the forced movement of Tanzania's farmers to agricultural communes by the Nyerere government in the 1970s. "Measured simply by population movement the policy succeeded, moving 90 percent of the rural population into newly established agricultural communes. But these produced only 5 percent of the nation's crops, and the disruption of traditional small hold farming soon turned one of Africa's leading food exporters into one of its neediest importers, rescued from bankruptcy only by World Bank loans."[81]

This is the social-cultural context of Ela's call for a new wave of liberation in Africa. He was troubled by "the apparently meaningless existence, the extreme and paralyzing poverty, the violation of basic rights, the colonial and neocolonial violence, [and] the multinational exploitation" that have become commonplace.[82] It is also the context of his plea that the church must do more than demand "conformity with European cultural norms."[83] In fact, Ela's theological reflections on these avoidable social and political ills were "not so much directed toward fixing the national political and economic systems as it is directed against the church itself, its own self-understanding, history, and mission."[84] What Ela expects of the church is for the church to embody an alternative.[85] What, after all, is the meaning of solidarity and friendship in a continent where misery and oppression are

77. Ibid.
78. Ibid.
79. Ibid.
80. Ibid., 35.
81. Ibid.
82. Katongole, *The Sacrifice of Africa*, 105.
83. Hoekema, "Faith and Freedom in Post-Colonial African Politics," 39.
84. Katongole, *The Sacrifice of Africa*, 106.
85. Ibid.

rife?[86] How might one speak of salvation in a continent caught in the throes of a struggle with imperialism? Has paper independence not become an obstacle to the self-assertion of the African personality and recognition of their real identity?[87] In concrete terms, how can the Church witness to the Gospel in an African society where bureaucratized elites plunder the helpless masses of such a great portion of the national income?[88] How can the church respect African cultural identity when Africa is caught in the clutches of foreign companies that destroy the very concept of self-identity?[89] These are critical questions that Ela thinks must be answered before genuine inculturation can take place.

B. Theological Locus of Liberation

Ela sees Western-style theology as serving mainly imperial agenda because Christianization and colonization, at least as far as Africa was concerned, "marched shoulder to shoulder."[90] In his view, the evangelization of Africa was carried out mainly by missionary institutes who have traits of the West, i.e., Western influence, Western thought systems, Western institutions, and Western traditions. As part of this Western thought systems, he thinks that these missionary institutes employ the same imperial image of Christ that were used as "an alibi for all the crusades."[91] He thinks the same inner logic is operative in the colonial enterprise in which Christianity and colonization march shoulder to shoulder to places designated pagan by the Church's hierarchy. When they arrived at these so called pagan places "the 'Christian' nations were more preoccupied with the accumulation of riches than with spreading the light of the Gospel."[92] Ela, therefore, questions "whether a white church implanted among blacks" can effectively root the "faith and gospel in Africa."[93] Again Ela's term for putting an end to this kind of exploitation is *liberation*—bringing an end to that brand of theology that has

---

86. Ela, *African Cry*, 62.
87. Ibid., 131.
88. Ibid.
89. Ibid.
90. Ibid., 107.
91. Ela, "The Memory of the African People and the Cross of Christ," 33.
92. Ibid.
93. Ela, *African Cry*, 106.

been used in the exploitation of Africa in the guise of evangelization.[94] "To what extent," he wrote, "is the situation of the churches of black Africa not a neocolonial situation, analogous to that of stymied societies living in a situation of strict dependency on the great decision-making centers, which are the monopoly of the countries of the northern hemisphere?"[95] He even wonders whether or not the churches of the so called third-world, since they have been deprived of their texture, are not simply "third churches?"[96]

According to John Mbiti (b. 1931), Ela, in a sense, sees the oppressor as the Latinized structures, traditions, and theology of the Roman Catholic Church.[97] His critique here again is two pronged: he is as critical of Church structure as he is of his fellow African priests. The missionary priest may be "a man of the rite, living in a universe of 'holy days' in which ordinary life was absent,"[98] the African priest is equally impotent and inept if he is unable to unlock how the historical dimension of God's scheme pertains to the African. Ela was referring primarily to the translated version of Church catechism used by African priests in instructing the faithful. Ela's angst is that the catechism is codified in European thought system and pattern that does not speak to the African. The inability to make the gospel speak to the modern African makes "catechesis abstract, dry, doctrinal, moralizing, legalistic, prescriptive and aimed at meekly reciting the text."[99] This makes the activity of the Church in Africa seem like an "assembling part" that tries to replicate an imported model of the "mother plant.[100] It is for this reason again that Ela argues that liberation, not cultural adaptation, ought to be the obligatory locus of theological research.[101] He suggests that just as the West has succeeded in synthesizing faith and reason after centuries of wrestling with the subject, the task of theology from Africa should be how to synthesize faith and liberation.[102] "It is no longer enough to pose the questions of faith on the level of culture alone," he writes, "we must also pay

---

94. Ibid.
95. Ibid.
96. Ibid.
97. See Mbiti, "Ascents in African Theology," 106.
98. Ela, African Cry, 70.
99. Ibid., 71.
100. Ibid.
101. Ela, "Christianity and Liberation in Africa," 140.
102. Ela, "The Church—Sacrament of Liberation," 138.

attention to the mechanisms and structures of oppression at work."[103] The theological language inherited from the West, he argues, "does not speak to us, it does not move our hearts, [and] it does not communicate our thoughts."[104] The African church is, therefore, faced with two inexorable alternatives: continue with the way things are and slip into anachronism and become a stranger to the real questions of today's Africa or become prophetic and daring and revise, not only of the language of theology, but also "all its forms, and all of its institutions, in order to assume the African human face."[105]

The Paradox of the Eucharist

Ela decries what he sees as "the paradox of the Eucharist" in the Christian communities of Africa because he thinks the unfortunate split between inculturation and liberation finds its locus in the liturgy.[106] He thinks the liturgical adaptations undertaken by many in the wake of political independence has proven to be anything but superficial. For him, the manner of celebrating the Eucharist is not only alienating, it also reveals "the domination at the heart of the faith as lived in Africa, within a Christianity that refuses to become incarnate in our peoples."[107] A context here may be helpful. In the Thomistic theology in which Ela was trained, a distinction was made between the *Matter* of a sacrament (sensible object) and the *Form* of a sacrament (words used by the minister). For the Eucharistic sacrifice, bread and wine are the Matter of the sacrament and the words the priest says over the bread and wine during consecration are the Form of the sacrament. Ela finds both the Matter and Form of the Eucharist to be problematic. Bread and wine, he points out, come from European agricultural products. Wheat and grapes, are not staples of sub-Saharan Africa. The use of these non-traditional African agricultural products, for Ela, has many implications, which cannot be taken lightly.

---

103. Ela, "Christianity and Liberation in Africa," 140.
104. Ela, "The Church—Sacrament of Liberation," 138.
105. Ela, *African Cry*, 134.
106. Ibid., 1.
107. Ibid., 5.

The Problematic of African Theology of Inculturation

1. **Economic Implication:**

   Imported foreign agricultural products used in the liturgy send a wrong message to Africans—that they cannot produce crops that can serve the same purpose. The Church law that forbids the use of similar products puts Africans at more disadvantage. What this means is that places that can produce similar products are discouraged because the Church's liturgical laws forbid their use. Economically then, Africans are on the wrong end of the trade deal "because they are made to import the Eucharistic elements of bread and wine, elements that could be replaced by viable African alternatives such as millet."[108]

2. **Perpetuation of Dependency**

   In addition to the economic implications of not allowing the use of African products in the Eucharist, there is also the problem of perpetual dependency which the refusal to use viable alternatives creates. Ela suggests that the refusal "to allow the celebration of the Eucharist using grains other than wheat in regions where wheat is not grown is to condemn communities to celebrate salvation in Jesus Christ in dependency on Mediterranean culture."[109]

3. **Disparagement of African Symbols**

   As the source and summit of the Christian life, the Eucharist has a very powerful symbolism. One of these symbolism is the agricultural products of bread and wine that the priest refers to in the prayers of the Eucharist as "fruits of the earth and works of human hands." This powerful symbolism puts us in touch with our earthly stewardship and roots us deeply in our environment. Ela points out that when the priest calls the origin of the symbols of bread and wine "fruit of the earth," it "conveys the message that the agricultural efforts of the vast majority of the African population are not under consideration for a role in Christian symbolism."[110] For Ela, again this means that the Eucharist reveals the domination at the heart of the faith as lived in Africa.[111]

---

108. Ngong, "The Theologian as Missionary," 14.
109. Ela, *African Cry*, 5.
110. Ngong, "The Theologian as Missionary," 14.
111. Ela, *African Cry*, 5.

4. Lack of Openness to Non-Western Realities

For Africans meal is culturally significant because of the symbolism of the elements from which the meal is derived.[112] Ela argues that if the Eucharist is truly a meal or banquet as Christian theology says it is then the Eucharistic sacrifice should be of more significance for Africans for whom participation in meals or banquets is part and parcel of what it means to be a member of a community. Ela cites example the Kirdi people of North Cameroon for whom millet plays a basic role in social and religious life.[113] For the Kirdi, millet is culturally nutritive and constitutes part of their menu, just in the same way that bread and wine form part of the menu of many people in Europe. Why can millet then not be a substitute for bread for these people of the savanna for whom production of millet is tied to socio-economic life? Ela wonders whether the Church's insistence on bread and wine (European imports) as the sole Matter of the sacrament of the Eucharist is not indicative of the Church's lack of openness to non-Western realities? He wonders whether the manner in which African agricultural products are set aside does not reveal "a Christianity that becomes uneasy the moment it must deviate from a manner of existence proper to Europeans?"[114]

5. Why a Single Rite?

Ela does not see why there cannot be multiple rites in post-Vatican II Church. He points out that in spite of the rhetoric of liturgical pluralism, "a single rite is actually imposed on the ensemble of the Christian communities of black Africa: the Roman rite, whose substance must be respected integrally and faithfully."[115] The Roman rite represents for him an imposition. It "has not been of our choosing; it bears the mark of a culture not ours; it has not developed in function of our personality or of the genius of our people. And so the Eucharist in the life of the church has become the locus of our daily alienation."[116]

---

112. Ibid., 4.
113. Ibid.,
114. Ibid., 4–5.
115. Ibid., 3.
116. Ibid., 3–4.

The Problematic of African Theology of Inculturation

It is important to stress that Ela is not calling for "symbolic" or token adoption of African elements and practices for use in the liturgy. "Introduction of a few African elements and practices within worship or other church practices is not enough to reverse this alienation of an institution grounded in neocolonial imagination."[117] What he wants rather is a radical rethinking of "the entire structure of church life from the perspective of African history."[118] Without such a fundamental rethinking the whole quest for inculturation will become "a vast entertainment project, whose purpose is to distract the exploited masses from the struggles of the present."[119] It is on the strength of this argument that Ela speaks of the paradox of the Eucharist—that in the "essential action in which the whole faith of the Church is at stake, African Christians experience salvation in Jesus Christ in a situation of dependence."[120] Part of the paradox he refers to is the fact that "the church, in its current Eucharistic practice, reveals our alienation at the hands of a world that imposes its products on us not only generally, but in the very liturgy that actualizes our redemption."[121] It is also paradoxical that in trying to maintain uniformity in Eucharistic species the Eucharist is rendered meaningless for African Christians who are forced to engage in a cultural universe that has no link with the real life of African communities.[122] For example, "the symbolism of the Eucharist escapes the savanna people or the forest people because the meaning of wheat bread and grape wine in European culture escapes them."[123]

Ela, however, was not the first to call for replacement of European agricultural products with African ones. Two African bishops, one from Cameroon and the other from Chad, had earlier carried out an actual experiment substituting for the unleavened wheat bread and fermented grape wine of the Eucharist millet bread and millet beer, the staple food and drink of their regions in which they worked. Their experiment was condemned and brought to an end by the Vatican's instruction *Inaestimable Donum*.[124] Not deterred by this condemnation, Ela calls on the Church to

---

117. Katongole, *The Sacrifice of Africa*, 108.
118. Ibid.
119. Ela, *African Cry*, 129; cited in Katongole, *The Sacrifice of Africa*, 108.
120. Ela, *African Cry*, 2.
121. Ibid., 5.
122. Ibid.
123. Ibid.
124. Bowie, "The Inculturation Debate in Africa," 72.

exercise a critical function of faith, and not be an element of the established system.[125] He is not interested in any romanticization of the past, whether the romanticization is of ecclesiastical glory or African indigenous cultures, as his critical attitude towards political philosophies (like Negritude and Consciencism) purportedly deriving from African traditions shows. When he depicts *negritude* as "a system belonging to ivory tower intellectuals,"[126] his point is to show that the rhetoric of authenticity amounts to nothing in an environment of general dependence and insufficiency. The African, for him, has come a long way. "It is no longer a matter of having our rights (as Africans) acknowledged. It is a matter of exercising them."[127]

A Critical Evaluation of Ela's Theology

Jean-Marc Ela is an important voice in African Christian theology. His theological reflections must be taken seriously, if the search for a truly inculturated Church is to bear fruit. But his theology is not without some difficulties. His idea of history, which is uncritical, and his program of liturgical reforms have been very problematic. His Christology is also very controversial. He has been criticized for equating the oppressed with Jesus Christ in his theology.[128] "It is correct to say that God demonstrates profound concern for the oppressed, especially as seen in the Exodus, the prophets, and the life of Jesus, but to equate the oppressed to Jesus Christ is a theological misnomer." [129] Equating the oppressed with Jesus amounts not only to granting "messianic qualities" to the oppressed, but is also to confuse and blur the distinction between the oppressed and Jesus Christ.[130] There is also what critics have identified as Ela's extreme historicizing of the eschatological hope. While Ela is to be applauded for recognizing that the Christian life is moving in the direction of Christ in whom all converges, his insistence that salvation does not exist outside the world and history is hard to defend. "It is correct to insist that salvation must be made visible in the here and now but to limit it to the here and now negates an important

---

125. Ela, *African Cry*, 50.
126. Hoekema, "Faith and Freedom in Post-Colonial African Politics," 39.
127. See Magesa, Review of *African Cry*, 255.
128. Ngong, "The Theologian as Missionary," 17.
129. Ibid.
130. Ibid., paraphrasing Bosch, *Transforming Mission*, 443–44.

The Problematic of African Theology of Inculturation

aspect of the Christian faith."[131] The eschatological hope of Christianity—that there is another reality besides this visible and tangible world— cannot be reduced to this world.[132] There is also "Ela's calumniation of Western Christianity as a 'decadent and decomposing Church,'"[133] a calumniation that is not peculiar to him alone but common among African theologians: "Because of the historical problems that have characterized the relation between Africa and the West, many African theologians came to think that authentic African theology must repudiate Western theology, especially Western rationalism. It is indeed correct to insist that Christianity must be given an African color, but pitting African Christianity against Western Christianity insists on a false dichotomy, which… does not strengthen the case for African liberation."[134] Finally, there is the important fact that missing in Ela's discussion "are concrete indications of what is to, or can replace the foreign elements and how they ought to be implemented."[135] John Mbiti has correctly observed that while the theoretical side of Ela's work is convincing, "we are left in doubt on the practical side."[136] Would semiotics help ameliorate these shortcomings? In the next section we shall situate or correlate Ela's theology within the context of Bakhtinian notion of discourse and speech act in order to make him tenable.

These shortcomings notwithstanding, Ela's point that what is generally considered to be African theology was developed within the context of Western missionary practice and his point that the theological paradigm falls short because it does not take into consideration African cultures and traditions cannot be easily dismissed. It is this befuddlement that a theological paradigm meant to serve the needs of a people in a continent beset by poverty and incalculable human miseries lacks the mechanism to address or ameliorate their material needs that led him to suggest an alternative—a theology that fuses inculturation with liberation (an idea we shall take up, albeit in a semiotic way in chapter six). Ela is also to be commended for pointing out that since the encounter between Africa and the West has been characterized by oppression, domination, and exploitation, the Church has to do more than preach about the salvation of souls

131. Ibid., 17.
132. Ibid.
133. Ibid.
134. Ibid.
135. Mbiti, "Ascents in African Theology," 106.
136. Ibid.

hereafter, but be committed to improving the lots of African peoples.[137] The Church must "be a social force, a protest against the established order, the conscience of the conscienceless society, the voice of the voiceless."[138] But what Ela fails to point out is that the Church has also played a prophetic role in Africa. Many examples abound of the Church's prophetic and mediating role in African socio-political life. In apartheid South Africa for example, Churches operating under the umbrella of the South African Council of Churches (SACC), under the leadership of Desmond Tutu and Beyers Naude, together with the heroic actions and sacrifices of ordinary citizens of South Africa, made the country ungovernable for the apartheid leaders.[139] A little nuance here may be helpful. While *SACC's "prophetic" role in the struggle for liberation of South Africa is a good example of what it means for liberation to be part and parcel of inculturation, their heroic actions does not in any way diminish Ela's point because the response of different religious institutions in South Africa to the system of apartheid varied significantly from the overt or tacit support of the Dutch Reformed Church to the outright rejection of SACC.* The Dutch Reformed Church—the most powerful religious body in South Africa at the time not only supported the system of apartheid but also used the Bible to justify its claim that apartheid was integral to the mission of the Church. Most of the white minorities, including presidents and prime ministers of the apartheid regime, came from the Dutch Reformed Church. Many of the whites who appeared before the Truth and Reconciliation Commission for murder and violation of human rights at the end of apartheid[140] have confessed to receiving their "spiritual inspiration" from their Church.[141] This in itself validates Ela's point that the church cannot embark on a program of liturgical adaptation when the mass of the citizenry are in economic and political bondage. How, for example, can a theologian speak of inculturation and Africanization to a Black South

---

137. Ngong, "The Theologian as Missionary," 9.

138. See Healey, Review of *African Cry*, 36.

139. Ntarangwi, "African Christianity, Politics, and Socioeconomic Realities," 9.

140. The perpetrators of apartheid were offered conditional amnesty and were required to apply for amnesty individually. In their application they must show that violations of human right were politically motivated and appear in a public hearing to disclose the whole truth of their involvement in human rights abuses. See Gade, "Restorative Justice and the South African Truth and Reconciliation Process," 11.

141. The Dutch Reformed Church was expelled from the World Council of Churches (WCC) in the 1980s and only rejected apartheid as a sin in 1992, two years after the release of Nelson Mandela from jail.

African without making the liberation of the South African from the system of apartheid an integral part of the quest itself?

Christian theology must not only address political liberation, it must also attend to social and economic issues like poverty, famine, war, denial of women's rights, child exploitation, and the perennial struggle for justice. Like Black South Africans who saw political resistance against apartheid as part of the struggle for Africanization, Africans (sub-Saharan Africans in particular) in general see resistance to unjust colonial and postcolonial structures as something "rooted in religious symbols and narratives, especially the promises of God liberating the enslaved and the prophetic demands of justice."[142] This is what Ela was getting at when he insists that faith, in a climate of oppression, must engage politics or risk becoming meaningless. Ela's "preferential option for the poor" (to use a phrase that was adopted at Puebla, Mexico, in 1979 by the General Conference of Latin American Roman Catholic bishops and now commonly used in papal encyclicals, ecclesiastical conferences, and synods) should not be mistaken for *ressentiment* in Friedrich Nietzsche's (1844–1900) sense of "a subtle but powerful revenge of the weak against the strong."[143] Rather, Ela's commitment to the poor flows from that compassionate spirit (for both rich and poor) that should animate authentic Christian spirituality—the unrestricted act of understanding, valuing and loving that flows from the knowledge of God. It is, as it were, Ela's response to the question whether it is good and valuable "to live authentically in response to the questions which arise from the concrete historical circumstances in which one finds oneself."[144]

Ela's contention that there be no disjunction between inculturation and liberation seem today to be mainstream because contemporary Africans do not see disconnection between liberation and inculturation or faith and politics. A recent survey of Pentecostals in ten randomly chosen African countries carried out in 2007 shows that eighty- three percent, seventy-five percent, and sixty-three percent of Christians in Kenya, Nigeria, and South

---

142. Shore, "Christianity and Justice in the South African Truth and Reconciliation Commission," 169.

143. See Byrne, "Ressentiment and the Preferential Option for the Poor," 215. Byrne explains that it was in critiquing morality in general that Nietzsche took over the French word "ressentiment," which, although it literally means "re-feeling," connotes "a particular feeling that is being re-felt, namely impotence." Nietzsche, as Byrne correctly points out, used it to denote "a denigration of certain values arising out of recollected feelings of injury, insult, or impotence." See also Nietzsche, *On the Genealogy of Morals*.

144. Byrne, "Ressentiment and the Preferential Option for the Poor," 219.

Africa, respectively, expect religion to play a vital role in politics and public life.[145] In fact, "many Africans have asked church people to chair national conferences."[146] There are many examples from the 1980s to the present. In Benin Republic, Isidore de Sousa, the Archbishop of Cotonou was asked to preside over the national conference as president of the Haut Conseil de la Republique and oversee the transition process.[147] There was also the case of Basile Mve Engone, the bishop of Oyem, Gabon, and those of Sanouko Kpodzo, bishop of Atakpame, Togo, Ernest Kombo, bishop of Owando in the Congo, and Laurent Monsengwo Pasinya, archbishop of Kisangani of the former Zaire, now Congo Democratic Republic who all presided over national conferences that were designed to halt their countries slide to anarchy.[148] In South Africa Archbishop Desmond Tutu also chaired the post-apartheid Truth and Justice Commission in the 1990s. This suggests that the average African has confidence in the church. This confidence must be a catalyst for the church to pursue an inculturation theology that cannot be limited to the religious sphere alone, but rather a theology that penetrates all the areas of African life.[149] Archbishop Desmond Tutu has more recently espoused this view, suggesting that liberation and inculturation are not mutually exclusive. They are rather a "series of concentric circles of which Black theology is the inner and smaller circle."[150]

To take our apartheid-era example a step further, one of the criticisms leveled against the post-Apartheid Truth and Justice Commission is that justice was sacrificed to create a new South African government. The Truth and Justice Commission in fact "was the result of the political negotiation between Nelson Mandela's African National Congress and F. W. de Klerk's National Party, which ended over forty years of apartheid. In 1995, one of the first acts of Mandela's newly elected government was to sign into law the Promotion of National Unity and Reconciliation Act, the legislation that established the [Commission]."[151] Critics allege that the

---

145. Ntarangwi, "African Christianity, Politics, and Socioeconomic Realities," 6–7.

146. Bujo, *Africa Theology in Its Social Context*, 10.

147. Gifford, "Democratization and the Churches," 1.

148. Ibid.

149. Bujo, *Africa Theology in Its Social Context*, 10.

150. Bediako, *Jesus and the Gospel in Africa*, 49, quoting Tutu, "Black Theology and African Theology—Soul mates or Antagonists?," 54.

151. Shore, "Christianity and Justice in the South African Truth and Reconciliation Commission," 161.

Commission's amnesty provision was based on Christian concept of forgiveness and reconciliation, which greatly undermined traditional African notion of punishment and vengeance (retributive justice).[152] The Truth and Justice Commission in turn responded by pointing out how its path to peace and reconciliation has roots in African indigenous cultures through congruence with *Ubuntu*.[153] Ubuntu[154] is an ethic based on an African worldview and anthropology. The word derives from "the Zulu and Xhosa languages and has no direct English translation. It can be translated from the Xhosa axiom, *umuntu ngumuntu ngabanye bantu*, 'people are people through other people.'"[155] *Ubuntu* is the African notion of interconnectedness, "the idea that no one can be healthy when the community is sick. '*Ubuntu* says I am human only because you are human. If I undermine your humanity, I dehumanize myself.' It characterizes justice as community restoration – the rebuilding of the community to include those harmed or formerly excluded".[156] It is this connection to *Ubuntu* that is responsible for the tendency among African leaders (like Julius Nyerere in Tanzania and Steve Biko in South Africa)[157] to move towards Africanization—their own way of bringing an end to the experience of alienation and acculturation in the post-colonial era.[158] In like manner, we can also make the argument that Ela's notion of "liberation" is rooted in Ubuntu. His notion of "liberation," like Ubuntu, may be relatively new in African theological discourse, but the spirit is not; it is embedded in traditional African concept of interrelatedness. One thing that Ela did not point out that needs to be made explicit is that true African liberation is not possible without rediscovering deeply rooted traditional cultural values,[159] something we shall consider

---

152. See Wilson, *The Politics of Truth and Reconciliation in South Africa*; "Reconciliation and Revenge in Post-Apartheid South Africa; and Mamdani, "Reconciliation without Justice."

153. The idea that there is a congruence between justice and *ubuntu* is also presented in the Truth and Reconciliation Commission Report in the section entitled "*Ubuntu*: Promoting Restorative Justice."

154. See Gade, "The Historical Development of the Written Discourses on *Ubuntu*"; and Gade, "What is *Ubuntu*?"

155. Shore, "Christianity and Justice in the South African Truth and Reconciliation Commission" 166.

156. Yamamoto, "Race Apologies," 47–88.

157. See Nyerere, *Freedom and Socialism*; and Biko, *I Write What I Like*.

158. Gade, "The Historical Development of the Written Discourses on Ubuntu," 23.

159. Bujo, *Africa Theology in its Social Context*, 10.

in the next chapter in our discussion of reasons for the growth of African Independent Churches (AICs).

Conclusion

What we have in Jean-Marc Ela's "Shade-Tree" theology is a political and/or grass root theology intentionally done in the context of the African village. Its approach is experiential and context driven. It is meant to be an alternative to the abstract non-experiential theology that does not engage African life situations. Since theology, systematic theology at least, must address a particular situation and catalyzes an alternative situation that closely approximates the reign of God in human affairs,[160] Ela's approach is to show why it is futile to do African theology in a context far removed from the African social milieu. In Lonerganian terms, Ela is doing differentiation of consciousness—the self-knowledge that understands the different realms of meaning and knows how to shift from one realm of meaning to another.[161] In showing how African theology can move from the abstract European non-experiential context to a concrete one that engages the African in his or her specific cultural context, Ela attempts to move theology as done in Africa to a new stage of meaning—the level of reflective rational self-consciousness. His insistence that theology be approached in a way that speaks to real life-situations of the African is not only valuable and insightful, but is also validated by the science of semiotics that approaches cultures as a cultural system in which all parts of human life are interrelated in a meaningful way.[162]

Ela's call for rational self-consciousness and his attempt to bring African theology to the levels of the time, can benefit, as we shall show in later chapters, from the practical common sense approach suggested by Bernard Lonergan (1904–84). Like Lonergan who "emphasized history as a major concern, spoke eloquently and one might say prophetically about bias and its socially distorting influences, proclaimed the possibility of healing in history, and turned to economic theory partly at least out of a profound concern for the social order,"[163] Ela spoke about the possibility of healing in history but spoke of this possibility only in terms of "libera-

---

160. Doran, "Lonergan and Balthasar: Methodological Considerations," 63.
161. Lonergan, *Method in Theology*, 84.
162. See Geertz, "Religion as a Cultural System," 1–46.
163. Doran, "Lonergan and Balthasar," 83.

The Problematic of African Theology of Inculturation

tion." What he termed liberation is his way of overcoming all the biases (European and African) that have colluded to distort the social fabric of African life. Healing and redemption, for Ela, is tied to economic, social, and political development.

Ela raises some crucial questions that can help realize the new praxis of meaning that contemporary African situation demands: How do we re-evaluate the Christian message in a world of cultural pluralism in such a way that it does not become an alien or disrupting influence to African cultural identity? How is the African to live and express his or her faith so that the Christian faith does not become an alienating reflection of a foreign world behaving aggressively towards indigenous African customs and beliefs?[164] A semiotic approach to the theology of inculturation can validate Ela's key insights and ground transcendentally his main contention that liberation and inculturation not be viewed as two opposing forces for which the African is forced to choose between the one or the other. For the matter of theology of inculturation in Africa can best be sorted out semiotically. Ela's criticism that the brand of theology bequeathed to Africa was in large part based on abstraction and theory far removed from the worldview of the African, for example, can be understood clearly when juxtaposed with the insights of linguistic pragmatists. Their insights on the linguistic-pragmatic constitution of the subject as a social person makes it imperative to attend to the matter of subjectivity of language. The American philosopher and gender theorist, Judith Butler (b. 1956), for example, has correctly pointed out that if we think "that the analysis of social conditions doesn't include the analysis of psychic suffering or, conversely, that the analysis of psychic suffering involves the suspension of critical analysis of social conditions, then we're lost. Suffering is both the effect and modality of oppressive social conditions, so we cannot really think the conditions without the suffering."[165]

Ela's larger issue that a person as a social being is constituted in the concrete act of his or her way of doing theology and therefore that theology done in Africa must be intelligible and must speak to the issues of the poor and marginalized in Africa is very loaded and can also be sorted out semiotically. The Russian literary critic, philosopher and semiotician, Mikhail Bakhtin (1895–1975), speaking of novelistic discourse, suggests that it is

---

164. Ela, "Ancestors and African Faith: An African Problem," 34.

165. Bell, "New Scenes of Vulnerability, Agency and Plurality: An Interview with Judith Butler," 135.

a diversity of social speech types, diversity of languages, and a diversity of individual voices artistically organized. Drawing from Fyodor Dostoevsky's (1821–81) novels, Bakhtin develops "the theses of dialogism and polyphony, which deal with the harmonizing and autonomy of characters' voices and emphasize contextual relations."[166] Polyphony is his umbrella term for different interactive processes of all the different voices in artistic discourse. He sometimes uses the term "heteroglossia" for this interaction of voices that seek a harmonious whole, at times using the term as a theoretical model for dialogue.[167] "The individual speeches, genres, and languages with their own voices in a literary work strive for harmony, which unites the structure of the whole."[168]

Bakhtin calibrates "more systematically ideas about the different voices, otherness, and polyphony" inherent in novels,[169] speaking of a literary work as a whole as "a phenomenon multiform in style and variform in speech and voice. In it the investigator is confronted with several heterogeneous stylistic unities, often located on different linguistic levels and subject to different stylistic controls."[170] He also points out that throughout its historical existence every language has its own internal stratification: language of the authorities, languages that serve a given socio-political purpose of the day, languages of generations and age groups, professional jargon, generic language, etc. These, according to Bakhtin, are the indispensable prerequisites of the novel as a genre. The novel orchestrates all its themes, i.e., authorial speech, speeches of the narrators, inserted genre, etc, by means of social diversity of speech. For this reason, Bakhtin speaks of novel as having an inherent heteroglossia—what permits a multiplicity of social voices and interrelationships. "These distinctive links and interrelationships between utterances and languages, this movement of the theme through different languages and speech types, its dispersion into the rivulets and droplets of social heteroglossia, its dialogization—this is the basic distinguishing feature of the stylistics of the novel."[171]

---

166. Mladenov, "Unlimited Semiosis and Heteroglosia (C. S. Peirce and M. M. Bakhtin)," 441. See Bakhtin, *Problems of Dostoevsky's Poetics*.

167. Mladenov, "Unlimited Semiosis and Heteroglosia," 442.

168. Ibid.

169. Ibid.

170. Bakhtin, *The Dialogic Imagination: Four Essays*, 261.

171. Ibid., 263.

Pushing the concept of heteroglossia further, Bakhtin insists that every given sentence reflects, not only linguistic information, i.e., phonological, morphological, and syntactic, but also something about the speakers ideological commitments to a specific social structure, say for example class, tribe, or ethnic group.[172] Bakhtin calls this concept of the relationship of the speaker's ideology "voice." A speaker's "ideology is always formed in political conflict or tension with the ideology of another speaker positioned in a different social group, so that voice is also properly understood only in relation to dialogue, or a colloquy of voices, rather than monologue."[173] Bakhtin's idea of literary work as a speech act is similar to that of the American literary critic, Kenneth Burke (1897–1993) for whom a poem is not simply an expression of an emotion or an idea, "but a communicative act—a framework that turns the poem into a social act comprising an addressor, an addressee, their social relationship, the channel or medium of their communication, and the effects the poem may have on a wider social context."[174]

Bakhtin's concept of heteroglossia, i.e., the "many-language-ness of artistic discourse,"[175] does not presuppose two but three or more dialogue partners. Dialogue, as Michael Holquist reminds us, is not a dyadic or binary phenomenon but a polyphonic concept engaged in a relentless inquiry that for schematic purposes can be reduced to a minimum of three elements: an utterance, a reply, and a relation between the utterance and the reply. "It is the relation that is most important of the three, for without it the other two would have no meaning."[176]

In theological terms, the Bakhtinian notion of dialogue and speech acts provides a good context for understanding Ela's "shade-tree theology," Ela's own alternative to what he thought was abstract theology of Europeans. Ela, as it were, refuses to accept reduction of theological "voices" to a single one. Theological discourse (whether arcane or abstract), like a literary text, is an act of communication. It emerges out of a communicative context. It is also at one and the same time a response to someone's discourse and an anticipation of future response. Ela's "shade-tree theology" is his act of communication in response to other theological "voices."

---

172. Caton, *"Peaks of Yemen I Summon,"* 255.
173. Ibid.
174. Caton, "What Is an 'Authorizing Discourse?,'" 40–41.
175. Mladenov, "Unlimited Semiosis and Heteroglosia," 442.
176. Holquist, *Dialogism*, 28.

Just as no communicative act should be reified or seen as a morphological type, there is no room for a reified European theology in Ela's shade-tree theology.

Bakhtin had suggested that when someone else's ideological discourse is internally persuasive for us and acknowledged by us that such discourse may be of decisive significance in the evolution of an ideological consciousness.[177] Ela was guided by a similar principle that "dependence on views thought up by others ought to be replaced by context-committed insight, rather than propositions disconnected from the varying here and now."[178] A good case in point is the *Lineamenta* to the 1994 African synod that was prepared in Rome. In the same way he dismisses any theology that does not emerge from the African context, Ela deployed the document as lacking attention to the real problems affecting the continent because it does not "speak" the African language.[179]

Language, the basis of human communication, is always dialogic in nature. Heteroglossia, for Bakhtin, is "another's speech in another's language, serving to express authorial intentions but in a refracted way."[180] In the Bakhtinian notion of speech acts "what is realized in the novel is the process of coming to know one's own language as it is perceived in someone else's language, coming to know one's own belief system in someone else's system."[181] If what takes place within the novel is "an ideological translation of another's language and an overcoming of its otherness—an otherness that is only contingent, external, illusory,"[182] and if the ideological becoming of a human being is the process of selectively assimilating the words of others,[183] then Ela's "shade-tree theology" is an attempt to overcome an ideological divide in what he sees as mainstream European oriented theology. Mainstream theology, as he sees it, is theoretical and arm chair dilanttete, done from a position of privilege and power. "Shade-tree theology" is, for Ela, a viable alternative; it is oral, grass root, and addresses specific needs of people on the margins. Ela is seeking what Bakhtin calls "internally persuasive discourse," as opposed to "externally authoritative"

---

177. Bakhtin, *The Dialogic Imagination*, 345.
178. Hetjke, "Thinking in the Scene of Disaster," 62.
179. Bujo, *Africa Theology in Its Social Context*, 10.
180. Bakhtin, *The Dialogic Imagination*, 324.
181. Ibid., 365.
182. Ibid.
183. Ibid., 341.

The Problematic of African Theology of Inculturation

discourse that is affirmed through assimilation. Authoritative discourse, for Bakhtin, cannot be represented (easily acquired); it is only transmitted (forcefully enforced).[184] It is not grounded in reflective understanding and does not lead to self-affirmation of the knower.

> The importance of struggling with another's discourse, its influence in the history of an individual's coming to ideological consciousness, is enormous. One's own discourse and one's own voice, although born of another or dynamically stimulated by another, will sooner or later begin to liberate themselves from the authority of the other's discourse. This process is made more complex by the fact that a variety of alien voices enter into the struggle for influence within an individual's consciousness.[185]

Shade-tree theology is Ela's internally persuasive discourse in the Bakhtinian sense. It is Ela's way of affirming himself as a knower and intelligent inquirer, which theology that is authentic demands. He gives genetic priority to oral expression of theology over formal theoretical one because of the proximity of oral expression to the conscious act of understanding,[186] and by so doing draws a contrast between his theological method and those of the likes of Jacques Derrida (1930–2004) who privilege the written text over and above the oral.[187] Ela's context-based oral theology also falls within the purview of the last stage of Lonergan's functional specialty "communications." Communications, is the final stage in which theological reflections bear fruit because it is not apart from the preceding research, interpretation, history, dialectic, foundations, doctrines, and systematics.[188] Ela's insistence that "shade-tree theology" be oral or "communicated" has to do with the fact that, since it is not to be "transmitted," but "represented," it comes from where the faith lives, in the life-situation of the community of faith.[189] To speak of theology as oral, as the Ghanaian theologian Kwame Bediako explains, may give the misleading impression that the oral phase deals with a transition stage, a movement to academic or written theology—the real theology.[190] But the internally persuasive discourse, in the

---

184. Ibid., 344.
185. Ibid., 348.
186. See Rixon, "Derida and Lonergan on Human Development," 223.
187. See Derrida, *Limited Inc*.
188. Lonergan, *Method in Theology*, 355.
189. Bediako, *Jesus and the Gospel in Africa*, 17.
190. Ibid.

everyday rounds of our consciousness as Bakhtin has shown, "is half-ours and half-someone else's."[191] It is, in other words, always dialogical. Therefore, grassroots and academic theology, like the themes of liberation and inculturation, are not two polar opposites, but two sides of the same reality. "When the two aspects are working well, theology acquires its authentic character—as a task, not of scholars alone, but of a community of believers who share in a common context, and are committed to the task of bringing the Gospel into contact with the questions and issues of their context."[192] Grass root theology "liberates the academic theologian from the false burden of having to 'construct a theology' as if by himself or herself. For its part, academic theology has the important role of understanding, clarifying and demonstrating the universal and academic significance of grass roots theology in the interest of the wider missionary task of encountering the world with the Gospel."[193] In the chapters that follow we shall draw on the works of semioticians to elucidate the point that convergence or dialogue between academic theology and practical grass root oral theology is necessary for the construction of the theology of inculturation, African theology of inculturation in particular.

---

191. Bakhtin, *Dialogical Imagination*, 345.
192. Bediako, *Jesus and the Gospel in Africa*, 18.
193. Ibid., 18.

2

Single Story Narratives and Resilience of African Independent Churches

IN THE LAST CHAPTER we alluded to an often neglected but nonetheless significant trend in postcolonial African Church, the explicit involvement of the church in the public sphere. We used pin-pointed examples to show how the church has played significant roles in preventing a deadlock and averting anarchy in times of crisis.[1] Still Jean-Marc Ela thinks the Church has not done enough to liberate Africans from unjust social structures. He thinks the Church can do more than occasionally intervene and that the Church can play a more active role in the liberation of Africans from unjust social and political structures if the program of inculturation is given the attention it demands. He paves the way by constructing a political theology that tries to fuse the themes of liberation and inculturation, two themes that at times seem divergent. He wants to do for African theology what Johann Baptist Metz and Jurgen Moltmann did in Germany by re-contextualizing South American liberation theology in light of the unjust structures of German society.

One of Ela's main contributions is that he shows how it is no longer true to claim, as John de Gruchy did, that "theologians outside of southern Africa have not generally developed a critical political theology able to help the churches resist tyranny, overcome ethnic tension, and establish a just democratic order."[2] Ela's other main contribution is his shade-tree theology that contains both his program of liberation vis-à-vis inculturation and his alternative to European style academic theology. To amplify this important contribution to African Christian theology, we suggested

---

1. See Gifford, *African Christianity*, 21.

2. De Gruchy, *Christianity and Democracy*, 191, cited in Gifford, *African Christianity*, 30.

that Ela's theological reflections can benefit from the semiotics of Mikhail Bakhtin, particularly the Bakhtinian notion of language and speech acts. Discourse, for Bakhtin, is about dialogicality in the sense that every utterance is at one and the same time a response to a previous utterance and still an anticipation of a future objection. Bahktin also shows that power inheres in dialogical act in so far as one's discourse is framed as an anticipatory act with intent to influence someone else. Bahktin's privileging of heteroglossia (different ways of speaking) over monoglossia (one way of speaking) and his argument that we resist the temptation to move from a heteroglossic to monoglossic situation reinforces one of Ela's primary contentions that African Christian theology cannot forever remain a cloned European theology and that an African Christian theology that addresses the problem of the African in his/her specific social location is urgently needed, if Christian theology is to become meaningful to the African. Thus, in this chapter we take a fresh look at how a discourse or narrative is an attempt to frame an ideology and how semiotics can help African Christian theology resist the danger of monoglossia.

Search for a World Church

Ela was not the first to point out that the theology that was used in the European evangelization of Africa was monoglossic, to use Bakhtin's term. There were many others who sensed this danger and summarily dismissed the theology that was bequeathed to Africa in the wake of Christian expansion to Africa as "a prefabricated" and "book theology."[3] The general concern remains the same—that Christian theology risks becoming meaningless to the African, unless the Christian message is truly inculturated. The general feeling was that when the last European missionary left the African soil their African protégés continued their "book theology," essentially reducing African Christian theology to either what they were told by Europeans or what they read in books written by European theologians.[4] Similar concerns have been voiced collectively by theologians from developing nations who came together under the umbrella of Association of Third World Theologians (EATWOT). At their 1976 meeting in Dar-es-Salam, Tanzania, they denounced what they saw as existing "colonial

---

3. Bediako, *Jesus and the Gospel of Africa*, 16, quoting Idowu, *Towards an Indigenous Church*, 22.

4. Bediako, *Jesus and the Gospel of Africa*, 23.

exploitation" and Western Christian missionaries "services to Western imperialism."[5] They also protested what they saw as the other related problem—that rather than be a liberating force against suffering and violence, Western Christianity has been used to reconcile Africans and indigenous peoples to hardship in this life.[6]

EATWOT is not alone in their demand for a truly inculturated Church. Before the Second Vatican Council Karl Rahner had observed that "the actual concrete activity of the Church in its relation to the world outside of Europe was in fact the activity of an export firm which exported a European religion as a commodity it did not really want to change but sent throughout the world together with the rest of the culture and civilization it considered superior."[7] At the time of Rahner's writing the Catholic Church was revising its code of Canon law. Rahner raised many critical questions regarding both the application of Canon law and the entire Church's structure and style of governance: "will the new Code of Canon Law being prepared in Rome avoid the danger of being once again a Western Code that is imposed on the world Church in Latin America, Asia, and Africa? Do not the Roman Congregations still have the mentality of a centralized bureaucracy which thinks it knows best what serves the kingdom of God and the salvation of souls throughout the world, and in such decisions takes the mentality of Rome or Italy in a frighteningly naive way as a self-evident standard?"[8] In what seemed at the time to be radical and cutting edge, Rahner also spoke of cultures in the plural, recognizing that contemporary cultures are involved in a process of change at a rate and degree previously unknown and went on to suggest that the church must be inculturated if it is to be a world Church.[9] The truth is that there are some theoretical problems that need to be resolved before the Church can be truly inculturated and become a world church in the true sense of the word. The first might be a critical re-telling of African stories, because our lives and our cultures are composed of many overlapping stories.[10] Re-telling of these stories may lead to narratives that can help upturn past myths that have been constructed to

---

5. Gifford, *African Churches*, 31, quoting Torres and Fabella, *The Emergent Gospel*, 266.

6. Gifford, *African Churches*, 31.

7. Rahner, "Towards a Fundamental Interpretation of Vatican II," 717.

8. Ibid., 717–78.

9. Ibid., 718.

10. See Adichie, "The Danger of a Single Story."

aid the plundering of the continent. It is also hoped that re-telling of these stories will help overcome the dramatic breakdown of traditional African identities and boundaries that became commonplace following Berlin Conference (1882) and by so doing help clarify what makes African identities and realities unique in the modern world. As Eduardo Mendieta correctly observed, we are continuously involved in not only "negotiating our localities or positions vis-à-vis race, class, gender, and nationality, but also positionalities within a geopolitical system."[11]

Narratives, Discourse, and Injurious Speech

One of the functions of storytelling is the "ability to bring some theoretical concept down to earth so that it can be grasped at several levels."[12] When properly constructed stories can give a people a sense of order, identity, and meaning.[13] But the flip side is also that stories can morph into a myth that is believed and enlarged over time and become a form of violence. Violence is not only physical. Violence can and do take many forms. Violence can be about denigrating a people through narratives that psychologically destroy and diminish their dignity.[14] Oftentimes people coming out of colonial experience try to tell their own story their own way and by so doing reaffirm the identity they fear is being lost.[15] "When Greenland, despite its tiny population of fifty-six thousand and very limited income resources, voted in 2008 to loosen its ties with Denmark, the premier commented that at last Greenlanders could tell their own story to the world."[16]

One of the relics of Enlightenment thinking is the false notion that "the self is an autonomous, stable, structural entity composed of factors and traits that 'add up' to a total person without their active involvement and transcending their particular place in culture, language, and history."[17] The Nigerian writer and novelist, Chimamanda Adichie, captures this in her well narrated poem titled "the Danger of a Single Story."[18] Adichie backs up

11. Mendietta, "Identities," 409.
12. Arbuckle, *Culture, Inculturation, and Theologians*, 63.
13. Ibid., 64.
14. Ibid., 59.
15. Arcbuckle, *Culture, Inculturation, Theologians*, 65.
16. Ibid.
17. Ibid., 66,
18. See Adichie, "The Danger of a Single Story."

the Bahktinian claim that what takes place within narratives are ideological translations of another's language. She insists that when others tell our story it is usually not the whole story because often times something is left out. Using Africa as an example, Adichie correctly makes the point that when the African story is told by outsiders it is almost always exclusively told as that of a continent beset by violence, famine, poverty, wars, and diseases. While Adichie is not denying that the realities of war, famine, poverty, and disease are present in Africa, she insists that this cannot be the whole story and suggests instead a heteroglossic reading (to use Bahktinian term again) of African stories. She maintains that there is more to African story than these. Using her own life examples, she tells how our lives and cultures comprise of many overlapping layers of stories. For example, Adichie claims to have only found her own authentic cultural voice when she paid attention to the multi-layered stories of her culture. She warns that if we hear only a single story about another person or culture we risk a critical misunderstanding.

Adichie's upbringing, as she describes it in "The Dangers of a Single Story," was that of a conventional middle class Nigerian family. She was eight years old when her family secured the services of a male house help, named Jide. Adichie recounts how she felt pity for Jide's family because all she heard about Jide's family was how poor they were. It had not occurred to her that anyone in Jide's family was capable of doing anything else. Poverty was her only single story of Jide's family. But this soon changed when she (Adichie) and her mother visited Jide's family and she saw to her surprise that poverty was neither the defining story of Jide's life nor the defining story of their family.

Adichie, according to her own account, left Nigeria for the United States for studies when she was nineteen. In school she found out that her own roommate had a single story of Africa, like she (Adichie) had of Jide's family. Her roommate never thought Africans spoke English and so was shocked when she heard Adichie speak English. According to Adichie, her roommate also assumed that because she (Adichie) was coming from Africa that she did not know how to use common household things like stove and dish washer. So Adichie's roommate felt enormous pity for her even before she got to know her. According to Adichie, this was because her roommate had a single story of Africa—a story of catastrophe. The roommate's default position towards Adichie was that of a patronizing well-meaning pity. In the roommate's single story of Africa there was no possibility of Africans being similar to her in any way, no possibility of feelings more complex than pity, no possibility of a connection as equals in the community of persons. Adichie recalls that it was after she had spent some years in the US as an African that things began to crystalize for her and she began to understand her roommate's response to her. She herself then realized that had she not grown up in Nigeria, had all she knew about Africa been from popular images as her roommate did she too would think that "Africa was a place of beautiful landscapes, beautiful animals, and incomprehensible people fighting senseless wars, dying of poverty and AIDS, unable to speak for themselves, and waiting to be saved by a kind white foreigner."[19] She realized that she too would have seen Africa in the same way she in her own childhood days saw Jide's family, i.e., as being defined by a single story.

Adichie correctly points out in this poem that the origin of this single-story narrative, as far as Africa is concerned, goes back to Western historiography, particularly the writings of John Locke (1632–1704) and Georg Friedrich Hegel (1770–1831) who portrayed Africa as a place of negativity, darkness, and indifference. Their view of Africa was, in the words of the English poet and novelist Rudyard Kipling (1865–1936), "half devil, half child." Adichie claimed to have realized much later that her American college roommate must have heard different versions of this same single story all through her life. She draws from this that perhaps the way to create a single story is to portray a people as one thing and as only one thing and then tell the story over and over again and the people eventually become that thing.

Adichie's poem is also important on another level because it captures the connection between single-story narratives and power—the capacity to influence. It is impossible to talk about single-story narrative without talking about power because stories are defined by the principle of power: how they are told, who tells them, when they are told, and how many versions of the same story are told and retold.[20] These factors, according to Adichie, are really dependent on power. The French philosopher, philologist, and literary critic Michel Foucault (1926–84) is famous for distinguishing different kinds of power: position power, which is the ability to use power deriving from the status a person holds within an organization; coercive power, which is the ability to force people to act through fear of punishment; personal power, a person's capacity to influence because of his or her personal qualities; unilateral power, occurs when a person refuses to be influenced

19. Ibid.
20. Ibid.

by others; and reciprocal power, ability to influence and be influenced by others.[21] Adichie uses power somewhat differently from Foucault. Power here is the ability not only to tell the story of another person but to make it the definitive story of that person.[22] This ability, according to Adichie, works with a simple psychology: if you want to dispossess a people, you tell their story and start with "secondly." Start, for example, she buttresses, the story with the arrows of Native Americans and not with the arrival of the British and you have an entirely different story. Or start the story with the failure of African states and not with the colonial creation of African city-states and you have an entirely different story.[23] This is precisely why the Kenyan writer, Ngugi wa Thiong'o argued that "the biggest weapon" used by colonialism against indigenous people is "the cultural bomb... annihilating a people's beliefs in their names, in their languages, in their environment, in their heritage of struggle, in their unity, in their capacities and ultimately in themselves. It makes them see their past as one wasteland of non-achievement... It makes them want to identify themselves with that which is furthest removed from themselves."[24]

How do single stories harm us? What is the extent of our vulnerability to single-story narratives? Could the language hold the key to unlocking the extent of our vulnerability? If we are vulnerable because of the language in which single-story narratives are framed is that not a testament to the fact that we are in some sense linguistic beings and that our vulnerability is in some sense a consequence of our being constituted within the parameters of language?[25] The practice of exclusion and the language of exclusion go hand in hand. Most "exclusionary practices would either not work at all or would work much less smoothly if it were not for the fact that they are supported by exclusionary language and cognition."[26] In the next chapter we will explore the semiotic meaning of language in order to tease out how language, like sign, represents, depicts, and stands for something outside of itself. In her well written essay on the American war against terrorism in

---

21. See Foucault, *Power/Knowledge*; Foucault, *Discipline and Punish*; and *History of Sexuality*, cited in Arbuckle, *Culture, Inculturation, and Theologians*, 38.

22. Adichie, "The Danger of a Single Story."

23. Ibid.

24. Cited in Hillman, "Good News for Every Nation Via Inculturation," 346. See also Wa Thiong'o, *Decolonizing the Mind*, 3.

25. See Butler, *Excitable Speech*.

26. Volff, *Exclusion and Embrace*, 75.

the post 9/11 world, the American philosopher and gender theorist Judith Butler cautions against the frames we use to justify a given position, say for example war or violence. Butler also suggests that considerable attention be paid to the frames we use because "a frame for understanding violence emerges in tandem with the experience, and that the frame works both to preclude certain kinds of questions, certain kinds of historical inquiries, and to function as a moral justification for retaliation."[27] Butler suggests that it is "crucial to attend to this frame, since it decides, in a forceful way, what we can hear, whether a view will be taken as explanation or as exoneration, whether we can hear the difference, and abide by it."[28] Adichie's poem ("The Dangers of a Single Story") is best appreciated within the parameters of what Butler says about linguistic vulnerability and the interpellative power of the frames we use. Butler probes whether the power of language to injure follows from its interpellative power as well as how linguistic agency emerges from the scene of enabling vulnerability.[29] What Adichie calls "a single-story narrative" is that "injurious speech," which according to Butler, derogates and demeans. "Injurious speech" here is to be understood along the lines of what the African-American novelist Toni Morrison (b. 1931) calls "oppressive language." For Morrison, as for Butler, oppressive language does more than represent violence; it is violence itself.[30] "Oppressive language is not a substitute for the experience of violence. It enacts its own kind of violence. Language remains alive when it refuses to 'encapsulate' or 'capture' the events and lives it describes. But when it seeks to effect that capture, language not only loses its vitality, but acquires its own violent force."[31]

Injurious speech then raises the question of which words wound and which representations offend? The use of the term "wound" suggests, for Butler, that "language can act in ways that parallel the infliction of physical pain and injury."[32] Injurious speech, works like physical injury, like a "verbal assault." It produces "physical symptoms that temporarily disable the victim."[33] Butler suggests that aside the metaphor of physical injury, there is no description that is "proper" to linguistic injury. This lack of description

27. Butler, "Explanation and Exoneration, or What Can We Hear," 179.
28. Ibid.
29. Butler, *Excitable Speech*, 2.
30. Ibid., 6.
31. Ibid., 9.
32. Ibid., 4
33. Ibid.

is rather what makes it "more difficult to identify the specificity of linguistic vulnerability over and against physical vulnerability."[34]

The problematic of injurious speech raises for us the need to scrutinize, not only the words with which we address the other, but the mode of address itself—a mode that interpellates and constitutes the one addressed.[35] There is a sense in which one is either sustained or threatened through modes of speech and the frames we use. "To be injured by speech is to suffer a loss of context, that is, not to know where you are. Indeed, it may be that what is unanticipated about the injurious speech act is what constitutes its injury, the sense of putting its addressee out of control."[36] For as Butler explains, to be addressed injuriously is not only to suffer disorientation of one's situation, but also not to know the time and place of injury. Why should the mode in which one is addressed matter? Because to be addressed is not just to be recognized for what one already is, but to "exist" is to be recognized. If language can sustain, then it can also threaten one's existence. "The question of the specific ways that language threatens violence seems bound up with the primary dependency any speaking being has by virtue of the interpellative or constitutive address of the other."[37] Butler contends that even a statement made on the basis of grammar alone that appears to pose no threat may in the end become harmful when it emerges in the act of speaking for the reason that speech act says more or at times says differently that it means to say.[38] Butler suggests, therefore, that it is not easy to determine under what probability certain words will wound and under what circumstances. The "efforts to establish the incontrovertibly wounding power of certain words seem to founder on the question of who does the interpreting of what such words mean and what they perform."[39]

> To argue, on the one hand, that the offensive effect of such words is fully contextual, and that a shift of context can exacerbate or minimize their offensiveness, is still not to give an account of the power that such words are said to exercise. To claim, on the other hand, that some utterances are always offensive, regardless of context, that they carry their context with them in ways that are

34. Ibid.
35. Ibid., 2.
36. Ibid., 4.
37. Ibid., 5–6.
38. Ibid., 10–11.
39. Ibid., 13.

too difficult to shed, is still not to offer a way to understand how context is invoked and restaged at the moment of utterance.[40]

In sum, Butler shows how speech can act injuriously on the one it is directed, the same way that single-story narratives and the frames we use can and do create stereotypes. In both the vulnerability to the other constituted by the prior address or the single story is hardly easy to overcome.[41] The question regarding how the language we use affects others is connected to the question, how does the story we tell affect others? Can one say, as Butler queried, that someone else made up the speech or story or frame that we use and thereby absolve ourselves from blame? In other words, does citationality of discourse dissipate agency and responsibility?[42] Single-story narratives have their origins in bias, particularly what Lonergan calls dramatic bias—scotoma or prejudices that notoriously vitiate theoretical investigations and bias understanding.[43] As Adichie correctly points out, the problem with stereotypes is not that they are untrue but that they are incomplete. They make one story become the only story. Because it lacks a rounded and balanced view, it results in behaviors that generate misunderstanding in oneself and in others.[44] As Adichie carefully puts it, it robs a people of their dignity and makes recognition of our equal humanity difficult in so far as it emphasizes how we are different, rather than how we are similar.[45] It also robs "the development of one's common sense of some part, greater or less, of the corrections and the assurance that result from learning accurately... and from submitting one's own insights to the criticism based on other's experience and development."[46]

As blind spot, single-story narratives often emerge, not as conscious acts, but as something fundamentally unconscious. They lock people up in their own limited vision and deny them access to openness and development.[47] Single story narratives do damage to both objectivity and what Alice M. Ramos poignantly calls "ethics of knowing."[48] Single story narra-

40. Ibid.
41. Ibid., 26.
42. Ibid., 27.
43. Lonergan, *Insight*, 214.
44. Ibid.
45. Adichie, "The Danger of a Single Story."
46. Lonergan, *Insight*, 214–15.
47. Lonergan, *Method in Theology*, 217.
48. Ramos, *Dynamic Transcendentals*, 48.

tives, at their root, hinder not only knowledge, but objectivity of the truth as well. While human beings are conscious of themselves as truth seekers they often fail to see that the truth they grasp from time to time is only a limited reflection of the truth of the whole.[49] Often people "substitute their own subjective understanding of the truth of the whole, which is true enough in terms of their own experience, for 'objective' truth, that which is true even apart from their own (or anyone else's) experience."[50] The distortion of single story narrative, therefore, is akin to the "sight-seeing" (shortsightedness) that Aquinas suggests disposes a person to the vices of lust and cruelty regarding the way things seen are represented.[51] The actual meaning of events that have genuine existential significance in the life of a people always include something more than has been objectified.[52] To return to the question whether the citationality of discourse can absolve one from all responsibility? Butler's useful recommendation is that citationality of discourse works to enhance and intensify our sense of responsibility. "The responsibility of the speaker does not consist of remaking language ex nihilo, but rather of negotiating the legacies of usage that constrain and enable that speaker's speech."[53] To such "negotiation" we turn next.

Attempt at a Balanced Story

Long before the scramble for and partition of Africa (1876–1914), Great Britain "had been exploiting Africa without great opposition and without bothering to govern it for some decades before the scramble."[54] The

---

49. Bracken, "Authentic Subjectivity and Genuine Objectivity," 300.

50. Ibid.

51. Ramos, *Dynamic Transcendentals*, 59. See *Summa Theologiae* II-II. q.167, a.2, ad 2. Aquinas tried to safeguard the objectivity of knowledge by arguing that it is not our knowledge that determines the existence of being but that beings exist independent of our knowing them. In other words, our knowledge is not the measure of things, since things are known only according to the mode of the knower. Our knowing things, therefore, cannot be taken to be their measure in any absolute sense. Referring to the truth of things, Aquinas says things are considered true only to the extent that they conform to the divine mind. For a simplified discussion of the theme or theory of measure in Aquinas and its relationship to infinite and finite beings, see Ramos, *Dynamic Transcendentals*, 27–46.

52. Rahner, "Towards a Fundamental Theological Interpretation of Vatican II," 716.

53. Butler, *Excitable Speech*, 27.

54. Gifford, *African Christianity*, 2.

scramble, which lasted about three decades, was precipitated by mounting pressures from France and Belgium. With the scramble came colonialism, which introduced Western schools, European languages, and European administrative structures.[55] Among its many effects was "the totally artificial boundaries which united at least two but usually many more recognizably distinct 'peoples,' and conversely divided homogeneous groups between two or more different countries."[56] There are also other negative legacies of colonialism beyond the heterogeneity of citizens:

> Colonial administrations were both centralized and authoritarian. Just as important, the rulers manifested a sense of superiority over those they ruled, and power was experienced as coming from above rather than flowing from below. Thus the ruled developed a sense of the state as an alien institution, to be feared but also to be deceived and exploited, since it existed on a plane above the people whom it governed, beyond any chance of control.[57]

Although generally speaking, colonialism had its general features, its effect affected different areas differently, depending on which Western power was controlling the area and which mineral resources could be extracted in the area.[58] By the time most African countries were granted independence, i.e., the end of colonialism (1957–68), "independence coincided with a most important global phenomenon, a period of unparalleled economic growth (1945–75) which achieved the most dramatic, rapid and profound revolution in human affairs of which history has record."[59] The optimism of political and economic liberation that came in the years following independence either did not materialize or it did not take long before things went awry. The reason for the failure of the nation states is beyond the scope of this work.[60] Our point here is to set the context for the colonial state and the postcolonial ones that replaced them. Colonial states, as Paul Gifford correctly captures it,

> had been above all about control: they were essentially about securing the obedience of an alien people. They were hierarchical,

55. Ibid., 3.
56. Ibid.
57. Ibid.
58. Ibid.
59. Ibid., 4.
60. For a detailed discussion of reasons for the failure of the newly independent African nations, see Gifford, *African Christianity*, 5–20.

with their primary aim being the maintenance of order. Moreover, as the colonial states had to pay for themselves, they were geared to extracting resources from the domestic economy, or from the trade flowing from the economy's incorporation into the global trading system. Only after that was the state concerned with the provision of services. So the African state from birth was essentially an agency for control and extraction. There was never any merging of state and society as common expressions of shared values. Thus there has been little in the way of legitimacy, or popular commitment to public institutions.[61]

The historical nonfiction work *The Ghost of Leopold*, by the American journalist Adam Hochschild, underscores the basic fact that the African state was from birth an agency of control and extraction. In this well-written work Hochschild reconstructs colonial atrocities in what was then the Congo Free States (formerly Zaire and now Democratic Republic of the Congo) in the nineteenth and early twentieth century.[62] The Congo Free States were conceived as a pet project of the Belgian monarch, King Leopold II, whose avarice and greed made him to divest the country of its riches and natural resources. The irony here should not be missed. While he held the people in bondage and took to plundering the resources of this region (ironically named the Congo Free States) Leopold was portraying himself at the same time in Europe as a humanitarian. Hochschild estimates that he murdered about ten million Congolese. This and similar stories must be told and retold to get at a nuanced view and avoid "the dangers of a single-story."

Emmanuel Katongole has brilliantly used the event of the Congo Free States as a context or starting point for re-telling the African story. Because "*King Leopold's Ghost* lays claim, not to the unearthing of a forgotten catastrophe, but rather, to an intertextual tradition of humanitarian narratives that Hochschild appropriates, extends, transvalues, and reformulates for the contemporary historical moment"[63] Katongole thinks that the story itself can serve many good lessons, particularly these five:

1. **Colonial Impact, Social Memory, and Forgetfulness**
   The brutal rubber policies that Leopold adopted in the rain forest left many Congolese with raw memories that remained with

---

61. Ibid., 4.
62. See Hochschild, *King Leopold's Ghost*.
63. De Mul, "The Holocaust as a Paradigm for the Congo Atrocities," 601–2.

them for the rest of their lives, something Hochschild saw as the "most murderous part of the European Scramble for Africa."[64] Katongole draws from this that the violence and brutality in Leopold's Congo were not isolated or pathological incidents that can be taken as exceptions, but part of the grand design of Africa's initiation into modernity. Thus, just as *King Leopold's Ghost* ceases to be a book about the Congo, but rather a metaphor for Africa, the "violent memories" were also not limited to King Leopold's Congo, but became "the sort of memories that accompanied colonialism in other parts of Africa."[65]

> Since I knew that such memories do not simply go away or die with the initial victims, I was anxious to know how and in what ways those memories live on. In fact, the more I thought about this connection, the more obvious it became that the key actors of Africa's post-independence history—Idi Amin, Bokassa, Mobutu, and Mugabe—were but colonial "types," that is, mimetic reproductions of colonial actors like Kurtz, Leopold, and Ian Smith. One cannot understand these actors without locating them in a social history.[66]

What we need to do, therefore, is "engage the layers of memory through which the performance of the colonial imagination continues to live in the present."[67] Where are the resources for engaging these memories? Katongole suggests that the resources are to be found in cultural patterns—questioning and interrogating cultural forms "in order to uncover the patterns of performances through which the memory of history lives on."[68]

2. The Lies of Noble Ideals

Europe never got the chance to hear the truth of the true mission of Leopold in the Congo because he portrayed himself as "philanthropic monarch" and a "great emissary of civilization," in Africa, "notions that not only framed the Europeans' vision of Africans as savage and primitive, but shaped their own identity

---

64. Hochschild, *King Leopold's Ghost*, 280.
65. Katongole, *The Sacrifice of Africa*, 11.
66. Ibid., 12.
67. Ibid.
68. Ibid.

and vision of themselves as noble and civilized."[69] Europe did not get to hear the truth of Leopold's project because "the truth will be too dark to tell."[70] Thus, not being able to hear the truth, for Katongole, shows how "ideals like 'democracy,' 'development,' 'civilization,' and 'progress' have become such tantalizing but misleading notions, forming the basic imaginative canvas yet obscuring reality."[71]

3. **Politics of Greed and Plunder**

The driving force behind Leopold's project in the Congo was personal ambition and greed, ironically today the Democratic Republic of the Congo "operates by the same law of plunder and greed."[72] Before the death of King Leopold, who destroyed all public records of the Congo Free State, he ceded the administration of his pet project to the Belgian government who renamed the Congo Free State (1887–1908) the Belgian Congo (1908–60). At independence in 1960 the Belgian Congo was renamed the Democratic Republic of the Congo under the leadership of its first president Patrice Lumumba (1925–61). In 1971 it was renamed Zaire (1971–97) under the leadership of Mobutu Sese Seko (1930–97). In 2006 it was again renamed the Democratic Republic of the Congo under the leadership of the current leader Joseph Kabila, the son of the former leader Laurent Kabila (1939–2001). The constant rancor and external formalities of name change has made Katongole to observe how the actors change but the script remains the same.[73]

> Moreover, the more I thought about these connections, the more the Congo's story became a lens through which I was beginning to understand other African countries. For whether it is Uganda, Zimbabwe, Liberia, or Sierra Leone (as the recent Blood Diamond so clearly depicts), one confronts the same story of the politics of greed, dispossession, and state brutality, with perhaps the only difference being the degree of sophistication. As Michela Wrong points out, the Congo is but "a paradigm of all that

69. Ibid., 13.
70. Ibid.
71. Ibid., 14.
72. Ibid., 15.
73. Ibid.

> was wrong with post-colonial Africa." For the Congo's combination of rich natural and human resources and economic and political collapse reflects the tragic waste, selfish ambition, greed, and crippled potential that is the story of many African countries. What perhaps sets the Congo apart, according to Wrong, is the radicalization of a certain kind of "negative excellence": "It is as if Congo has embodied within its history the faults of any normal African state and pitched them one frequency higher."[74]

Katongole argues that "any suggestions for a way forward that do not confront this founding narrative of modern Africa are misleading at best."[75] This narrative, if left unquestioned, will continue to haunt modern Africa because it will continue to produce a social history that makes plunder, greed, and violence appeal all too natural.[76]

4. The Wanton Sacrificing of Africa

Adam Hochschild's book depicts how King Leopold indiscriminately conscripted the Congolese to his rubber plantation. The lives of the Congolese were meaningful only in relation of their value to the rubber project.[77] Katongole sees the same indiscriminate devaluation of African lives as extending to the postcolonial era. To the extent that "this dispensability of African lives had been accepted and came to be expected as part of the official, normal way of nation-state politics, postcolonial successors to the colonial project have had no qualms perpetuating the same wanton sacrificing of lives in pursuit of their political ambitions and greed."[78]

> Even as I began to see these connections between African politics and the sacrificing of African lives, as well as the expectation and even anticipation of African's disposability, I was also beginning to see theologically that a new claim regarding African lives is being announced and enacted: namely, that these are not unique precious, sacred lives; these are Africans, mere bodies to be used, mere masses to be exploited. That this theological claim

---

74. Ibid., 15–16. See also Wrong, *In the Footsteps of Mr. Kurtz*, 10–13.
75. Katongole, *The Sacrifice of Africa*, 16.
76. Ibid.
77. Ibid.
78. Ibid., 17.

has come to be widely assumed is obvious from the casualness with which the wastage of African lives is accepted.[79]

The way forward, according to Katongole, is not an interruption, but a confrontation of the forces inducing the wanton destruction of African lives.

5. The Visible Invisibility of Christianity

Even though the time of Leopold's project coincided with the era of Christian missionary evangelization in the Congo, "the role of Christianity remained largely invisible" in *The Ghost of Leopold* where missionaries were depicted as mere observers on the battlefield.[80] According to Hochschild,

> The missionaries had come to the Congo eager to evangelize, to fight polygamy, and to impart to Africans a Victorian sense of sin. Before long, however, the rubber terror meant that missionaries had trouble finding bodies to clothe or souls to save. Frightened villagers would disappear into the jungle for weeks when they saw the smoke of an approaching steamboat, on the horizon. One British missionary was asked repeatedly by Africans, "Has the Savior you tell us of any power to save us from rubber trouble?"[81]

The near invisibility of Christianity was largely due to the assumptions on which Western Christianity was built—that the realm of the spiritual (the domain of Christianity) was to be regarded as distinct from the material realm (the domain of politics), the "version of Christianity that the missionaries accepted and worked out of, and into which they evangelized their African converts."[82] The version of Christianity that is powerless in the face of Leopold's rubber terror cannot do much in the shaping of the future of modern Africa. Christianity, according to Katongole, has "to find a way of overcoming this Western heritage, to move beyond the narrow spiritual and pastoral areas

---

79. Ibid.
80. Ibid., 18.
81. Hochschild, *King Leopold's Ghost*, 172, cited in Katongole, *The Sacrifice of Africa*, 20.
82. Katongole, *The Sacrifice of Africa*, 19.

to which it is consigned and claim full competence in the social, material, and political realities of life in Africa."[83]

Although a lot has changed since the early days of independence, Africa, as Katongole correctly observed, "is still trapped in the same triangle of modernity, violence, and plunder as the Congo was under King Leopold's civilizing mission."[84] The question that was put before the British missionary: "Has the Savior you tell us about any power to save us?" is fundament to inculturation. Granted we have yet to define what we mean by the term "inculturation," the term itself can aid out attempt to address both the single-story narratives of Africa and also serve as a corrective to the "toothless Christianity" that acted no more than an observer in the face of Leopold's rubber terror. Inculturation may then be a way to tell one's story, by oneself, and for oneself, with a view to restoring the dignity one has been denied. It can also be an attempt to empower and make Christianity meaningful in a particular cultural context. Because one can be led astray by a story wrongly told and wrongly interpreted, inculturation therefore seeks to scrutinize the narrative, language, as well as the philosophical and theological underpinnings of all narratives.

If narratives are stories that can "provide people with a sense of order, identity, and meaning within and beyond time,"[85] then narratives can be used in religion to enlighten, engage, provoke, and validate one's lived experience within one's religion. Outside of the Catholic tradition, some have taken to doing just this. In telling their own story in their own terms, they have also empowered and emboldened their members with the power of the Savior to save Africans from "rubber trouble." This group is collectively known as the African independent and African Initiated Churches (AICs). Their validation of Christianity in the context of African cultures (inculturation if you will) is somewhat different from what obtains in the Catholic Church. The AICs, as their manifesto shows, draw a sharp contrast between European Christianity and their own version of African Christianity. They see European mission of Christianity as "deeply rooted in European culture with the stigma of colonialism, paternalism and foreignness, and their attempt to denounce the African religion as barbaric," in contrast to the

---

83. Ibid.
84. Ibid., 20.
85. Arburckle, *Culture, Inculturation, and Theologians*, 64.

AICs mission "which is deeply rooted in African culture but without any stigma."[86] To this we turn next.

AICs: Who, What, When, Why, and How?

The AICs emerged out of the socio-cultural and political conflict posed by colonialism, on the one hand, and Christendom, on the other.[87] In a sense, the AICs are a cultural resistance and religious protest against imported and formalistic and rationalistic theology on African soil.[88] According to the manifesto of the Organization of African Independent Churches (OAIC),[89] the AICs "try to live Christianity with our own national clothing, in harmony with our own cultural heritage, seeking vehicles of worship that make the Christian faith alive to us as Africans. We have evolved our own liturgy and hymnology, our own doctrinal emphases. In yearning for spiritual satisfaction, and psychological and emotional security, we re-introduced an 'emotional depth' into Christianity."[90] At least five churches from the AIC tradition are members of the World Council of Churches (WCC).[91] Numerous others belong to the All Africa Council of Churches (AACC).[92]

---

86. Ositelu, *African Instituted Churches*, 45.

87. Pato, "The African Independent Churches," 29.

88. Anderson, *African Reformation: African Initiated Christianity in the 20th Century*, 219.

89. According to Ositelu, the Organization of African Instituted Churches (OAIC) was founded in Cairo, Egypt in 1978, at the invitation of leader of the Coptic Orthodox Church in Egypt, Pope Shenouda, and was attended by leaders of AICs from seven countries. The second conference in 1982 was attended by representatives from seventeen countries. "The conference approved a Constitution, which required member bodies to be Trinitarian, based on the Old and New Testaments and confessing Jesus Christ as Lord and Savior." See Ositelu, *African Instituted Churches*, 79.

90. Ibid., 81.

91. Ibid., 44. The five churches are the African Israel Nineveh Church that was founded by Paul David Zakayo Kivuli (1896–1974) in Kenya, the Church of the Lord (Aladura) that was founded by Josiah Ositelu in Ogere-Remo, Nigeria, Eglise de Jesus Christ sur Terre by Simon Kimbangu in Lutendele, Democratic Republic of Congo (former Zaire), the Harist Church of Cote d'Ivoire, by William Wade Harris, and the African Church of the Holy Spirit of Kenya in Kakanega, Kenya.

92. According to Ositelu, the All Africa Conference of Churches (AACC) was founded in 1963 as a fellowship of Christian Churches that confess Jesus Christ as God and Savior. See Ositelu, *African Instituted Churches*, 83.

Some theologians, mainly from the historical or mainline churches, have not taken seriously the contributions of AICs to African theology.[93] Part of it is because of the lingering question regarding whether the AICs are a legitimate church or a sect. Some have even raised question regarding how "Christian" are the AICs.[94] There is also the matter of their theology, which can at times seem troubling. Many of the leaders of the Pentecostal and Charismatic brand of AICS in particular lack formal theological training. The general criticism is that these churches often expound a theology of success and power at the expense of a theology of the cross.[95]

While some of the criticisms are legitimate, it is not in any way helpful to make a sweeping generalization of this movement that "has so much variety and is constantly adapting and changing."[96] Researchers in the field have long recognized the need to move beyond description and classification in the study of AICs.[97] "The mere description and interpretation of the belief systems of the AICs does not explain why they exist in the forms in which they do. The prevalent descriptions and interpretations tend to be ahistorical, creating the impression that AICs have an origin independent of socio-historical developments."[98]

In general terms, various words have been used to refer to the independent or African initiated churches. Some refer to them negatively as "schism," "sect," "nativistic," "messianic," "separatist," or "syncretic,"[99] while others positively refer to them as a revolution or renewal.[100] Among the latter is Allan Anderson who suggests that in the current climate where the phenomenon of AICs has irrevocably changed the face of Christianity in the continent it no longer makes sense to refer to the AICs as sects and the

---

93. AICs can stand for African Independent Churches, African Instituted Churches, African Initiated Churches, African Indigenous Churches, or African Initiatives in Christianity. Here we shall use the terms interchangeably. There are those like John Pobee and Gabriel Ositelu II who object to the use of the term "African Independent Churches." See Pobee and Ositelu II, *African Initiatives in Christianity*.

94. See Gilliland, "How 'Christian' are African Independent Churches?," 259–72.

95. Anderson, *African Reformation*, 240.

96. Ibid 238.

97. Pato, "The African Independent Churches: A Socio-Cultural Approach," 24. See Hastings, *A History of African Christianity 1950–1975*, 69–85; and Kruss, "A Critical Review of the Study of Independent Churches in South Africa," 26.

98. Pato, "The African Independent Churches," 24.

99. Anderson, *African Reformation*, 10.

100. Ibid., x.

European mission-founded churches as "mainline" churches. Using the example of South Africa as a case in point, Anderson argues that the reverse is rather the case, i.e., AICs have become "mainline" churches. What the AICs have done to the African church, according to him, should be seen as an African reformation.[101]

The truth is the AICs are not monolithic or homogenous. There are "many thousands" or varieties of AICs today in sub-Saharan Africa.[102] The various types are however, not mutually exclusive.[103] Although it is beyond the scope of this work to go into details about the many varieties of this fast growing and ever increasing group, a distinction between African Independent Churches and African Initiated Churches is still in order. According to Anderson, the phrase African Independent Churches (understood as a church founded in Africa, by Africans, and primarily for Africans) was the first acceptable neutral term for the movement.[104] Later, as many other churches founded by European missionaries in Africa became "independent" of European control terms such as "African indigenous churches" and "African instituted churches" were invoked to distinguish these churches from autonomous churches that were formed decades earlier.[105] "After the African states began to emerge one by one from colonial domination in the fifties and sixties, there was new impetus towards 'Africanization' of Christianity. Many Europeans mission-founded churches began to talk about and move towards inculturation and seek to be seen as 'indigenous.'"[106] According to Anderson, the term "African indigenous churches" is an inadequate term because "most AICs are not completely free from 'foreign' influence and can't be regarded as 'indigenous' in any normative sense."[107]

---

101. Ibid., 120.

102. Ibid., 10.

103. Ositelu, *African Instituted Churches*, 39.

104. Anderson, *African Reformation,* 10. Anderson suggests that the Nubian church, just south of Egypt, which survived until the eighteenth century was, most likely, the first African independent church of Latin Christianity. "Apart from the Nubian church, the first church initiated by Africans for Africans was probably the ancient Ethiopian Church, a distinctly African church that managed to survive the conquering Muslim armies from the north. It was founded by Egyptian Copts, it had strong Jewish characteristics, it was independent of any European church, and was presided over by the emperor" (45).

105. Ibid., 10.

106. Ibid., 10–11.

107. Ibid., 11.

AICs have played a significant role in the expansion of Christianity to the south. A lot has been made about "the center of gravity" in the Christian world moving "inexorably southward," with Africa, Latin America, and Asia as the leading frontiers.[108] The American historian and scholar, Philip Jenkins, estimates that of the 2 billion Christians worldwide, 530 million live in Europe, 510 million in Latin America, 390 million in Africa, and about 300 million in Asia.[109] In Africa in particular AICs represent the cutting and dynamic edge in the new shift.[110] They are increasingly becoming a major force in African Christianity, with the largest phenomenon experienced in Southern Africa, West Africa, Central Africa and Eastern Africa.[111] In 1900, for example, there was an estimated total of 42,000 AICs members in Africa. By 1985 the number rose sharply to 29 million, representing about 12 percent of the total Christian population in Africa. The estimated number for the year 2000 was 54 million, i.e., 14 percent of the total Christian population in Africa.[112]

The phenomenon of AICs demands our attention, not only because of their ever increasing number, but also because their growth in many cases is at the expense of the mainline churches, Catholicism in particular.[113] To cite an example from South Africa, in 1950 about 80 percent of the black South Africans belonged to the mainline Christian churches, while only about 14 percent belonged to the AICs. In 1980 the number of the mainline Christian churches dropped to 52 percent and that of the AICs rose

---

108. See Jenkins, *The Next Christendom*, 1.

109. Jenkins, *The New Faces of Christianity*, 9.

110. Anderson, *African Reformation*, ix.

111. Kealotswe, "The Rise of the African Independent Churches," 205. For detailed study of AICs in Southern Africa, see Barrett, *Schism and Renewal in Africa*; for West Africa, see Turner, *African Independent Church*; and for Central and Eastern Africa, see Kimbangu, *An African Prophet and his Church*.

112. Anderson, *African Reformation*, 7. The Aladura Church has a strong presence in the United States and Great Britain following migrations from Nigeria, Sierra Leone, and Liberia.

113. Ibid. There are, according to Anderson, no country in Africa has as many church denominations as South Africa where there as many as six thousand AICs. "The apartheid government that emerged in 1948 adopted a policy of 'non-interference' in the affairs of African churches, which in effect meant encouraging the development of churches that were totally 'independent' of what were sometimes seen as troublesome mission churches. The development of AICs was seen as in complete harmony with the apartheid ideology, which opposed any sort of social mixing, including integrated churches" (93, 103).

to 27 percent. In 1991 the number of the mainline churches dropped to 41 percent, while that of the AICs rose to 36 percent. Today the AICs are estimated to be the predominant church movement among Black South Africans.[114] The trend is not limited to South Africa but is representative of most of sub-Saharan Africa. About two-thirds of AICs members, for example, "are found in the three countries of South Africa, the Congo (Kinshasa) and Nigeria, where the proportion of AICs to the total Christian population is much higher than in other countries, with the possible exception of Swaziland, Zimbabwe, Kenya and Ghana."[115] The bottom line of AICs comes down to inculturation, indigenization, contextualization, and innovative approaches to mission theology.[116] They help shed light on "the relationship between gospel and culture, the contextualization of Christianity, new forms of mission strategy, a radicalized experiment of an indigenized Christianity, intercultural communication of the Christian gospel, the encounter between Christianity and another living religion."[117]

For a long time the historical or mainline Christian churches in Africa looked disdainfully at the AICs.[118] Their distrust for these churches stem from many factors: the lack of education of their pastors, their syncretic practices, and indecent theology, etc. In spite of these, the AICs are proliferating at a remarkable rate, "growing faster than our staid more western type of churches."[119] The fact that more people in several parts of Africa belong to the AICs speaks volume. "In the past three decades the percentage of people belonging to the 'mainline' churches has declined quite considerably, which raises disturbing questions, among others, about the content and relevance theological training and the curricular of theological institutions in Africa."[120] The AICs can no longer be properly referred to as mere protest movements if they are seen by the ordinary people to be meeting their needs. It seems that they are on to something that the mainline churches have yet to discover, "which speaks to epistemology and ontology, the questioning, the hopes and fears of Homo Africanus."[121]

114. See Oosthuizen et al., *Afro-Christianity at the Grassroots*, ix.
115. Ibid., x.
116. Anderson, *African Reformation*, 11.
117. Ibid.
118. Tutu, "Foreword," vii.
119. Ibid.
120. Anderson, *African Reformation*, 245.
121. See Pobee, "Foreword," ix.

According to the former Anglican Archbishop of Cape Town, Archbishop Desmond Tutu, "reluctantly, if privately, we had to admit that it appeared there was a need that these [AIC] churches were meeting which our own churches with their more cerebral theologies and dignified liturgies were certainly failing to do."[122] In South Africa for example, Black South Africans continue to find a home in the AICs because they realize their true identity in these independent churches. The independent churches provide a charismatic healing ministry that addresses their concerns about witchcraft and ancestry related spells and illnesses.[123] They also provide hospitality not found in the mainline churches. According to Archbishop Tutu, "a newcomer into the urban conurbations of our townships bewildered and lost, needing a warm welcoming environment and reassurance in a hostile setting, was more likely to gravitate to these new creations than join our huge and often unwelcoming congregations with their daunting anonymity."[124] Furthermore, Tutu suggests that when the urban setting threatens personal disintegration, the independent churches and their way of doing things provide healing and "a bridge between what they came from, the familiar, and what they were experiencing in this great unknown."[125] There is also the added fact that the AICs "stress the elements of healing that is relevant to Africans with its conviction that through faith in Jesus, through the Word, the Gospel answers all man's problems."[126] The mainline churches, to their detriment, tend to scorn the healing ministry,[127] perhaps as part of the deliberate attempt "to put the lid on any distinctive developments and to channel African church life back into the stereotype patterns of the West."[128] It is either that they lack insight into African cultures and the effect of culture on the whole life, i.e., sociological, political, and religious, or that they make no serious attempt to investigate the interrelationship of these factors as the AICs have done.

---

122. Tutu, "Foreword," vii.

123. See Maboea, "Causes for the Proliferation of the African Independent Churches," 121–36.

124. Tutu, Foreword," vii.

125. Ibid.

126. Maboea, "Causes for the Proliferation of the African Independent Churches," 125.

127. Tutu, "Foreword," vii.

128. Maboea, "Causes for the Proliferation of the African Independent Churches," 125.

Resilience of African Independent Churches

Any Lessons for the "Mainline" Churches?

The AICs, as we have pointed out, are not a monolithic or homogenous group, but an ever expansive and multifaceted entity. There is, for example, among the churches that are lumped under the general umbrella of AICs, a distinctive movement—a new and rapidly growing form of African Christianity that emerged in the 1970s called Newer Pentecostal and Charismatic Churches (NPCs).[129] This movement, which is concentrated mainly in big cities and urban centers, is "fast becoming one of the most significant expressions of Christianity on the continent."[130] To understand African Christianity in all its varieties one cannot but pay attention to this and many other countless movements like it in the AICs. To suggest that we pay attention to this movement does not amount to romanticizing or idealizing them as a paradigm for inculturation. Far from it. There are many things that AICs do, for example, that are subject to criticism—facile reading of Scripture, constant friction, schism, and breakaway groups, propagation of "prosperity gospel" characteristic of NPCs in particular, etc. The criticisms notwithstanding, AICs cannot be ignored and they themselves know it. As they emphatically stated in the manifesto of OAIC, "we cannot be ignored anymore. Indifference will not make us disappear."[131]

A responsible theological evaluation of the AICs requires that a superficial acceptance be as intolerable as an unfair condemnation of these churches.[132] The AICs have something distinctive and unique (like theology in oral narrative and theology that takes the African worldview seriously) that is quite different from the other expressions of Christianity found in the mainline churches. It is difficult to deny that they portend what an indigenous expression of Christianity can produce. They put together a form of Christianity that appeals to a new generation of Africans and are backed up by the fact that the peculiarity of the African worldview requires an

---

129. Anderson, *African Reformation*, 167. Anderson writes that "the entrance and pervading influence of many different kinds of NPCs on the African Christian scene now makes it even more difficult, if not impossible, to put AICs into types and categories" (168).

130. Anderson, *African Reformation*, 167. NPCs "are often sharply critical of the older AICs, particularly in what they perceive as the African traditional component of AIC practices, which are sometimes seen as manifestations of demons needing 'deliverance'" (184).

131. Ositelu, *African Instituted Churches*, 81.

132. Gilliland, "How 'Christian' are African Independent Churches?," 259.

understanding of Christ that meets that need. After all, who Jesus is in the African spirit universe must not be severed from what he does and can do in that world.[133] What then can the mainline churches learn from the AICs?

1. Innovation and Inculturation

According to Archbishop Desmond Tutu, the AICs "have been a wonderful goad to our acknowledging that while the Gospel comes in judgment of much in our African ways, it also comes to fulfill what is good, that we are loved and redeemed by God not under pseudonyms but as who we authentically are—Africans with our peculiar gifts and weaknesses."[134] Most of the Africans who belong to the mainline churches, in Archbishop Tutu's assessment, have come to realize that they have been suffering from a strange schizophrenia. "They were expected to be 'circumcised' into occidental persons in the manner of their worship, their beliefs [and] their theology before they could be integrated into their church community. They had to deny their African-ness to become genuine Christians. Their African *Weltanschauung* was denigrated and virtually all things African were condemned as pagan and to be destroyed root and branch."[135]

The AICs have no doubt made some interesting and innovative adaptations to some traditional African practices and religious beliefs like divination, traditional medicine, healing, polygyny, traditional patterns of leadership, and ancestors. They, like the mainline Churches, reject the traditional practices of witchcraft, divination, and ancestor rituals as a means of solving problems. "Whereas missionaries generally saw the practices as ignorant superstitions to be obliterated systematically by education, AICs saw them as expressions of real social malevolence and manifestations of evil spirit and sorcery."[136] They AICs not only appeal to the Bible for a radical solution to the African spirit world that threatens human social life, but also proclaim a gospel of deliverance from evil spirit. They proclaim this gospel of deliverance in symbols and experiences that ordinary African people

---

133. Bediako, *Jesus and the Gospel in Africa*, 22.
134. Tutu, "Foreword," vii.
135. Ibid., vii–viii.
136. Anderson, *African Reformation*, 194.

are familiar. "The AICs provide many examples of an innovative approach, whereby traditional cultural and religious ceremonies have been adapted and transformed to have Christian meanings. Rituals and symbols adapted from both the Western Christian tradition and the traditional African religions (and sometimes, completely new ones) are introduced. Usually these have local relevance and include enthusiastic participation by members and lively, ecstatic worship."[137]

2. Divination and Prophetic Healing

A key feature of African Traditional Religions (ATRs) is the practice of seeking the cause of evil through divination and the power to deal it and avert future reoccurrence—a phenomenon the early Christian missionaries designated "prophetism."[138] The AICs were "the first to build the bridge between primal religion and African Christianity by appropriating resources from the gospel to deal with this typical African religious practice."[139] There is, according to Anderson, an increasing acknowledgment even among Western scientists today that there are two types of diseases in Africa: the "natural diseases" that can be cured by natural means, including appeal to Western medicine and "African diseases" (understood by Africans in the context of their cosmology) that can only be cured by "supernatural" means and infusion of power on the individual by medicine man.[140] Africans usually appeal to diviners to diagnose and solve the "spiritual problem," i.e., problem of witchcraft, sorcery, evil spirits, and spirit possessions. AICs are almost universally opposed to traditional divination (consultation with diviners and healers for access to power through the use of charms and medicines).[141] Despite this negative attitude, AICs have not left the needs addressed by the diviners unattended. AICs have prophets and healers who fill the vacuum by taking over the vital duties of the

---

137. Ibid., 195.
138. Omenyo, "Man of God Prophesy unto Me," 30.
139. Ibid.
140. Anderson, *African Reformation*, 198.
141. Ibid., 195.

diviner.[142] "Many AICs have effectively substituted the power wielded by diviners by their message of the power of the Spirit, enabling them to treat 'African' problems. Sorcery and witchcraft, evil spirits and ancestor possession are usually encountered by these churches as problems that must be overcome by the Spirit rather than by any other power."[143]

3. Ancestral Beliefs and Practices

For many sub-Saharan Africans for whom the religious practices associated with the ancestors are the most important aspect of their religious life and worldview the ancestors are benevolent guardians and protectors of the family unit and clan.[144] There is the widespread belief that ancestors speak to the people through dreams and diviners and that those who ignore the bidding of the ancestors are severely punished. "Their sanctions have a fearful control over people's lives, and most seem to practice ancestor rituals in order to be rid of disturbing visitations."[145]

AICs respond to the phenomenon of ancestors in two ways.[146] The first is by *confrontation*. Many AICs, according to Anderson, reject the ancestor observances. They teach that these are not ancestors at all, "but demons that need to be confronted and exorcized, for they only bring further misery and bondage. They have no power over Christians, because Christians have the greater power of the Spirit, which overcomes Satan's power."[147] The second response is one of *accommodation* and concession, a more tolerant and ambivalent response.[148] They teach that the ancestors are to be respected and obeyed because they act as mediators of God, angels, witnesses in heaven, or even mediators between the people and God.[149] Accommodation, according to

---

142. Ibid., 197–98. Anderson correctly points out that there is now a growing recognition among churches in Africa and African theologians that the problems taken to the diviners need to be responded to.

143. Ibid., 201–2.

144. Ibid., 202.

145. Ibid., 203.

146. Ibid.

147. Ibid.

148. Ibid., 204.

149. Ibid.

Anderson, is not however, the predominant reaction to ancestor ritual among AICs. The common reaction is a Spirit-inspired confrontation by which they replace traditional beliefs with Christian teachings. The AICs "may have a greater awareness of the African spirit world and therefore make a greater contribution to contextualization in this area."[150] The AICs, "especially in their prophetic therapy and prescriptions, provide the protection and guidance formerly sought from ancestors."[151]

4. **Indigenized Liturgy**

A distinguishing feature of Pentecostal liturgy is active participation of every member of the congregation. Their liturgy has "social and revolutionary implications in that it empowers marginalized people, takes as acceptable what ordinary people have in the worship of God and thus overcomes 'the real barriers of race, social status, and education.'"[152] The flexibility of their liturgy and the emphasis on the immediate presence of God, alongside a preaching message that promises solutions for ordinary life problems like illness and fear of evil spirit, make Pentecostal AICs liturgy readily acceptable to the people.[153] "In Africa, Pentecostal AICs have changed the face of Christianity because they have proclaimed a holistic gospel of salvation that includes deliverance from all types of evil oppression like sickness, barrenness, sorcery, evil spirits, unemployment, and poverty. This message may not have engaged always effectively with the more structurally oppressive political and economic monopolies, but the needs of Africa have been addressed more fundamentally that the rather spiritualized and intellectualized legacy of European and North American missions."[154]

---

150. Ibid.
151. Ibid., 205.
152. Ibid., 207.
153. Ibid.
154. Ibid, 210.

Conclusion

This chapter has argued that the issue of political self-determination is tied to power that inheres in stories about Africa, particularly the way they are told. "Stories not only shape how we view reality but also how we respond to life and indeed the very sort of persons we become."[155] Stories also shape not only our values, our aims, and our goals, but also define the range of what is desirable and what is possible for us. They are not mere fictional narratives meant for our entertainment, but are part of our social ecology. "They are embedded in us and form the very heart of our cultural, economic, religious, and political worlds.... This is why a notion like "Africa" names not so much a place, but a story—or set of stories about how people of the continent called Africa are located in the narrative that constitutes the modern world."[156] Missionaries who bring the gospel to the mission land always bring with it, and understandably so, their own, stories, their own context, and their own worldview. Inculturation is an imperative if the exigencies of the old context (missionary perspective) and the new (the place the gospel is being preached) are to be met. This will require "a dialectic of mutual critique, affirmation and transformation between the received gospel and the culture. The past of both traditions need be challenged from the perspective of present experience and the present memory of the past of both traditions."[157]

Christianity has become part and parcel of Africa's story and a key element of Africa's "civil society."[158] A paradox has emerged in the story of the Christianity within the global south and the north. "In the West Christianity, while arguably a key source of modernity, has declined in its public significance as modern society has taken shape. In Africa it may be that Christianity is assuming an increasing significance in the creation of a modern, pluralistic African society."[159] The African Initiated Churches, African Instituted Churches, and African Independent Churches (AICs) have helped to fuel the surge of Christianity in African public life by the manner they tell the Christian story using African cultural values. Why should the universal Church care about AICs? Perhaps because AICs are no longer

---

155. Katongole, *The Sacrifice of Africa*, 2.
156. Ibid., 2–3.
157. Okoye, "Inculturation and Theology in Africa," 65.
158. Gifford, *African Christianity*, 20.
159. Ibid.

only in Africa. Members of AICs who migrate to Europe and America go with their faith and are radically altering the Euro-American religious landscape and the nature of Christian mission.[160] Even in South America, AICs "are the fastest growing churches, even more than the Pentecostals in South America."[161]

AICs are African expression of Christianity—a phenomenon too impactful to be ignored that some have compared it to great to the Protestant Reformation, dubbing it the African Reformation.[162] Is it possible that such a phenomenon of African origin has provided us with an alternative way of envisaging how Christianity might gain root and expand even further in Africa? Might this phenomenon not have raised important questions regarding the relationship between the gospel and culture that demands our attention? Whether or not one agrees with the theology or style of ministry of the AICs, a rapidly expanding religious movement like theirs demands our attention.[163] As Anderson correctly puts it, the fact that the AICs are witnessing remarkable growth in membership while the mainline churches are experiencing decline means that the mission methods of the AICs should be examined. "There must be something that they are 'doing right' from which all Christians can learn in the ongoing task of proclaiming the gospel. And conversely, there must be something that western missionaries failed to do or did wrongly which resulted in such a huge response."[164] The AICs are thriving where the historical or mainline churches are struggling—to provide a contextualized Christianity in Africa.[165] Their main significance lies in their uninhibited indigenization of Christianity.[166] Their bread and butter is not in a highly formalized theology, but in "praxis and a spirituality in which a theology is profoundly implicit."[167] In Botswana, for example, the most common reason for the rise of the AICs and the reason "which made them challenge the missionary founded churches is their integration and transformation of the religious beliefs and practices of Bostwana and embracing

160. Creumbley, *Spirit, Structure, and Flesh*, 3.
161. Ositelu, *African Instituted Churches*, 81.
162. See Anderson, *African Reformation*, 7.
163. Ibid., 247.
164. Ibid., 246.
165. Ibid., 237.
166. Ibid., 217.
167. Ibid., quoting Hastings, *A History of African Christianity 1950–1975*, 54.

them in their expressions of Christianity."¹⁶⁸ It is reasonable to argue, for these and other reasons, that "more than any other form of Christianity in Africa, the Pentecostal 'Spirit' AICs have given uniquely African character to their faith. In certain respects, they have attained the goals towards which formal African theology still struggles."¹⁶⁹ Thus, Anderson is correct to point out that it is no longer justifiable to blame the Europeans; the fact that the AICs continue to gain strength at the expense of the mainline churches has implications for these churches.¹⁷⁰ Africa's new prominence in the world Church "is not a call for African self-congratulation, but for sober reflection and faithful witness on the part of the African Christian church."¹⁷¹

The shift in the center of gravity in the Christian world demonstrates that Christianity has become a non-Western religion, "which means, not that Christianity has become irrelevant, but rather that Christianity may now be seen for what it truly is, a universal religion., and that what has taken place in Africa has been a significant part of this process"¹⁷² For the African, the shift unambiguously makes "clear that modern European values are not universal but rooted in the particular history of Scottish and French enlightenments. These values are rightly criticized by non-Western Christians."¹⁷³ Thus, one important implication of this shift is that there is a need for a new "hermeneutic of communication, where the desire to understand [African] Christians and the desire to be understood by them meet."¹⁷⁴ Would a semiotic approach to an African theology of inculturation not help us to uncover this hermeneutic of communication, which might in turn lead to a hermeneutic of recovery? Perhaps we should first probe what insights we can garner from metapragmatic use of language by cultural anthropologists with a view to utilizing their postmodern understanding of culture.

---

168. Kealotswe, "The Rise of the African Independent Churches," 219.

169. Anderson, African Reformation, 218.

170. Ibid, 246.

171. Bediako, *Jesus and the Gospel of Africa*, xvii.

172. Ibid., 3.

173. Wijsen, "Global Christianity," 159.

174. Ibid., 158. Wijsen argues that "1) that the challenge of the shift of the Christianity's center of gravity is the intercultural communication between Northern and Southern Christians, 2) that the struggle between Northern and Southern Christians is a struggle about the values of modernity, and 3) that European theologians cannot simply return to pre-modern values, stick to modern universalism or be satisfied with postmodern relativity, but move beyond modern values and develop further a trans-modern hermeneutic" (150–51).

3

Metapragmatic Use of Language

THEORETICAL LINGUISTS PROVIDE A matrix within which a theory of culture that is consistent with a semiotic approach to culture can be built. Language, as the Russian linguist and literary theorist Roman Jakobson (1896–1982) has suggested, must be investigated in all the variety of its functions.[1] Apart from providing a communication system, language confers on a people a distinctive identity, avails them with resources for managing information, gives them a sense of belonging, and provides them resources for dealing with innovation. This chapter will embark on an investigation of language use in the context of postmodern criticism that culture or identities are never final or settled but always involved in a dynamic process of becoming with a view to discovering how a metapragmatic use of language furthers our semiotic approach to a theology of inculturation. "Postmodernism" was a term that was coined in the 1930s as a reaction to both modernism and classical culture. Its hermeneutics, which essentially is one of suspicion, "eschews both the Enlightenment myth of progress and any form of Romantic nostalgia for a pristine past beyond restoration in present or future as well."[2] Although the German philosopher and revolutionary thinker, Karl Marx (1818-83) and the Austrian neurologist and founder of psychoanalysis, Sigmund Freud (1856-1939) were major players in postmodern criticism of religion and the arts, the key figure in postmodernism still remains the German philosopher, philologist, and cultural critic, Friedrich Nietzsche. Nietzsche called "into question not just Enlightenment rationalism but the Romantic reaction to that rationalism ushered in by [Jean-Jacques] Rousseau"[3] whose political philosophy influenced modern social and po-

---

1. Jakobson, "Closing Statement," 353.
2. Lawrence "The Fragility of Consciousness," 55.
3. Ibid.

litical thought since the time of the French revolution. To be clear, postmodernism is not the same as the "linguistic turn" in social anthropology (which we shall examine next) nor is it the same as the "cultural turn" in anthropology (which we shall examine in the next chapter). It however, overlaps intellectually with a number of their concerns.[4]

Before the postmodern critique of the arts was extended to the branch of social anthropology now known as linguistics, a speaker's reflexive account of how he or she (and others) use language used to be seen as "anecdotal" and as an empirically unreliable linguistic data that is "contaminated" by the speaker's own consciousness.[5] But recent groundbreaking effort by linguists to conceive reflexive activities of language and language use metapragmatically has completely altered the way we view language and language use, paving the way for integrating reflexive linguistic activities into social and cultural analysis.[6] This metapragmatic conception sees language as a guide to the scientific study of culture.[7] "Each language encompasses several concurrent patterns which are each characterized by a different function."[8] One can locate an interdependence of diverse structures within a unity of language, an over-all code that itself represents a system of interconnected sub-codes.[9]

According to Susanne Langer (1895–1985), the concept of meaning in all its varieties, i.e., sign, symbols, denotation, signification, and communication, is a dominant contemporary philosophical concept that any serious study of religion cannot ignore.[10] Sign, symbols, denotation, signification, and communication are now studied by linguistics. The study of science of linguistics has injected into contemporary discussion of culture the understanding that in every cultural matrix is to be found a link between language, thinking, and cognition. People use the language they speak in a variety of ways, primarily to express the activities of the mind. There are, however, two common characteristics of language that linguists point to. "One is that the reality of language, as a general rule, remains unconscious; . . . we have no more than a very faint and fleeting awareness

---

4. Suny, "Back and Beyond," 1482.
5. Inoue, *Vicarious Language*, 17 (see n12).
6. Ibid.
7. Sapir, "The Status of Linguistics as a Science," 209.
8. Jakobson, "Linguistics and Poetics," 352.
9. Ibid.
10. See Langer, *Philosophical Sketches*.

of the operations which we accomplish in order to talk. The other is that, no matter how abstract or how specialized the operations of thought may be, they receive expression in language."[11] In other words, "thinking and speaking are activities distinct by nature, associated for the practical necessity of communication, but which both have their respective domain and their independent possibilities, those of language consisting of the resources offered to the mind for what is called the expression of thought."[12]

The value of linguistics for anthropology and cultural studies has long been recognized by experts in the field.[13] Edward Sapir (1884–1939) suggested that "it is an illusion to think that we can understand the significant outlines of a culture through sheer observation and without the guide of the linguistic symbolism which makes these outlines significant and intelligible to society."[14] Any attempt to understand culture without the aid of language spoken in that society is, according to experts in linguistic study, "amateurish as the labors of a historian who cannot handle the original documents of the civilization which he is describing."[15] The "cultural turn," which we shall take up in the next chapter, was largely due to the influence of Clifford Geertz who not only rejected positivist approaches to human experience, but insisted on "the centrality of meaning, the historically and culturally specific constructions of understanding and feeling."[16] Why the "turn?" Of what significance was it? What was the desired outcome? We can only answer these questions after exploring the contributions of linguistic to cultural anthropology.

In this chapter, therefore, we probe the contributions the study of language can make to our understanding of human nature and the culture in which a person lives. Recent discoveries in cybernetics and communication sciences lend credence to this, fueling the idea that the era of artificial separation of disciplines is passé—that it is no longer a badge of honor for a discipline to demonstrate its absolute independence of the others.[17] One of the merits of new developments in cybernetics and the communication sciences is that these discoveries are beginning to free the

11. Benveniste, *Problems in General Linguistics*, 55.
12. Ibid.
13. Sapir, "The Status of Linguistic as Science," 207–14.
14. Ibid., 209.
15. Ibid.
16. Suny, "Back and Beyond," 1483.
17. Chomsky, *Language and Mind*, 1.

scientific imagination from the shackles of isolationism and challenge long standing convictions, "premature orthodoxy," and "stultifying dogma" that characterize, according to Noam Chomsky, the artificial separation of the disciplines.[18]

The Sapir-Whorf Hypothesis

Here we examine two cardinal hypothesis or principles deriving from two renowned linguists, Edward Sapir and Benjamin Lee Whorf (1897–1941) who very early on grasped the relationship between language, thought, and reality. Sapir-Whorf hypothesis is so called because of the relatively cordial association between Sapir and Whorf. Their hypotheses show us how language is a valuable guide to understanding social reality and culture and how the "network of cultural patterns of a civilization is indeed in the language which expresses that civilization."[19] Brief biographical information of the two thinkers may be helpful.

Edward Sapir was born in Lauenburg, Germany, on January 26, 1884. His parents emigrated to the United States when he was five years old. He attended Columbia University where he studied Germanics and Semitics for his Bachelors and Masters degrees. For his doctorate he studied primitive languages and anthropology under the legendary German-American anthropologists, Franz Boas (1858–1942), receiving his PhD in 1909. Sapir concentrated his research on the study of several northern Indian groups: Nootka and Athapascan, with attention to the psychological and psychoanalytic patterns in linguistic and cultural behavior. His study led him to the view that language is a psychologic-symbolic phenomenon.

Sapir worked as research assistant at the University of California (1907–8) and taught as instructor of anthropology at the University of Pennsylvania (1909–10). He left Pennsylvania after two years for Canada to take up position at the newly established division of Anthropology in Ottawa. While in Canada he did fieldwork among the Nootka Indians of Vancouver, a research project that greatly shaped his thinking in ethnology.[20] He also read two influential works in Ottawa that would lay the seed of his future thinking on personality and culture: Carl Jung's *Psychological Types* (1921) and C. K. Ogden and A. I. Richards's *Meaning of Meaning* (1900). Sapir's

18. Ibid.
19. Sapir, "The Status of Linguistic Science," 209.
20. Benedict, "Edward Sapir," 466.

"intensive studies of various Athabascan languages, continued in later years with a highly refined study of Navaho, gave him the material with which to explore processes of linguistic change with rigorous methodology and to construct an Ur-Athabascan language in the best philological manner."[21]

Sapir also taught anthropology and general linguistics at the University of Chicago (1927–31). It was at Chicago that he began to pay close attention to personality development—the interface of personality and culture, which led to the idea of cultural creation of meaning. His work, widely read in psychiatry and psychoanalysis, "paved the way toward a fruitful union of the disparate disciplines of psychology and anthropology."[22] Sapir left Chicago to accept a position in anthropology and linguistics at Yale University (1931–39). His studies in Indo-Germanics and Semitics "resulted in insights of singular importance which were fully appreciated by linguists in these fields, and which were embodied in brief but carefully documented papers. Among the most significant was the discovery of a relationship between Tibetan and Tocharian."[23] Sapir, in these studies, "brilliantly applied the phonemic approach which he had been instrumental in developing and which already has proved a source of fresh vigor to the discipline of linguistics."[24] In a glowing tribute to Sapir, Franz Boas wrote that "the strictness of phonetic methods and the general adoption of phonemic principles in the study of primitive languages are largely due to him."[25]

Sapir's close ally, Benjamin Whorf, was born in Winthrop, Massachusetts, on April 24, 1897. Whorf had his early education in Winthrop and after graduating from high school in 1914 proceeded to the Massachusetts Institute of Technology (MIT) to study chemical engineering. He received his Bachelor of Science in chemical engineering in 1918. After graduation he worked for a fire preventing engineering company in Hartford, Connecticut, rising to the prestigious ranks of Special Agent (1928) and Assistant Secretary of the company (1940).

Working as a businessman, Whorf developed interest in linguistics, researching "the lost writing system of the Mayas and the study of the languages of the Aztecs of Mexico and the Hopis of Arizona."[26] The initial

21. Ibid.
22. Mandelbaum, "Edward Sapir," 133.
23. Benedict, "Edward Sapir," 468.
24. Ibid.
25. Boas, "Edward Sapir," 59.
26. Whorf, *Language, Thought, and Reality*, 1.

spark that led to this interest in linguistics was religiously motivated. By his own account, this interest in linguistics did not come until 1924 when he became "increasingly concerned about the supposed conflict between science and religion."[27] Whorf's religious upbringing was Methodist Episcopalian. He saw some of the religious teachings he received as conflicting with some issues in science. As he got steep in the issue, Whorf began to believe "that the key to the apparent discrepancy between the Biblical and the scientific accounts of cosmogony and evolution might lie in a penetrating linguistic exegesis of the Old Testament,"[28] a realization that led him to begin the study of Hebrew language in 1924. Whorf also believed that "fundamental human and philosophical problems could be solved by taking a new sounding of the semantics of the Bible."[29]

Whorf's foray into the Hebrew language led to the discovery of an important nineteenth-century work, *La langue hebraique restituee*, by the French dramatist, philologist, and mystic, Antoine d'Olivet (1768–1825). The English translation of this work was published in 1921. It was probably this translation that Whorf read, leaving a lasting imprint in him.[30] To be clear, it was not really the biblical exegesis of d'Olivet that Whorf was concerned about but the method and the "root-sign" that d'Olivet uncovered. Whorf thought the "root-sign" was a foreshadowing of what linguists today call phoneme.[31]

The discovery of d'Olivet's work was almost like the impetus Whorf needed to delve deeper into the study of languages. It reawakened his interest in Mexican antiquities and lore—Aztec language and Maya hieroglyphs which he began studying in 1926 and 1928.[32] It was while studying these that he met Edward Sapir in 1928. Sapir would become the second major influence in Whorf's study of linguistics. Before meeting Sapir, Whorf had

27. Ibid., 7.

28. Ibid.

29. Ibid.

30. Ibid., 8. D'Olivet suggested that "the hidden meanings of the Book of Genesis could be elucidated by an analysis *au fond* of the structure of the triliteral Hebrew root" and that each letter of the Hebrew alphabet "contained an inherent meaning."

31. Ibid., 9. Linguists distinguish the concept of phoneme from "sound" and "phonetic element." Phoneme is "a functionally significant unit in the rigidly defined pattern or configuration of sounds peculiar to a language" and it is "an objectively definable entity in the articulated and perceived totality of speech." See Sapir, "The Psychological Reality of Phonemes," 46.

32. Whorf, *Language, Thought, and Reality*, 10.

read Sapir's *Language* (1921). After series of other personal encounters with this renowned scholar, in 1931 Whorf enrolled in Sapir's course in American Indian linguistics at Yale when Sapir took a position there as professor of Anthropology. "Although Whorf nominally enrolled for a program of studies leading to the doctorate, he never sought or obtained any higher degree; he pursued his studies for pure intellectual ends."[33]

Whorf had a lot of success in linguistics and anthropology, which he combined with his business career. He consistently turned down several offers of academic and research positions because he thought "his business situation afforded him a more comfortable living and a freer opportunity to develop his intellectual interests in his own way."[34] Sapir helped Whorf to develop interest in oligosynthesis,[35] binary grouping,[36] and several other linguistic theories. Whorf later became a lecturer in anthropology in 1937–38 at Yale.[37] In the field of linguistics, Whorf is best known for his linguistic analysis of Hopi.[38] In general terms, Whorf advanced the idea that thinking is relative to the language learned and that "there is no one metaphysical pool of universal human thought. Speakers of different lan-

---

33. Ibid., 16.

34. Ibid., 5.

35. "Oligosynthesis is a name for that type of language structure in which all or nearly all of the vocabulary may be reduced to a very small number of roots or significant elements, irrespective of whether these roots or elements are to be regarded as original, standing anterior to the language as we know it, or as never had independent existence, theirs being an implicit existence as parts in words that were always undissociated wholes." See Whorf, *Language, Thought, and Reality*, 12.

36. Binary grouping is a principle Whorf thought to inhere in the structure of Hebrew root words. According to Whorf, "a binary group is a group of Semitic roots having in common a certain sequence of two consonants, containing all the roots with this sequence in one language, and having these roots with but few exceptions allocated to a FEW CERTAIN KINDS OF MEANING." See ibid., 13.

37. Ibid., 16.

38. According to Lakoff, Whorf was wrong on many aspects of Hopi. For example, Whorf had claimed that English had rich metaphorical systems, which for him was not a good thing because he considered metaphors to be false and misleading. It is not that metaphors, for him, do not have positive values but that they arise from what he called *synesthesia*, which, although could connote something that has no positive value, properly means "confusion of thought." When he encountered Hopi, Whorf thought Hopi had no metaphors, an indication, in his thinking, of Hopi superiority to English. "Hopi is replete with metaphor, especially in its temporal system. Whorf was also wrong about the Hopi concept of time. He had claimed that Hopi did not have anything like a Western concept of time... Hopi does have a concept of time—and a rich system of temporal metaphors." See Lakoff, "Whorf and Relativism," 325.

guages see the Cosmos differently, evaluate it differently, sometimes not by much, sometimes widely."[39]

Whorf is viewed variously as a relativist and as an objectivist.[40] With respect to fact, he is relativist because he "believed that languages, as a matter of fact, had different and incommensurable conceptual systems."[41] But with respect to value, Whorf was an objectivist because he "believed that there was an objectivist reality, and he thought that some but not other conceptual systems built into language were capable of fitting it with reasonable preciseness. He believed that languages differed in their conceptual systems, but he believed that some languages were more accurate—and therefore better for doing science—than others."[42] George Lakoff writes:

> Whorf's objectivism came from two sources: he was a fundamentalist Christian, and he was trained as a chemical engineer at MIT in the 1910s. His interest in linguistics arose from the discrepancy between his two sources of objective truth: science and the Bible. He believed that the discrepancy was due to a misunderstanding of the original biblical text as a result of its having been translated into Indo-European languages. A new understanding of the semantics of the Bible, he thought, would remedy the discrepancy. He came to view English and other Indo-European languages as having a conceptual system that was misleading because it did not accurately fit the objective world.[43]

Hypotheses Considered

The first hypothesis of Sapir-Whorf is that all higher levels of thinking are dependent on language. The goal of language, as Whorf articulated it, is the same as the goal of linguistics, i.e., meaning, and that the real concern of linguistics "is to light up the thick darkness of the language, and thereby of

39. Whorf, *Language, Thought, and Reality*, x.

40. Although there is no one acceptable meaning of relativism in linguistic terms, for some the term is "a bête noire, identified with scholarly irresponsibility, fuzzy thinking, lack of rigor, and even immorality." Some who consider themselves "as committed to science assume that scientific thinking requires an objectivist world view—a commitment to there being only one 'correct' conceptual system." See Lakoff, "Whorf and Relativism," 304.

41. Lakoff, "Whorf and Relativism," 324.

42. Ibid.

43. Ibid., 324–25.

much of the thought, the culture, and the outlook upon life of a given community with the light of this 'golden something,' as I have heard it called, this transmuting principle of meaning."[44] Sapir adds that it is an illusion to think that people adjust to reality without the use language or that language is merely an incidental means of communication or reflection. "Human beings do not live in the objective world alone, nor alone in the world of social activity as ordinarily understood, but are very much at the mercy of the particular language which has become the medium of expression for their society."[45] The social reality or the "real world" of a group "is to a large extent unconsciously built up on the language habits of the group."[46] No two languages, according to Sapir, "are ever sufficiently similar to be considered as representing the same social reality. The worlds in which different societies live are distinct worlds, not merely the same world with different labels attached."[47] Language, therefore, is primarily a cultural or social product. For a people in a given community, their whole life is mirrored by the words they use and even simple acts of perception "are very much at the mercy of the social patterns called words."[48]

For Sapir, an outstanding characteristic of any language is that of its formal completeness. "We may say that a language is so constructed that no matter what any speaker of it may desire to communicate, no matter how original or bizarre his idea or his fancy, the language is prepared to do his work."[49] All human activities, according to Sapir, may be thought of as either functional in the immediate sense or as symbolic, or even as blend of the two.[50] Thus, language can be thought of as the symbolic guide to culture,[51] or "a socialized type of human behavior."[52]

Working out of a neo-grammarian school of historical linguistics, a tradition quite different from the behaviorist tradition of Sapir-Whorf, the American linguist and cognitive scientist, Noam Chomsky (b. 1928)

---

44. Whorf, *Language, Thought, and Reality*, 26.
45. Sapir, "The Status of Linguistics as a Science," 209.
46. Ibid.
47. Ibid.
48. Ibid., 210.
49. Sapir, "The Grammarian and his Language," 153. Sapir explains that formal completeness has nothing to do with the richness or poverty of the vocabulary.
50. Sapir, "The Status of Linguistics as a Science," 211.
51. Ibid.
52. Ibid., 213.

makes some remarks that shed a little more light on this first hypothesis.[53] In *Language and Mind*, a work in which he probed the contributions the study of language makes to our understanding of human nature, without specifically referring to either Sapir or Whorf, Chomsky suggests that there are "respects in which language mirrors human processes or shapes the flow and character of thought."[54] Arguing that language can be conceived as a particular relation between sound and meaning, Chomsky suggests that sound and meaning do not necessarily equal communication. He also argues that an essential but often ignored characteristic of human behavior not found in modern developed theory of communication, like sound spectrograph, computer, and automaton, is the fact that only humans have the ability to use language. Underlying language use, Chomsky observes, are "abstract mechanisms of some sort that are not analyzable in terms of association and that could not have been developed by any such simple means."[55] He suggests that to understand human language "we must isolate and study the system of linguistic competence that underlies behavior but that is not realized in any direct or simple way in behavior."[56] To this end, Chomsky finds helpful the findings of the sixteenth century Spanish physician, Juan Huarte who discovered that the word for "intelligence," *ingenio* may have come from the same Latin root for "engender" or "generate," which holds clue to the nature of the mind. "One may discern two generative powers in man, one common with the beasts and plants, and the other participating in spiritual substance. Wit (ingenio) is a generative

---

53. The American linguist Leonard Bloomfield (1887–1949) led the development of structural linguistics in the United States. See Bloomfield, *Language*. His work was continued by Chomsky. One of the main criticism against them is that they tend to separate the study of meaning from the analysis of linguistic form. The neo-grammarian school dominated the field of linguistics in the late nineteenth century. They generally "advocated a strictly 'genetic' explanation of language, viewing individual sounds of a particular language as having 'evolved' from sounds at an earlier stage. These sound changes were caused, either by the nature of the articulatory apparatus, or by diffusion and borrowing through contact in war or trade." They also see the aim of linguistic description as working "backwards through methods of comparative (and language internal) reconstruction to an earlier stage of history—the so called 'proto' language" (see Caton, "Contributions of Roman Jakobson," 224–25).

54. Chomsky, *Language and Mind*, 1.

55. Ibid., 3.

56. Ibid., 4.

power. The understanding is a generative faculty."[57] Huarte distinguishes three levels of intelligence, which Chomsky finds useful:

- The first level, which is the lowest of the three levels, is what is called "docile wit," the empiricist position—justifies the maxim that there is nothing in the mind that is not first transmitted through the senses.
- The next level is normal intelligence; it goes beyond the empiricist position of sense experience—that normal human mind is able to engender within itself and by its own power the principles by which knowledge rests. [This generative ability is what Descartes thought was lacking in animals and automaton because they lack the use of language as normal instrument of thought.]
- The highest level goes beyond normal intelligence; it is an "excise of creative imagination"

The difference between the first level (docile wit) and the second level (normal intelligence) is what distinguishes humans from animals.

The 3 Levels of Intelligence

Level 1 Docile Wit	Level 2 Normal Intelligence	Level 3 Highest Level
It is the empiricist position—justifies the maxim that there is nothing in the mind that is not first transmitted through the senses.	Normal intelligence: goes beyond the empiricist position of sense experience—that normal human mind is able to engender within itself and by its own power the principles by which knowledge rests	Goes beyond normal intelligence; it is an "excise of creative imagination"

57. Ibid., 9.

A Semiotic Approach to the Theology of Inculturation

Level 1 Docile Wit	Level 2 Normal Intelligence	Level 3 Highest Level
		The difference between the first level (docile wit) and the second level (normal intelligence) is what distinguishes humans from animals.

The second hypothesis of Sapir-Whorf is the principle of linguistic relativity—that the structure of language one habitually uses influences the manner in which one understands one's environment and behaves with respect to it.[58] The hypothesis dispels any notion of the existence of the so called primitive languages. It suggests rather that all languages operate in an entirely parallel but different worlds and that understanding the linguistic structure of a language, say Twi or Greek or Efik or Latin, is a prerequisite for understanding the mind of the Twis, Greeks, Efiks, and Latins. Differences between languages therefore, according to this hypothesis, accounts for the differences in the way events are reported. Take the Greek philosopher, Aristotle, for example, using his native Greek language, Aristotle posited the existence of ten categories he identified as substance, quantity, quality, relation, action, passion, place, time, posture, and habit. He spoke of these as the inventory of properties or predications that may be made about being:

> Each expression when it is not part of a combination means: the *substance,* or *how much,* or *of what kind,* or *relating to what,* or *where,* or *when,* or *to be in a position,* or *to be in a condition,* or *to do,* or *to undergo.* "Substance," for example, "man," "horse";—"how much," for example, "two cubits," "three cubits";—"of what kind," for example, "white," "educated";—"relating to what," for example, "double," "half," "larger";—"where," for example, "at the Lyceum," "at the market";—"when," for example, "today," "last year";—"to be in a position," for example, "he is lying down," "he is seated";—"to be in a condition," for example, "he is shod," "he is armed";—"to

---

58. Whorf, *Language, Thought, and Reality,* 23.

do," for example, "he cuts," "he burns";—"to undergo," for example, "he is cut," "he is burned."[59]

The French structuralist, linguist, and semiotician renowned for his work on Indo-European languages, Émile Benveniste (1902–76), has offered a helpful critique of Aristotle in refuting the notion that there are in fact only ten categories as Aristotle suggested. According to Benveniste, what Aristotle stated as a priori concepts and what he thought were absolutes that organize all human experience are primarily categories of language. The linguistic structure of Greek, which Aristotle spoke, predisposed his notion of being and "made it possible [for him] to set up 'being' as an objectifiable notion."[60] Although Aristotle was merely contrasting *episteme* from *doxa*, *sophia* from *phronesis*, and necessity from contingency, he was doing this by "simply identifying certain fundamental categories of the language in which he thought."[61]

Bienveniste's insight brings us back to the relationship between categories of thought and categories of language. Thought has a preeminent and independent position with regard to language.[62] But it is language that provides the fundamental configuration of the properties of things that the mind recognizes. While thought might claim to set up universal categories, "linguistic categories are always categories of a particular language."[63] According to Benveniste, "no matter how much validity Aristotle's categories have as categories of thought, they turn out to be transposed from categories of language."[64] While no type of language can by itself alone foster or hamper the activity of the mind, the structure of language is such that it is informed by signification—to think is to manipulate the signs of language.[65] A peculiar quality of an utterance is that it has a performative quality, "that of being self-referential, of referring to a reality that it itself constitutes by the fact that it is actually uttered in conditions that make it

---

59. Benveniste, *Problems in General Linguistics*, 57, citing Aristotle's *Categories*.
60. Ibid., 62.
61. Ibid., 57.
62. Ibid., 56.
63. Ibid.
64. Ibid., 61.
65. Ibid., 64.

an act."[66] An utterance taken as a whole is, therefore, more specifically (not a sentence or proposition) an act.[67]

In sum, the Sapir-Whorf hypotheses, significant as they were, fell out of favor in the 1940s and were dismissed for a variety of reasons before they were eventually rehabilitated and brought up for reconsideration by linguistics and cognitive psychologist like George Lakoff (b. 1941) and the University of Chicago professor of linguistics and anthropology, Paul Friedrich. The details of their critique need not detain us here. What is important for our purpose is that these linguists and cognitive psychologists reworked the Sapir-Whorf hypotheses emphasizing how individuals are influenced by the metaphors they use to explain phenomena—making meaning.

Meaning-Making

The groundbreaking work of Sapir-Whorf is the basis for speaking of "the linguistic turn" in anthropology that rejects any hard, fixed, essentialist notion of human nature. The linguistic turn helps us understand that human identities, like language, are fluid, multiple, highly contestable and in need of constant development. Thus, the Sapir-Whorf hypothesis that posits a relationship between categories of meaning within a language and the mental categories speakers of the said language use to describe the world has profound implications beyond linguistics. "It suggests that understanding meaning—in all its different dimensions—is as important as understanding phonetics, syntax, and grammar, the most common dimensions of linguistic analysis prior to Sapir's work."[68] The hypothesis also implies "that different languages mark different systems of perception and that the differences between societies' cultural behavior are communicated by and

---

66. Ibid., 236. According to Benveniste, a group known as Oxford philosophers devote themselves to analysis of ordinary language with the goal of freeing it from abstractions and conventional frames of reference. They demand that we scrutinize the words we use because a person can be blinded by a wrongly interpreted word. A leading member of the Oxford tradition is J. L. Austin who distinguishes three kinds of utterances: performative utterance (imperative utterances or utterances that perform an action), declarative utterance (assertion of fact), and constative utterance (utterances that are neither true nor false).

67. Austin, *How to Do Things with Words*, 20.

68. Moore, *Visions of Culture: An Introduction to Anthropological Theories and Theorists*, 88.

Metapragmatic Use of Language

codified in the structure of linguistic meaning."⁶⁹ Chomsky validates this point by making a valuable distinction between competence and performance in a language system used by a people in his theory of grammar. "Competence" is what all societies or peoples have in their native language system.⁷⁰ Out of that competence they are able to generate an endless variety of correct sentences which other speakers of the language find intelligible.⁷¹ The actual sentences generated in the process is what Chomsky calls "performances." There are certainly good, "well-formed performances, and incorrect, ill-formed performances. Any native speaker can instinctively recognize the difference between the two kinds of performances, but may not be able to account for the difference perceived."⁷²

Language is, therefore, about making meaning. Meaning is embodied in human intersubjectivity and is carried in art, in signs, in symbols, in language, and in the lives and actual conducts of human persons.⁷³ The codes or set of rules that govern the use of sign center around the three areas of syntactic (sets of relationships between signs that govern their movement through cultural system), semantics (content or meaning of the message), and pragmatics (rules that govern communication and range of intelligibility of what is being communicated).⁷⁴ While it is these three rules and the interaction of signs or group of signs that mutually define each other that produces a culture,⁷⁵ the semantic or meaning-related structure of language itself helps us to understand how various cultures view a meaningful life. The Sapir-Whorf hypotheses, for example, show how words have their meaning within sentences and that meaning is not separable from individual existence. "Meaning can be approached through language, but it is not the product of language."⁷⁶ Reality is meaningfully structured prior to it being grasped in language. Language can either grasp or miss the semantic structure of reality.⁷⁷ Lonergan brilliantly demonstrates this by distinguishing four functions of meaning.

69. Ibid., 89.
70. Schreiter, *Constructing Local Theologies*, 114.
71. Ibid.
72. Ibid.
73. Lonergan, *Method in Theology*, 57.
74. Schreiter, *Constructing Local Theologies*, 50.
75. Ibid.
76. Pannenberg, *The Historicity of Nature*, 151.
77. Ibid.

A first function of meaning is cognitive. Bernard Lonergan illustrates this carefully using the metaphor of a child's transition from the world of infancy to adulthood. An infant's world is no more than a world of sensory perception: touching, grasping, hearing, seeing, feeling, etc. It is a world of immediacy—of hunger and satisfaction, of thirst and inebriation, of sleeping and waking, etc. But an adult person does not live in a world of immediacy, but that mediated by meaning. The world mediated by meaning is a world of language and concepts. As one's language develops, words begin to denote, for the person, "not only what is present but also what is absent or past or future, not only what is factual but also the possible, the ideal, [and] the normative."[78]

Besides the cognitive function, meaning is also efficient. We are involved in acts of meaning through engagement in our various religions, histories, and specific ways of life, art-forms, and cultural traditions. Meaning is also constitutive because acts of meaning that are constituted are not immutable. "They adapt to changing circumstances; they can be reconceived in the light of new ideas."[79] Finally, meaning is also communicative. It can be communicated artistically, linguistically, or symbolically. What a people hold as their common meanings are passed on from one generation to another through communication.[80] Often times what holds a community or group together is their common meaning. Common meaning is realized, according to Lonergan, "by decisions and choices, especially by permanent dedication, in the love that makes families, in the loyalty that makes states, in the faith that makes religions. Community coheres or divides, begins or ends, just where the common field of experience, common understanding, common judgment, common commitments begin and end."[81]

Lonergan shows how the meaning that enters into the fabric of human living varies from place to place and from one generation to another. It means, therefore, that meaning is "subject to cumulative development and cumulative decline."[82] The question of meaning then, when correctly understood, is inseparable from the question of truth a community holds dear to itself. "To the concept of truth belongs the unity of all truth, that is, the simultaneous existence, without contradiction, of each individual truth

---

78. Lonergan, *Method in Theology*, 76–77.
79. Ibid., 78.
80. Ibid.
81. Ibid., 79.
82. Ibid., 81.

with all other truths."[83] Each individual, as a being shaped by a particular history, is also shaped in "interaction with the traditions of the communities in which he happens to have been born and, in turn, these traditions themselves are but the deposit left him by the lives of his predecessors."[84]

Can Language Mediate Culture?

The Sapir-Whorf hypotheses provided the backdrop for the much heralded semiotic turn in anthropology heralded by Charles Sanders Peirce (1839–1914) and Josiah Royce (1855–1916) and after them Susanne Langer—that the world is accessed through signs and symbols and words have no value except as symbols.[85] Language is a form of social sign. It is a powerful, supple, and adaptable symbolism.[86] Working out of the Sapir tradition, a tradition that views language as a heuristic whose "forms predetermine for us certain modes of observation and interpretation,"[87] Langer shows how language "first and foremost grows out of the tendency to see reality symbolically. It is rooted in primitive forms of aesthetic attraction and mysterious fear, an originary 'aesthetic sense of import.'"[88]

Why do we possess language to begin with? What is the relevance of the human-animal contrast relative to language? Langer answers that human beings possess language because they "all have the same psychological nature, which has reached, in the entire human race, a stage of development where symbol-using and symbol-making are dominant activities."[89] As a high form of symbolism, language makes possible the transformation of the world into concepts. This transformation is the primary semiotic motor driving language.[90] According to Langer, "the transformation of experience into concepts, not the elaboration of signals and symptoms, is the motive of language. Speech is through and through symbolic; and only sometimes signific."[91] Thus, Langer suggests that the roots of language are

---

83. Pannenberg, *The Historicity of Nature*, 160.
84. Lonergan, *Method in Theology*, 81.
85. Langer, *Philosophy in a New Key*, 75.
86. Ibid., 73.
87. Ibid., 126.
88. Innis, *Susan Langer in Focus*, 50–51.
89. Langer, *Philosophy in a New Key*, 142.
90. Innis, *Susan Langer in Focus*, 53.
91. Langer, *Philosophy in a New Key*, 126.

A Semiotic Approach to the Theology of Inculturation

in the affect-laden or the affect-drenched dimension of experience that non-human animals and humans share.[92] "Further, it is the ability, for example, to construct a symbolic gesture that leads to language as we know it. There is a difference in principle between an intentional genuflection and the emotional quaver of a suppliant's voice."[93]

For the sake of clarity, we need to distinguish the two important streams in anthropological theory that have inspired the shift to cultural relativity: the structuralist and the interpretive streams. The interpretive stream is more suited for a theology of inculturation. That is not to say one can dismiss the value of structuralism altogether. The interpretive school is in fact indebted to the structuralist school and many semioticians (one arm of the interpretive school) have acknowledged their indebtedness to Levi Strauss, the founder of the structuralist school. This is why some have taken to calling structuralism the "godparent" of semiotics.[94] The structuralist notion of linguistic sign was reformulated in the latter part of the twentieth century, thanks to the efforts of Roman Jakobson whose refinement of structuralism came with "an explicit and far-reaching criticism of Saussure, in spite of his acknowledged debt to the Swiss master."[95]

a. The Structuralist Tradition

The structuralist school was inspired by the French anthropologist, Claude Lévi-Strauss (1829–1902) who assumed that language is basically a structured and structuring part of culture.[96] Strauss was one of the first people to call attention "to the diverse 'sensory codes' through which information may be transmitted,

---

92. Innis, *Susan Langer in Focus*, 51.

93. Ibid.

94. Schreiter, *Constructing Local Theologies*, 51.

95. Caton, "Contributions of Roman Jacobson," 224. Jacobson refuted Saussure's notion of the sign as too linear. While he commended Saussure for working out a system of signification, he faults him for not adequately drawing out its further implications for language theory. According to Caton, for Saussure, the purpose of communication was referential, but as we now know "reference is not the only, nor even the primary goal of communication. Nor does structural system serve all goals. Rather, in Jacobsonian/Prague School model, language is composed of many different kinds of subsystems, each subsystem being the means to accomplish a particular goal or purpose of communication. Language is viewed as a 'system of systems' with cross-cutting properties such as binariness, hierarchy, and paradigmatic and syntagmatic oppositions" (231).

96. Mukerji and Schudson, "Rethinking Popular Culture," 18.

and how they may be combined and mutually 'translated.'"[97] Strauss and his followers argued that it is language system that gives order to the experience of individuals, in addition to providing them with the means of generating complex cultural forms.[98] All societies, simple and complex ones alike, have "complex cultures because all societies have relatively complex language systems."[99] Structuralists hold the view:

> that the human mind universally orders the flux of experience into binary oppositions: male/female, sacred/profane, pure/impure, in/out, kin/other, and most of all, nature/culture. People make sense of the world through these binary categories and make use of the sense data of the world—plants, animals, colors, human bodies, weather, geography—to arrive at cognitive order. Things that seem to bridge categories are "anomalous" and take on special powers of danger, magic, or heightened meaning. Religious systems and myths are cultural constructions that elaborate a society's cognitive categories. The cognitive categories hold social, moral, and intellectual significance.[100]

The structuralist approach places great emphasis on the cognitive experience of a social group because religion, for the structuralist, is not so much about the spirit as it is about the mind.[101] Strauss understands the use of myth in religion, for example, as an instance of "not how men think in myths but how myths operate in men's minds without their being aware of the fact."[102]

b. The Interpretive Tradition

The interpretive stream differs from the structuralist tradition in many ways. While the structuralist school emphasizes "cognitive organization," for example, the interpretive tradition emphasizes "patterns of feeling or sentiment."[103] In terms of method, the interpretive school also differs from the structuralist in the sense in the sense that it tries to understand human experience

---

97. Turner, *From Ritual to Theatre*, 9.
98. Mukerji and Schudson, "Rethinking Popular Culture," 18.
99. Ibid.
100. Ibid., 19.
101. Ibid.
102. Levi-Strauss, *The Raw and the Cooked*, 12.
103. Mukerji and Schudson, "Rethinking Popular Culture," 20.

from the point of view of the subject and by so doing avoids the danger of taking things out of context, as the structuralists tend to do.[104] The interpretive tradition owes a lot to the efforts of Charles Sanders Peirce and Clifford Geertz who place a lot of premium on signs and our ability to interpret them. We shall consider Geertz's views in the next chapter, in other to see more clearly why he "takes the capacity for and reliance on the symbolic as the defining feature of the human species"[105] and why he suggests that symbols "exercise a cybernetic control over human behavior, expressing the social and the personality systems of a culture without being merely expressive."[106]

Geertz was preceded by Peirce in the interpretive school. Peirce's ground work on sign was important for the thinkers that followed him. Peirce speaks of sign as a *representamen*, "something which stands to somebody for something in some respect or capacity."[107] A sign addresses somebody and creates in the mind of the person "an equivalent sign, or perhaps a more developed sign."[108] Peirce calls the sign which the sign creates in the mind the "interpretant" of the first sign. The "interpretant" stands for something, the object. Thus, a sign, for Peirce denotes an object that is perceptible, imaginable, or even unimaginable. For something to qualify to be a sign it must "represent" something else, its object. A sign may have more than one object. "If a sign is other than its object, there must exist either in thought or in expression, some explanation or argument or the context, showing how—upon what system or for what reason the sign represents the object or set of objects that it does."[109]

Peirce suggests that every sign virtually has a "precept," i.e., a precept of explanation embodying how it is to be understood as an "emanation" of its object.[110] The sign only represents and says something about the object it represents. An object here may be

104. Ibid., 20.
105. Ibid.
106. Ibid.
107. Peirce, *Collected Papers*, 135.
108. Ibid.
109. Ibid., 136.
110. Ibid., 137.

either a real-world object (like a mighty house) or an event (the coronation of the village chief) or an idea.[111] The object of the sign is "that with which it presupposes an acquaintance in order to convey some further information concerning it."[112] Peirce distinguishes three kinds of signs within a sign he calls icon (a sign which refers to the object it denotes by which of the characters it possess on its own), index ("a sign which refers to the object that it denotes by virtue of being really affected by that object"), and symbol ("a sign which refers to the object that it denotes by virtue of a law, usually association of general ideas, which operates to cause the symbol to be interpreted as referring to that object").[113] A sign then may be termed an icon, an index, or a symbol. Caton explains how this modality works:

> The sign bears some resemblance to the object it stands for. A map, for example, is an icon of a certain geographic space. In an indexical mode, the sign does not necessarily bear any physical resemblance to the object it stands for, but it must be in existential relationship with it (spatially or temporally contiguous to it). The map refers in the indexical mode when it is held up before the geographic space it stands for. Finally, the symbol refers to its object in all the ways icons and indexes do not. In a symbol, the relationship between the sign and its "object" is established by cultural convention or law.[114]

Thus, the Peircean tripartite mode of icon, index, and symbol shows "how signs may be intrinsically or existentially connected to what they stand for and yet may still be ontologically distinct."[115]

Another major figure and significant influence in the interpretative tradition is the British cultural anthropologist, Victor Turner (1920–83). Turner spent three years living in grass huts in the African villages of Ndembu, Lamba, Kosa, and Gisu in Zambia, an experience that brought home to him the power of symbols in human communication. The experience also made Turner realize that the power of symbols inheres "not only

111. Caton, "Contributions of Roman Jacobson," 235.
112. Peirce, *Collected Papers*, 137.
113. Ibid., 143.
114. Caton, "Contributions of Roman Jacobson," 235.
115. Caton, "What Is an 'Authorizing Discourse?,'" 37.

in the shared lexicons and grammars of spoken and written languages, but also in the artful or poetic individual crafting of speech through persuasive tropes: metaphors, metonyms, oxymora, 'wise words' (a Western Apache speech-mode), and many more."[116] When Turner speaks of communication through symbols, he is not limiting it to spoken words. He writes about how in every culture everyone "uses the entire sensory repertoire to convey messages: manual gesticulations, facial expressions, bodily postures, rapid, heavy, or light breathing, tears, at the individual level; stylized gestures, dance patterns, prescribed silences, synchronized movements such as marching, the moves and 'plays' of games, sports, and rituals, at the cultural level."[117] Turner calls these "social drama." Social drama takes place at all levels of social organization from the state to the family.

The structuralist and the (line of Peircean) interpretive tradition of sign complement each other, together rounding up "a holistic conception of semiotics."[118] Together with later additions and refinements of Clifford Geertz, the semiotic conception of sign would become very valuable for understanding culture and doing the work of inculturation. What they tell us in a nutshell is that language mediates culture in so far as it is the collaboration between the group of signs that mutually define each other and the rules governing the use of signs that produce culture. What semiotics does in this whole quest is "to describe and explain the signs, their interaction, the rules that govern them, and the complex that we call culture which emerges from all of this."[119]

Language—Indexicality of Ideology and Condition for Culture

In language lies the connection between cognition, perception, and cultures that are revealed in symbolic forms.[120] It is in the quest to appreciate these connections that both the structuralist and interpretative traditions of anthropology together aim at global cultural understanding. Together, to use the expression of Wilhelm Dilthey (1833–1911), they seek to "understand other people and their expressions on the basis of experience and

---

116. Turner, *From Ritual to Theatre*, 9.
117. Ibid.
118. Caton, "Contributions of Roman Jacobson," 235.
119. Schreiter, *Constructing Local Theologies*, 50.
120. Turner, *The Ritual Process*, v.

Metapragmatic Use of Language

self-understanding and the constant interaction between them."[121] Claude Levi-Strauss, to his credit, is among the first to capture this relationship between language and culture, pointing how necessary it is when we study a culture, to know the language and how necessary it is to understand what is meant by the population and also how necessary it is to have some knowledge of the culture besides the language.[122] Our concern here is not with the problem of causal relations, i.e., whether it is language which influences culture or whether it is culture that influences language. That investigation, as helpful is it may be, is beyond the scope of this project. Our concern rather is to tease out the dynamic interplay and the mutual influences between language and culture. We prescind from the assumption, as Levi-Strauss correctly puts it, "that between culture and language there cannot be no relations at all, and there cannot be 100 percent correlation either. Both situations are impossible to conceive."[123] Or as Lonergan puts it, "to be educated linguistically and to become human are found to be interchangeable."[124]

Language not only molds the developing consciousness of a people, it also structures their world.[125] Language gives us a clue into a people's social construction of self because embedded in every language are ideologies people hold about themselves, their world, who they are, and their place in the world. What is termed linguistic ideology in contemporary linguistic anthropology is a specific kind of discourse within language use—a reflexive meta-level statements about the way we use language.[126] It is defined by Michael Silverstein (b. 1945) as "sets of beliefs about language articulated by users as a rationalization or justification of perceived language structure and use."[127] Shedding more light on the concept further, Miyako Inoue explains that the concept of linguistic ideology concerns how both the structure and use of language, as well as beliefs about language, are conceived as interconnected dialectically in such a way that the one necessarily constitutes the other.[128]

---

121. Turner, *From Ritual to Theatre*, 18, quoting Dilthey, *Selected Writings*, 218.
122. Levi-Strauss, *Structural Anthropology*, 67.
123. Ibid., 79.
124. Lonergan, *Method in Theology*, 97.
125. Ibid., 71.
126. Inoue, *Vicarious Language*, 17.
127. Silverstein, "Language Structure and Linguistic Ideology," 193, cited in Inoue, *Vicarious Language*, 17.
128. Inoue, *Vicarious Language*, 17–18.

Language, ipso facto, leads to emergence of culture. Or put differently, cultural objects exist in and derive from a "code" or "language," i.e., that in the grammar of language "a 'sender' 'encodes' a 'message' in a given 'medium' that a 'receiver' or 'audience' then 'decodes.'"[129] Language, according to Levi-Strauss, can be said to be a condition of culture in two different ways:

> First, it is a condition of culture in a diachronic way, because it is mostly through the language that we learn about our own culture—we are taught by our parents, we are scolded, we are congratulated, with language. But also from a much more theoretical point of view, language can be said to be a condition of culture because the material out of which language is built is of the same type as the material out of which the whole culture is built: logical relations, oppositions, correlations, and the like. Language from this point of view, may appear as laying a kind of foundation for the more complex structures which correspond to the different aspects of culture.[130]

If language opens us up to a people's ideologies and leads to emergence of culture, the question then arises: (i) what do we mean by ideology? And (ii) what do we mean by culture? Since the question regarding what we mean by culture is a matter for the next chapter, only a tentative answer is required here. Steven Caton has done an important ethnographical work that addresses the difference between the reproduction of the cultural system and its emergence in communicative action. According to Caton, since it is the case that communicative action reproduces the cultural systems of symbols and meanings that is critical to social interaction, "it cannot be the case that culture has to be created *de novo* each time or be negotiated or emerge in every new transaction." [131] On the other hand, since a cultural system is not entirely given or presupposed, "there are situations in which intersubjective understanding must be created in communicative action."[132] For this reason, Caton suggests the following four types of social contexts as contexts in which an emergent notion of culture might be apropos:

1. Contexts of socialization and acculturation whereby cultural patterns emerge in the adolescent's repertoire of behaviors.

---

129. Mukerji and Schudson, "Rethinking Popular Culture," 11.
130. Levi-Strauss, *Structural Anthropology*, 68–69.
131. Caton, *Peaks of Yemen I Summon*, 260–61.
132. Ibid., 261.

2. Contexts of socioeconomic change whereby traditional systems no longer become adequate model or precedent for social actions. Instead new patterns emerge in the place of the older ones, or in the least blend and coexist ambiguously with them.

3. Contexts in which misunderstandings, which may or may not lead to serious conflicts, arise in sociopolitical interactions, leading to a new way of understanding or apprehension.

4. Contexts of social reconstruction that often take place after natural disasters or wars. This leads to the formation of larger national and social entities.[133]

The emergence of culture in social action will be elaborately discussed in the next chapter when we examine the semiotic approach of Clifford Geertz who was a leading figure in the reconstitution of the boundaries between anthropology and the social and behavioral sciences in the second half of the twentieth century.[134] Geertz's delineation of culture as a system of symbols and their meanings will also shed more light on the idea that peoples' ideologies are embedded in their language. Language is not just a system of abstract grammatical categories, but a worldview that is ideologically saturated. According to Mikhail Bakhtin, "every concrete utterance of a speaking subject serves as a point where centrifugal as well as centripetal forces are brought to bear."[135]

> Aristotelian poetics, the poetics of Augustine, the poetics of the medieval church, of "the language of truth," the Cartesian poetics of neoclassicism, the abstract grammatical universalism of Leibnitz (the idea of a "universal grammar"), Humboldt's insistence of the concrete—all these, whatever their differences in nuance, give expression to the same centripetal forces in socio-linguistics and ideological life.[136]

When we speak of language as "ideology," it should by no means be understood in the Marxist sense of something terrifying or "mystifying," i.e., that "the dominant class or group tries to impose its own notion—always a partial one—of reality on the rest of society, thereby achieving

---

133. Ibid.
134. See Ortner, *The Fate of "Culture,"* 1.
135. Bahktin, *The Dialogic Imagination*, 272.
136. Ibid., 271.

social preeminence and political predominance."[137] Rather, ideology here is meant to be understood along the lines delineated by Mikhail Bakhtin and Pavel Medvedev (1892–1938), Charles Sanders Peirce, and Valentin Nikolaevich Volosinov (1895–1936), and after them Lev Semyonovich Vygostky (1896–1934). They all show that language is a particular point of view on the world; that ideas cannot exist unmediated by material signs and how ideology is inseparable from communication.[138] Bahktin shows how language, at any given moment of its historical existence, "is heteroglot from top to bottom: it represents the co-existence of socio-ideological contradictions between the present and the past, between differing epochs of the past, between different socio-ideological groups in the present, between tendencies, schools, circles and so forth, all given a bodily form."[139] As Volosinov tersely expressed it, "the reality of the inner psyche is the same reality as that of the sign" and "understanding is a response to a sign with a sign."[140] Volosinov writes in *Marxism and the Philosophy of Language*:

> A sign does not simply exist as part of a reality—it reflects and refracts no other reality. Therefore, it may distort that reality or be true to it, or may perceive it from a special point of view, and so forth. Every sign is subject to the criteria of ideological evaluation (i.e., whether it is true, false, correct, fair, good, etc.). The domain of ideology coincides with domain of signs. They equate with one another. Wherever a sign is present, ideology is present, too. Everything ideological possesses semiotic value.[141]

Volosinov suggests that since "word is the ideological phenomenon par excellence," nowhere does the semiotic quality of sign appear fully and clearly as in language.[142]

As valuable as the ideas expressed in *Marxism and the Philosophy of Language* are, the authorship of the work still remains unclear. There are some who think the work was written by Volosinov, a student of Bakhtin and a Communist Party functionary, others think it was written by Bakhtin who chose to publish it under Volosinov's name because he Bakhtin was

137. Caton, *"Peaks of Yemen I Summon,"* 262.

138. Ibid.

139. Bahktin, *The Dialogical Imagination*, 291.

140. Caton, *"Peaks of Yemen I Summon,"* 262, quoting Volisinov, *Marxism and the Philosophy of Language*, 26 and 11.

141. Volosinov, *Marxism and the Philosophy of Language*, 10.

142. Ibid., 13.

Metapragmatic Use of Language

not viewed favorably by the Communist Party, while still others think it was jointly written by Bakhtin and Volosinov.[143] The book proposes the existence of two kinds of ideologies: an official ideology, "which emanates from various state apparatuses and other institutions of power,"[144] and a behavioral or an everyday or unofficial ideology, "which emerges through social interaction and in what they call dialogue."[145] The book, according to Caton,

> make the important point that the study of ideology had been confined largely to official ideology and that its operations in everyday behavior, especially linguistic behavior, had been neglected. But this neglect or oversight is unfortunate, for one can only understand how the official ideology sustains itself and leads to some sort of regulated social practice through the behavioral (dialogical) one. Indeed, according to their thinking, it is the everyday or behavioral ideology that "authorizes" the official one—and vice versa, for the two are in dialectical relation to each other. However, because it is a dialectical relation, the behavioral ideology may also implicitly "comment on" or "frame" the official ideology in ways that subtly undermine or subvert rather than merely authorizing it.[146]

In their concern for dialogue or the grammatical or linguistic ways in which dialogue is instantiated, the author or authors of *Marxism and the Philosophy of Language*, referring specifically to behavioral ideology, suggest that "a person, while speaking, is at once replying to a previous 'said' of discourse (either her own or someone else's) and anticipating a reply or answer to her own, and insofar as the stretch of speech may be said to contain these multiple voices of self/selves and other(s), it is 'poly-vocal.'"[147]

In various respects, both Bakhtin and Volosinov connect dialogicality with power, suggesting that understanding speech act helps one to understand how power operates.[148] The larger point here is, "that if one wants to understand religious practice, one has to understand it as a construction."[149] One, therefore, must "be attentive to the ways in which a discourse can

---

143. Caton, "What Is an 'Authorizing Discourse'?," 51.
144. Ibid.
145. Ibid.
146. Ibid.
147. Ibid., 52.
148. Ibid.
149. Ibid., 56.

constitute itself metapragmatically . . . And it is this creative or emergent process that one must grasp if one is to understand, in turn, how power is constituted in action."[150]

Implication of Linguistic Pragmatism for a Theology of Inculturation

The matter of how meaning is organized and communicated in a culture has profound theological import and very significant for a theology of inculturation. Inculturation is a dynamic interaction of the three elements of gospel, church, and culture, a dynamic interaction that Robert Schreiter correctly conceives as having a dialectical relationship. The gospel raises questions about the community or indigenous society. The church poses questions about how the community's relationship to the larger church ensures faithfulness to received and cherished tradition and how this relationship guarantees unity of the church at large. Both the church and gospel interact with culture with a view to making the gospel and culture at home in that culture.[151] How, for example, should a culture that has just received the gospel incorporate or receive church doctrine when that doctrine "is given in a form for which there is no cultural analogue in the local situation?"[152] How does such a culture resolve its question when the church's "only experience with its concern was under quite different circumstances?"[153] What are the criteria, if it is possible to outline them, of genuine Christian identity?[154] It demands then that church and gospel listen to a culture "to discover its principal values, needs, interests, directions, and symbols."[155] Listening to culture demands finding a balance between "respect of the culture and the need for change within culture."[156] It demands also development of what Clifford Geertz calls "thick description."[157] Thick description in theological terms demands that one finds a way of identifying Christ already present and active in culture as well as finding creative ways of bringing Christ

---

150. Ibid.
151. Schreiter, *Constructing Local Theologies*, 22–23.
152. Ibid., 96.
153. Ibid., 97.
154. Ibid., 98.
155. Ibid., 28.
156. Ibid., 29.
157. See Geertz, *The Interpretation of Cultures*.

into culture.¹⁵⁸ But this also presupposes that the culture has had a genuine encounter with the Christian tradition. We shall treat Geertz's description more fully in the next chapter. But the point here is that a theology of inculturation cannot neglect the valuable insights of postmodern thinkers and theoretical linguistics on culture. Theoretical linguistics' idea on language as a medium of communication and meaning-making follows along the lines of post-modern attempts to understand culture as fluid, "mutually interactive, internally contested, and indeed always prone to entropy, viral diseases, and even breakdown, as history attests."¹⁵⁹ In their "various attempts to 'stop the show, 'freeze the flux,' and 'release the truth-police'" postmodern thinkers reject any totalizing understanding of reality.¹⁶⁰ Their program of deconstruction was geared towards bringing an end to reification of thought or ideas that characterized both modernity and classical culture. They exalted "the heteromorphous nature of life, thought, and speech," in contradistinction to the universalizing tendencies of previous centuries.¹⁶¹ According to Thomas Guarino, "by unmasking horizons rooted in our factical situatedness—social location, ideological determination, cultural embeddedness, saturated reason, paradigm-bound rationality, contextualized knowledge, and the ontological productivity of history—postmodernity has become a militant protest and call to arms against universalizing tendencies."¹⁶² Working out of Nietzsche's idea that social and cultural set-ups, like politics, economic, and technological set-ups, are in the final analysis matters of convention that are precarious, fallible, and revisable, the postmodern thinkers championed the idea of plurality and difference.¹⁶³ It is the works of Nietzsche. Marx, Freud, Heidegger, etc. that sparked corresponding thought in the field of anthropology and linguistics, giving rise to Sapir, Whorf, Peirce, Austin, Langer, etc., who all "reject foundationalist ontologies of all types because these [ontologies] seek to 'close down' effective history, to end historical consciousness."¹⁶⁴

158. Schreiter, *Constructing Local Theologies*, 29.
159. Arbuckle, *Culture, Inculturation, and Theologians*, xii.
160. Guarino, "Postmodernity and Five Fundamental Theological Issues," 654.
161. Ibid., 655.
162. Ibid.
163. Lawrence, "The Fragility of Consciousness," 78.
164. Guarino, "Postmodernity and Five Fundamental Theological Issues," 656.

A Semiotic Approach to the Theology of Inculturation

In light of postmodern critique, theology must "evaluate its classical self-understanding, particularly its notion of ontology."[165] As Robert Schreiter carefully pointed out regarding the need to develop new conceptual categories to meet the needs of local context, "any catechist who has tried to explain to a religion class the complexities of Chalcedonian Christology will realize that some of the Chalcedonian questions are no longer questions to many contemporary local churches, even though these may be normative for them."[166] Postmodern critique makes us aware of the need for theology to engage in what Schreiter calls a sociology of theology.[167] Sociology of theology is akin to sociology of knowledge, "which is concerned with how ideas and systems of thought relate to their social contexts."[168] A sociology of knowledge tries to answer questions like: "Why is it that certain ideas or ways of thinking become prevalent at a particular point in time? How does an idea become outmoded? What wo we mean when say that an idea appears prematurely or ahead of its time?"[169] The answer, according to Schreiter is not far-fetched for the following reasons:

1. Some forms of thought are embedded in social conditions but they are not unilaterally determined by them because ideas can shape culture as much as culture can shape ideas.

2. Religion has a complex set of relations (legitimation, socialization, conservation, and innovation) to culture.[170]

3. Religion is far more than a set of doctrines or ideas; it is also a way of living in a world of human relationships.[171]

4. Although a particular form of thought may predominate in a culture at a given point in time, it nevertheless can live side by side with other thought forms.[172]

---

165. Ibid., 659.
166. Schreiter, *Constructing Local Theologies*, 32.
167. Ibid., 80.
168. Ibid., 78.
169. Ibid., 79.
170. Ibid.
171. Ibid.
172. Ibid.

5. "The relations between forms of thought and social conditions are such that they rarely allow for exhaustive description."[173]

We already saw (in chapter one) how Jean-Marc Ela took a leading role in critiquing the Christological metaphors he inherited from western missionaries. Ela was in essence posing a postmodern question and doing at the same time a kind of sociology of theology required for a theology of inculturation—that particular thought forms, like the Christological categories used at Chalcedon, are culture based, and that new thought-forms that are related to one's culture may be more helpful today in expressing the same ideas that Chalcedon expressed at the time. One of those who have addressed postmodern concerns in a way that is consistent with semiotic approach to culture in the field of Catholic theology and whose ideas we shall explore later (in chapter six) to develop a semiotic theology of inculturation was Bernard Lonergan who in bringing a balanced and nuanced understanding showed that while classicism was "not mistaken in its assumption that there is something substantial and common to human nature and human activity, its oversight is its failure to grasp that something substantial and common also is something quite open."[174] There is no denying the fact that the program of deconstruction of postmodern thinkers can lead to extreme relativism,[175] but such extremism has no place in a theology of inculturation and would in fact be antithetical to the objectivity that semiotics stands for. Perhaps one point we can draw from their program of deconstruction, which is pertinent to our semiotic approach to an African theology of inculturation, may indeed be "that Marx and Nietzsche expressed a more profound and effectual appreciation of the sinfulness of modern social and cultural structures than their Christian contemporaries had done."[176]

Conclusion

Carl Starkloff in a helpful essay on "Inculturation and Cultural Systems" has compared the infusion of the term "inculturation" into theological discourse to the proverbial stone cast into a pond because its ripples are

---

173. Ibid.
174. Lonergan, *Doctrinal Pluralism*, 8.
175. Lawrence, "The Fragility of Consciousness," 78.
176. Ibid.

now felt throughout the Christian world.¹⁷⁷ In chapter six we shall show how these ripples have factored into how one might construct a semiotic approach to an African theology of inculturation. Our task in this chapter has been limited to integrating insights of linguistic metapragmatics to the study of inculturation and by so doing do, in Lonerganian terms, "profound exigence" or the "contemporary exigence" that is required to bring theologians in contact with experts from other fields.¹⁷⁸ Since one of the characteristic features of our time is "ever increasing change due to an ever increasing expansion of knowledge," to use Lonergan's own words, "to operate on the level of our day is to apply the best available knowledge and the most efficient techniques" to meet both the needs of the Church and those of humankind.¹⁷⁹ This has been our quest to this point. The linguistic turn to metapragmatics—the practice of representing what is said (or imagined to be said) in a statement, text, discourse, or sign has the "capacity to transport spatially and temporally what is said from one context to another as a carrier in an endless loop of contextualization, decontenxtualization, and recontextualization."¹⁸⁰ This metapragmatics, understood in Jacques Derrida's sense of "iterability," i.e., ability to be viable and repeated in one context to another, is important for inculturation. "Iterability" is Derrida's way of speaking of the universal capacity of the sign—the ability of the sign to be repeated in *differance*. "Citationality" is equally his other way of speaking of "the ability of an utterance to be extracted from one context and contextualized in another."¹⁸¹ Thus, a sign, in Derrida's way of understanding the term, "carries with it a force that breaks with its context.... This breaking force (*force de rupture*) is not an accidental predicate but the very structure of [what is signified.]"¹⁸²

Lonergan's own analysis of inner word in *Verbum* also implicitly affirms the role played by language in perception and imagination leading up to acts of insight.¹⁸³ The Christian message can be conceived as an "iterable" sign in that it has a universal capacity, a capacity that also has "citationality,"

---

177. See Starkloff, "Inculturation and Cultural Systems," 69.
178. Lonergan, *Method in Theology*, 367.
179. Ibid.
180. Inoue, *Vicarious Language*, 20.
181. Ibid.
182. Derrida, *Limited INC*, 9.
183. Lawrence, "The Fragility of Consciousness," 84. See also Lonergan, *Verbum*; Lonergan, *Word and Idea in Aquinas*, 1–11, 151–53, and 155.

in that it can be taken from one cultural context and replicated or contextualized in very meaningful way in another cultural context. Citationality, as Derrida explains, not only "produces copies in difference," it is also "identical from one instance to another, but each instance is also different."[184] Lonergan also shows how, as intelligent, reasonable, and responsible human beings we can "use language to get beyond ourselves in knowing reality and in transforming it. This in no way occludes all the ways in which it is also true to say that language uses us perhaps even more than we use it."[185] We have already shown (in chapter one) how the Bakhtin-Volosinov metapragmatic idea that discourse, as "speech within speech," "speech about speech," or "utterance within utterance," "utterance about utterance," is helpful for inculturation.[186] "It is a way to take others' voices into one's utterance, and, by doing so, to construct and, potentially, to transform them."[187] It brings to light the need for authenticity or withdrawal from unauthenticity that Lonergan suggests brings to light the need for still further withdrawals.[188] To truly respond to others' voices one must ensure "the elimination of oversights and misunderstandings,"[189] that way "genuine religion is discovered and realized by redemption from the many traps of religious aberration."[190] In a nutshell, Lonergan shows how "by being more attuned to the way the structure and dynamism of consciousness mutually 'horizon' language, we may be more responsible and care-full in our utterances and actions."[191]

---

184. Inoue, *Vicarious Language*, 23.
185. Lawrence, "The Fragility of Consciousness," 85.
186. Volosinov, *Marxism and the Philosophy of Language*, 115.
187. Inoue, *Vicarious Language*, 18.
188. Lonergan, *Method in Theology*, 110.
189. Ibid.
190. Ibid.
191. Lawrence, "The Fragility of Consciousness," 85.

4

"Cultural Turn" and the Problematic of Inculturation

IN THE NEXT CHAPTER we shall attempt an elaborate clarification of the meaning of inculturation, a word as we shall see that has been historically linked with the Society of Jesus (the Jesuits). The Jesuits have a long tradition of adapting the Christian message to the various cultural situations they encounter. Ever before the word inculturation became a common word in the theological vocabulary, the Jesuits were already using it to denote a way of seeking relationship between faith and culture in their missionary enterprise. One of their best efforts at articulating what they mean by the word inculturation came at their general meeting in 1974 in which they issued a paltry, but nonetheless important two paragraph decree, on "The Work of Inculturation of the Faith and Promotion of Christian Life."[1] As important as this decree was, it still did not clarify the meaning of word inculturation. The decree, however, recommended that the Superior General of the Jesuits seek "expert assistance" to clarify for the congregation the true meaning of this important theological term. When Pedro Arrupe became the superior general of the Jesuits he took upon himself the task of implementing the decree of the General Congregation as demanded by the 1974 document. After seeking "expert assistance," Arrupe drew from sources that include Vatican II document *Lumen Gentium* (Pastoral Constitution of the Church in the Modern World) and *Evangelii Nuntiandi* of Pope Paul VI to clarify the meaning of this term that has a long and varied usage in Jesuit history. Although the common thrust of the ecclesial documents from which Arrupe drew was the "evangelization of cultures," neither one of the docu-

---

1. See Society of Jesus, *Documents of the Thirty-First and Thirty-Second General Congregation of the Society of Jesus*, 439–40. See also Starkloff, "Inculturation and Cultural Systems," 66–81.

"Cultural Turn" and the Problematic of Inculturation

ments used the term inculturation. Since a clarification of the meaning of the term inculturation inevitably involves a clarification of the meaning of the term "culture," Arrupe made it clear "that he was understanding 'culture' as these documents defined it, and made no further elaboration."[2] To rely exclusively on ecclesial documents, as Arrupe did, for the meaning of culture is fraught with many problems. "In the documents of Vatican II and subsequent ecclesial documents 'culture' is most frequently to be understood in its classicist sense."[3] Even *Gaudium et Spes* (The Pastoral Constitution of the Church in the Modern Word) that has the most direct references to culture can be confusing because it uses culture in both its empirical sense and classicist sense.[4]

In this chapter we attempt a cultural hermeneutic, what is known in social and behavioral sciences as the "cultural turn," with a view to getting at the empirical meaning of culture, since a clarification of the meaning of the term helps our understanding of inculturation. A critical understanding of culture is important, both for the reason that culture is an essentially contested concept and also for the reason that it is "a multiply defined one, multiply employed, ineradicably imprecise. It is fugitive, unsteady, encyclopedic, and normatively charged."[5] According to Clifford Geertz for whom the study of culture is "the understanding of understanding,"[6] there are those "for whom only the really real is really real, who think it vacuous altogether, or even dangerous, and would ban [the term culture] from the serious discourse of serious persons."[7] A critical understanding of culture is therefore crucial to our subject, keeping in mind however Alfred Lang's admonition that "attempts at defining culture in a definite way are futile."[8] Our cultural critique is aimed at attempting an answer to a two-pronged question: If there is only little in the moral domain that transcends culture and history how might it be possible for a people to be both different from us with regard to their social norms and still be entitled to have a good valuation of their social norms at the same time? And does cultural critique

---

2. Starkloff, "Inculturation and Cultural Systems," 68. See also Gallagher, *Clashing Symbols*, 36–55.
3. Arbuckle, *Culture, Inculturation, and Theologians*, 140.
4. Ibid.
5. Geertz, *Available Light*, 11.
6. See Geertz, *Local Knowledge*, 5.
7. Geertz, *Available Light*, 11.
8. Lang, "Thinking Rich As Well As Simple," 389.

not presuppose that one separates the provincial aspects of his or her moral judgment from non-provincial ones?[9]

The "cultural turn," to be clear, is not the same as "culture matters" or "bringing culture back in." Beyond any mnemonic devise, the cultural turn resists the "foundationalist de-contextualization," i.e., their ahistorical and essentialist assumptions about human nature.[10] There is no consensus as to who first effected the "turn," but a number of texts have been mentioned as responsible for the cultural turn. Among these are the American literary critic Hayden White's (b. 1928) *Metahistory: The Historical Imagination in the Nineteenth Century Europe* (1973) and the French poststructuralist Michel Foucault's *Discipline and Punish: The Birth of Prison* (1977). There are also many others, like the French literary theorist and semiotician Roland Barthes (1915–180), the French sociologist Pierre Bourdieu (1930–2002), the French philosopher and deconstructionist Jacques Derrida, the American physicist and philosopher of science Thomas Kuhn (1922–96), the American philosopher Richard Rorty (1931–2007), the American anthropologist Marshall Sahlins (b. 1930) and the Welsh novelist and critic Raymond Williams (1921–88). The most significant influence in the "cultural turn" however, is the American cultural anthropologist, Clifford Geertz who, although in theory separates culture (a system of symbols) from society (a system of social relations), in practice seeks to understand their mutuality.[11]

Geertz, whose insight we shall consider next, is our principal interlocutor here. His influential essay "Religion as a Cultural System,"[12] which follows his interpretive or hermeneutical approach to culture has been seriously attacked by Talal Asad in his widely read work *Genealogies of Religion*.[13] In his reading of Geertz's work, Asad understands Geertz as advancing a "universal" or "trans-historical" definition of religion as a cultural system, a definition that Asad interprets as purporting to perennially hold on to an ontological essence of religion.[14] Asad "scrutinizes the various constituent parts of the definition in an effort to demonstrate that it cannot, in fact, work in the way that Geertz claims it does. But he takes aim at the definition largely in order to show that Geertz's entire theoretical approach,

---

9. Shweder, "The Resolute Irresolution of Clifford Geertz," 204.
10. Suny, "Back and Beyond," 1484.
11. Mukerji and Schudson, "Rethinking Popular Culture," 20.
12. See Geertz, "Religion As a Cultural System," 176–217.
13. See Asad, *Genealogies of Religion*.
14. See Caton, "What Is an 'Authoring Discourse?,'" 33.

sometimes called interpretive, sometimes hermeneutic anthropology, is confused, if not downright wrong."[15] While Asad was right in holding that definition, by itself, is the historical product of discursive process and that there cannot be a universal definition of religion because its constituent elements are historically specific, the problem is that Asad substantially mischaracterizes Geertz's project. The fact is, as Steven Caton correctly points out, Geertz is not making a universalist claim in the essay in question and "explicitly says he is not."[16] While it is beyond the scope of this work to attempt a rebuttal of Talal Asad's criticism of Geertz's interpretive work, it is useful to point out in passing that such a refutation has been done by Steven Caton in "What Is an 'Authorizing Discourse?'" Needless to say that Geertz's portrayal of how signs are used in social context and how cultural meaning is constituted through them remains useful,[17] as we show next.

Clifford Geertz (1926–2006)

Clifford Geertz was born in San Francisco, California. He had a difficult early life because his parents were divorced when he was three. According to Geertz's own account of the event, he was "dispatched" afterwards to live alone with an older woman in a northern California countryside. This was during the Great Depression. When he turned seventeen he enlisted in the US Navy (1943–45). After World War II he was discharged (1946), and like many others who served in the U.S. military, Geertz took advantage of the G.I. Bill and attended Antioch College, OH (1946–50). He started with English, which at the time included literature, but later switched to philosophy. He graduated in 1950 with BA in philosophy.

After he graduated from college, not sure what to do next because of the hard economic conditions of the Great Depression, Geertz sought the

---

15. Ibid. Caton dismisses Asad's claims—that Geertz is a cognitivist and that what Geertz takes to be religion as a cultural system are things Geertz (unconsciously) think are embedded in Christian theology. Caton writes that he takes exception to "the characterization of Geertz as a cognitivist tout court, a move that is not a little ironic when one recalls what passed for cognitivist anthropology in the 1970s, a movement Geertz vehemently distanced himself from in interpretive essays published in 1973 . . . And it was such formalistic and cognitivist approaches to the study of culture that Geertz opposed—as he stated in his essay 'Thick Description'—for fear that his own might be mistaken for them" (38).

16. Ibid., 34.

17. Ibid., 33.

advice of his philosophy professor, George Geiger, who happened to be John Dewey's last graduate student. Geiger's advice to Geertz was this: "Don't go into philosophy; it has fallen into the hands of Thomists and technicians. You should try anthropology."[18] Through the influence of Geiger, Geertz secured a scholarship to study anthropology at Harvard under Clyde Kluckhorn, who at the time was "engaged with some colleagues in developing an experimental, interdisciplinary department there called 'Social Relations,' in which cultural anthropology was conjoined not with archaeology and physical anthropology . . . but with psychology and sociology."[19] At Harvard, Geertz studied under Kluckhorn, Alfred Kroeber, Talcott Parsons, Gordon Allport, Henry Murray, Frederick Mosteller, and Samuel Stouffer.

A team of Harvard graduates made up of two psychologists, five anthropologists, one historian, and one sociologist was to be sent to Java, Indonesia, for a field study. Geertz and his wife Hildred were invited to join the team. Geertz left for Pare (Geertz sometimes refers to it as Modjokuto), a small town on the Brantas river plain in Java in 1952. The Dutch who colonized the area had just left two years earlier after years of guerrilla insurrection, making Java part of the newly created Republic of Indonesia, which incidentally was experiencing its first military coup d'état at the time. Geertz and his wife spent two and half years there studying religion and doing fieldwork before returning to Harvard to write "a thesis on Javanese religious life under the direction of Cora DuBois, an eminent Southeast Asianist," the second woman professor in all of Harvard.[20] During his ethnographical work in a remote Balinese village, initially the villagers did not accept Geertz and his wife and treated them with suspicion. But the seeming hostility changed about ten days after their arrival when they attended a cockfight. The cockfight was raided by the police and Geertz and his wife ran from the police, like the villagers did. The turn of events came when Geertz and his wife were stopped and questioned by the police. The village chief came to their defense by telling the police that Geertz and his wife had nothing to do with the cockfight. From then on the villagers' attitude to Geertz and his wife changed to one of positive attitude. Thus, Geertz described the act of getting caught as leading to "a sudden and unusually complete acceptance into a society extremely difficult for outsiders to penetrate. It gave me the kind of immediate, inside-view grasp of an

18. Geertz, *Available Light*, 7.
19. Ibid.
20. Ibid., 9.

"Cultural Turn" and the Problematic of Inculturation

aspect of 'peasant mentality' that anthropologists not fortunate enough to flee headlong with their subjects from armed authorities normally do not get."[21] Geertz returned to Bali after defending his thesis and explains the substance of his experience as follows:

> 1. Anthropology, at least of the sort I profess and practice, involves a seriously divided life. The skills needed in the classroom or at the desk and those needed in the field are quite different. Success in the one setting does not insure success in the other. And vice versa. 2. The study of other peoples' cultures (and of one's own as well, but that brings up other issues) involves discovering who they think they are, what they think they are doing, and to what end they think they are doing it, something a good deal less straightforward than the ordinary canons of Notes and Queries ethnography, or for that matter the glossy impressionism of pop art "cultural studies," would suggest. 3. To discover who people think they are, what they think they are doing, and to what end they think they are doing it, it is necessary to gain a working familiarity with the frames of meaning within which they enact their lives. This does not involve feeling anyone else's feelings, or thinking anyone else' thoughts, simple impossibilities. Nor does it involve going native, an impractical idea, inevitably bogus. It involves learning how, as a being from elsewhere with a world of one's own, to live with them.[22]

Geertz held different fellowships and positions at a number of schools before landing a position in the Department of Anthropology at the University of Chicago in 1960. It was while teaching at the University of Chicago that a budget of terms around which the study of culture began to emerge for Geertz: "thick description," "model-of/model-for," "sign system," "episteme," "ethos," "paradigm," "criteria," "horizon," "frame," "world," "language games," "interpretant," "*sinn zusamenhang*," "trope," "*sjuzet*," "experience-near," "family resemblance," "heteroglossia," and "structure."[23] Geertz believes that the answers to our basic questions—why? How/ what? Whither?—to the extent that they are answerable, are to be found, if one looks diligently, in the details of lived life experience.[24] In 1970 Geertz left Chicago to become professor of social science at the Institute of Advanced Study in Princeton, NJ (1970–2000). Geertz conducted extensive

21. Geertz, *The Interpretation of Cultures*, 416.
22. Geertz, *Available Light*, 15–16.
23. Ibid., 17.
24. Ibid., xi.

ethnographical work in Southeast Asia and North Africa, particularly Morocco throughout his career.[25] His most famous ethnographical work is his analysis of Balinese cockfight that he titled "Deep Play: Notes on the Balinese Cockfight."[26]

> When I first observed the cockfight, I had no idea at all of what was going on. If you have seen one cockfight you have seen them all, but the Balinese were passionate about them, and I could not figure out why. Hence, I tried to clarify what was going on because I did not understand it. A pure description might point toward gambling, but it was clearly more than that. What I wanted to do was to understand or clarify the fight, to understand how the participators might understand it and, at the same time, try to show how such an analysis should be done. The cockfight analysis is thus a model or an example of how to do this kind of work. You try to make sense of it, i.e., make sense that they make of it. Try to understand how they make sense of their world. In that way, it is phenomenological and hermeneutic. It is an attempt to understand things from the native's point of view. Nevertheless, it is on our terms, i.e., the observer's.[27]

Geertz had many influences. His hermeneutics was inspired somewhat by Hans-Georg Gadamer (1900–2002), but more by Paul Ricoeur (1913–2005). The influence of their hermeneutic can be found in Geertz's phenomenological approach.[28] But there is also a difference in their various approaches, as Geertz noted in an interview: "I work empirically. Both Ricoeur and Gadamer are interested in the general possibility of knowledge, which I have learned a lot from, but it is not what I am doing. I am trying to get at some knowledge about some 'thing.' I am trying to have an applied phenomenology and applied hermeneutics to really do a hermeneutic job on whatever it is that I am trying to understand."[29] There is also the influence of John Dewey (1859–1952), one from whom Geertz learned "that thought is conduct" and a social act.[30]

One of Geertz's principal influences was the British analytic philosopher, Ludwig Wittgenstein (1889–1951). It was from Wittgenstein that he

25. See Geertz et al., *Meaning and Order in Moroccan Society*.
26. Geertz, *The Interpretation of Cultures*, 412.
27. Micheelseen, "I Don't Do Systems," 10.
28. See Geertz, *Negara*, 103–4.
29. Micheelseen, "I Don't Do Systems," 5.
30. Geertz, *Available Light*, 21.

"Cultural Turn" and the Problematic of Inculturation

discovered "a philosophy—one that opposed to big-systems thinking and ideas about universally fixed essences."[31] Thus, due to the influence of Wittgenstein, Geertz would refer to himself simply as an ethnographer "and a writer of ethnography" who does not do system. His interest, like that of Wittgenstein, was the role of ideas in behavior, the meaning of meaning, and the judgment of judgment.[32] Geertz thinks that Wittgenstein's "attack upon the idea of private language, which brought thought out of its grotto in the head into the public square where one could look at it, his notion of language game, which provided a new way of looking at it once it arrived there—as a set of practices—and his proposal of 'forms of life,'" seem almost custom design for his (i.e., Geertz's) sort of anthropological work.[33] He writes about this indebtedness to Wittgenstein:

> If it is true, as has been argued, that the writers we are willing to call master are those who seem to us finally to be saying what we feel we have long had on the tip of our tongue but have been ourselves quite unable to express, those who put into words what are for us only inchoate motions, tendencies, and impulses of mind, then I am more than happy to acknowledge Wittgenstein as my master. Or one of them, anyway.[34]

Geertz's other major influence was Max Weber (1864–1920) whose idea of religion and culture Geertz appropriates in his semiotic work. In all however, Geertz considers himself eclectic with regard to his theoretical assumptions and influences:

> It is eclectic in the sense that they are different people, but they all have a similar focus, i.e., symbol, meaning, or the philosophy of mind. [Talcott] Parsons introduced me to Weber's work, so I have to some degree a Parsonian view of Weber. The interpretation of Weber and, therefore, the discussion about Weber is of course whether he really believed in a social science with a scientific approach to culture, or if he believed in an interpretive one. I think one can read him either way—although I use him from the interpretive perspective. I am more interested in the sociology of religion than types of faith and so on. Langer, Wittgenstein, Schutz, and Ricoeur are all interested in *meaning* in some sense. Ryle was interested in the philosophy of mind. So I do not think it is an

---

31. Shweder, "The Resolute Irresolution of Clifford Geertz," 201.
32. Ibid., x.
33. Ibid., xii.
34. Ibid., xi.

eclectic list. There are many people not there—all the positivists are missing. It is of course eclectic in disciplinary terms, but the list has an inner consistency.[35]

Critics sometimes refer to Geertz as the father of skeptical postmodern social science and radical deconstruction, a label Geertz refutes and claims he has no need for. To his credit, Geertz thinks postmodernism is "past its sale date" and "a dead end" in terms of future development. Nevertheless, Geertz does accept the critique of postmodernism, which he thinks has helped clarify some fundamental concepts like culture and interpretation, but dismisses postmodernism as a program.[36] Geertz does not subscribe to the evolution of culture, as some postmoderns do. He speaks instead of the evolution of the brain and the growth of culture. "I do not believe in cultural evolution—culture changes and grows, and maybe by some standard, it evolves," he stated in an interview. "I do believe that culture is involved in our brain's evolution. However, culture does not evolve in the Darwinian sense."[37]

In order to properly locate Geertz, i.e., in relation to his contribution to cultural anthropology, it is helpful to understand the intellectual fault lines in American social anthropology. There are, according to Richard Shweder, three distinguishable intellectual territories or fault lines in American social anthropology since the early 1980s when, according to him, the field of cultural anthropology became partitioned or even fractured. There is the territory of what he calls the moral activists. This is the fault line of those "who view anthropology as a forum for political struggles against sexism, racism, homophobia, capitalism, and neocolonialism. These moral activists have a very strong sense of what is universally right and wrong, and there is very little about which they are irresolute."[38] Then there is the skeptical post-modernists who read "objective" accounts of ethnographic realities corrosively and as part of their critique of "essentialism," question the existence of identifiable cultural groups and attempts to identify

---

35. Micheelseen, "I Don't Do Systems," 5.
36. Ibid., 13.
37. Ibid.
38. Shweder, "The Resolute Irresolution of Clifford Geertz," 196–97. Geertz's essay, "Thick Description: Towards an Interpretive Theory of Culture," according to Shweder, is often wrongly cited and mischaracterized as a key text by those who think of Geertz as a skeptical postmodern deconstructionist.

characteristic features of the members of any culture.³⁹ Finally, there is the neo-positivists "who view cultural anthropology as a value-neutral discipline and who generally subscribe to the view that whatever patterns exist in social life are 'law like' and can be understood with reference to universal explanatory theories."⁴⁰ According to Shweder, "it is fair to say that Geertz never lived in, and rarely visited, any of these three intellectual territories."⁴¹ Geertz does not see human nature as having a fixed kernel. His rule-of-thump generalization for anthropology is that any sentence that begins with "All societies have . . . is either baseless or banal."⁴² He sees polarities and dichotomies like subjective vs. objective and particulars vs. universals sacred vs. profane, supernatural vs. natural and trans-empirical vs. empirical as old and alien Western notions, which are not necessarily applicable in all places.⁴³ Culture pertains to created signs and symbols that are found in peoples' behaviors and the task of the anthropologist is to sort out "the structures of signification." When other cultures seem different to us it is because we lack "familiarity with the imaginative universe within which their acts are signs."⁴⁴

It is because of Geertz's conviction that human cultures have similarities and differences that he attempts a fresh look at "the great integrative, totalizing concepts we have so long been accustomed to using in organizing our ideas about world politics, and particularly about similarity and difference among peoples, societies, states, and cultures."⁴⁵ These concepts—"tradition," "identity," "religion," "ideology," "values," "nation," "society," "state," and "culture," for Geertz, must be reconditioned or reconstructed "if we are to penetrate the dazzle of the new heterogeneity and say something useful about its forms and future."⁴⁶ In Geertz's own words:

> What we need are ways of thinking that are responsive to particularities, to individualities, oddities, discontinuities, contrasts, and singularities, responsive to what Charles Taylor has called "deep diversity," a plurality of ways of belonging and being, and that yet

39. Ibid., 197.
40. Ibid.
41. Ibid.
42. Geertz, *Available Light*, 135.
43. Micheelseen, "I Don't Do Systems," 12.
44. Geertz, *The Interpretation of Cultures*, 10.
45. Geertz, "What Is A State," 578.
46. Ibid.

can draw from them—from it—a sense of connectedness, a connectedness that is neither comprehensive nor uniform, primal nor changeless, but nonetheless real.[47]

The New Cultural Turn

Anthropology, as a discipline, according to Geertz, arose around the concept of culture and ever since anthropology, ironically, has been increasingly concerned about limiting, focusing, specifying, and containing its domination.[48] Geertz likens the concept of culture to a grandee idea that bursts suddenly into the intellectual landscape with a tremendous force. When such ideas burst into the intellectual landscape, they initially resolve many teething problems with a further promise of resolving later fundamental problems and even clarifying obscure issues. "Everyone gravitates to the new idea and do everything possible to exploit it, use it to make connections and even stretch its meaning to fit their purpose."[49] After a while, when everyone is familiar with the idea and it becomes "part of our general stock of theoretical concepts," and no longer as popular as it used to be, "our expectations are brought more into balance with its actual uses."[50] Although a few zealots may cling to the idea, "but less driven thinkers settle down after a while to the problems the idea has really generated. They try to apply it and extend it where it applies and where it is capable of extension; and they desist where it does not apply or cannot be extended. It becomes, if it was, in truth, a seminal idea in the first place, a permanent and enduring part of our intellectual armory. But it no longer has the grandiose, all-promising scope, the infinite versatility of apparent application it once had."[51]

Today the term "culture," according to Geertz, has "acquired a certain aura of ill-repute in social anthropological circles because of the multiplicity of its referents and the studied vagueness with which it has all too often been invoked."[52] Geertz would seek to provide an understanding of culture that avoids multiple referents and ambiguity. He departs from the old

47. Geertz, *Available Light*, 224.
48. Geertz, *The Interpretation of Cultures*, 4.
49. Ibid., 3. Geertz credits Susan Langer as the one from whom he borrowed the metaphor of grandee idea.
50. Ibid., 4.
51. Ibid.
52. Ibid., 89.

"Cultural Turn" and the Problematic of Inculturation

understanding of culture as a self-contained "super organic reality" to a new one. Instead of reifying culture, he suggests a semiotic understanding, agreeing with Max Webber that the human person is an animal suspended in webs of significance they spun. Geertz understands "culture to be those webs, and the analysis of it to be therefore not an experimental science in search of law but an interpretive one in search of meaning."[53]

Geertz draws from what the British philosopher Gilbert Ryle (1900–1976) calls "thick description." As Ryle uses the term, thick description "entails an account of the intentions, expectations, circumstances, settings, and purposes that give actions their meanings."[54] Ryle uses the illustration of two boys contracting the eyelids of their right eyes. One is doing it as an involuntary twitch and the other is doing as a conspiratorial signal to a friend. The two twitches are identical. An onlooker cannot tell which twitch is an involuntary action and which is a wink or even whether both or either is a twitch or a wink. Regardless of whether or not one is able to tell which is a twitch and which is a wink, the difference between the two is enormous. "The winker is communicating, and indeed communicating in quite precise and special way: (1) deliberately, (2) to someone in particular, (3) to impart a particular message, (4) according to a socially established code, and (5) without cognizance of the rest of the company."[55] The winker, on the other hand, has not contracted his eyelids and winked, but the twitcher has contracted his eyelids. "Contracting your eyelids on purpose when there exists a public code in which so doing counts as a conspiratorial signal is winking. That's all there is to it: a speck of behavior, a fleck of culture, and—viola! –a gesture."[56] Ryle adds more complexity to the story by assuming a third boy comes along and parodies the first boy's wink but does it in exact same way the second boy winked and the first twitched by contracting his eyelids. The difference here is that the third boy is neither twitching nor winking but parodying someone else for his amusement. Still he winks as if he is sending a message according to the socially established code, he is actually attempting to ridicule, not sending a message. Let us assume, says Ryle, that a fourth boy comes along and does the same thing, but this time not to parody but to pretend a conspiracy was in motion, etc, etc. "The dis-

---

53. Ibid., 5.

54. Greenblatt, "The Touch of the Real," 16, referencing Ryle, "Thinking and Reflecting," 465–96.

55. Geertz, *The Interpretation of Cultures*, 6.

56. Ibid.

tinction between a twitch a wink is secured by the element of volition that is not itself visibly manifest in the contraction of the eyelid; a thin description would miss it altogether. So too with the other layers of framing intentions that Ryle piles on: fake twitches, rehearsals of fake twitches, and so forth."[57]

Geertz uses this illustration to distinguish between what Ryle calls "thin description" (a parodist contracting his eyelids) and "thick description" (faking a wink to confuse an innocent into thinking a conspiracy was in motion). The right question to ask, according to Geertz, is not what the ontological status of wink is, but rather its import. In other words, is what is being communicated, ridicule or challenge, irony or anger, snobbery or pride?[58] The question as to whether culture is subjective or objective, idealist or behaviorist, impressionist or positivist, etc, is, for Geertz, a misplaced one. Using Ryle's illustration, Geertz suggests that culture is like a burlesqued wink. "Though ideational, it does not exist in someone's head; though unphysical, it is not an occult entity."[59] Human behavior, like twitches or phonation in speech or sonance in music, is a symbolic action. Culture is public because meaning is. For example, you can wink (burlesque) without knowing what counts as winking.[60] Culture, therefore, is not a private or psychological phenomenon or a characteristic of a person's mind or cognitive structure.[61] Rather, culture consists of "socially established structures of meaning in terms of which people do such things as signal conspiracies and join them or perceive insults and answer them."[62] This should not be taken to mean that culture is "a power, something to which social events, behaviors, institutions, or processes can be causally attributed [but] a context, something within which they can intelligibly— that is, thickly—described."[63] According to Geertz, human behavior must be attended to because it is through the flow of behavior (social action) that cultural forms receive their articulation.[64] There is no denying that cultural forms also get their articulation from various forms of artifacts as well, "but

---

57. Greenblatt, "The Touch of the Real," 16.
58. Geertz, *The Interpretation of Cultures*, 10.
59. Ibid., 10.
60. Ibid., 12.
61. Ibid., 13.
62. Ibid., 12–13.
63. Ibid., 14.
64. Ibid., 17.

these draw their meaning from the role they play in an ongoing pattern of life, not from any intrinsic relationships they bear to one another."[65]

Re-theorization of "Culture"

The word *culture*, according to A. L. Kroeber and Clyde Kluckhorn, who identified hundreds and multiple application of the meaning of the word, has always had a religious significance. The Latin word for culture, *cultura*, is derived from the Latin *cultus*, transliterated in English as "cult," meaning "worship."[66] Clifford Geertz's major contribution to anthropology is his re-theorization of the concept "culture," delineating how the concept has two interlocked dimensions, one ontological that answers the question, what is culture? And the other epistemological that answers the question, how can we know it?[67] Geertz adopts the semiotic approach—analysis of signs and symbols. There are multiple meanings and varied understandings of the semiotic approach. Geertz does not subscribe to the tradition that sees semiotic as a formal, scientific, abstract, objectivist discipline. His version of semiotic—as a general conception of the function of sign and symbol— is closer to that tradition deriving from the American mathematician, scientist and philosopher, Charles Sanders Peirce, a pragmatic tradition and phenomenological conceptual tradition Geertz finds appealing.[68] Thus, Geertz's semiotic approach sees culture as denoting "an historically transmitted pattern of meanings embodied in symbols, a system of inherited conceptions expressed in symbolic forms by means of which men communicate, perpetuate, and develop their knowledge about and attitude towards life."[69]

a. **Meaning**

Geertz does not define meaning but chooses instead to use it in different senses and contexts. "The concept of meaning, in all its varieties," writes Susan Langer (1895–1985), "is the dominant philosophical concept of our time. Sign, symbol, denotation, signification, communication—these notions are our stock in

---

65. Ibid.
66. See Kroeber and Kluckhorn, *Culture*, 62.
67. Ortner, *The Fate of "Culture,"* 6.
68. Micheelseen, "I Don't Do Systems," 7.
69. Geertz, *The Interpretation of Cultures*, 89.

trade."[70] Meaning, according to Langer, has psychological and logical aspects. Any account of meaning must hold these two intertwined aspects together without conflating them.[71] "Psychologically, any item that is to have meaning must be employed as a sign or a symbol; that is to say, it must be a sign or a symbol to someone. Logically, it must be capable of conveying a meaning, it must be the sort of item that can be thus employed."[72] These two aspects, according to Langer, are distinguished and at the same time related to each other. In some situations, the logical aspect is either implicit or is of the utmost importance in meaning-relations.[73] Geertz accepts Langer's distinction and adopts, as a paradigm for explaining meaning, the metaphor "that sacred symbols function to synthesize a people's ethos—the tone, character, and quality of their life, its moral and aesthetic style and mood—and their world view—the picture they have of the way things in sheer actuality are, their most comprehensive ideas of order."[74] Without cultural patterns the human person is functionally incomplete. We are genetically programmed to cultural patterns without which we would seem like a "formless monster with neither sense of direction nor power of self-control, a chaos of spasmodic impulses and vague emotions."[75] In exploring the meanings of the Balinese cockfight, for example, Geertz probes "what makes some cultural performances, some cultural experiences deeper, more intense, more gripping than others. This is the beginning of an analysis of why some rituals, texts, or symbols generate more meaning than others do."[76]

The experience of pain, bafflement, and moral paradox, raised by the problem of meaning, can at times lead to religious experience: belief in gods, devils, spirits or totemic principles, a religious experience that can be conceived as a form of "knowing." It is a "mode of seeing in that extended sense of 'see in which

70. Langer, *Philosophical Sketches*, 55.
71. Innis, *Susan Langer in Focus*, 36.
72. Langer, *Philosophy in a New Key*, 53.
73. Ibid.
74. Geertz, *The Interpretation of Culture*, 89.
75. Ibid, 99.
76. Swidler, "Geertz's Ambiguous Legacy," 302.

"Cultural Turn" and the Problematic of Inculturation

it means 'discern,' 'apprehend,' 'understand' or 'grasp.' It is a particular way of looking at life, a particular manner of constructing the world, as when we speak of an historical perspective, a scientific perspective, an aesthetic perspective, a common-sense perspective, or even the bizarre perspective embodied in dreams and in hallucinations." [77]

b. Symbols

Like his understanding of meaning, Geertz understanding of symbols follows in the tradition of Susan Langer and Charles S. Peirce's notion of symbols.[78] Langer distinguishes between signs and symbols, admitting in the process that there are instances in which a sign might have a sense of a symbol and vice versa.[79] She argues that something is not a sign in and of itself. A sign is always a sign to someone.[80] Signs arise only in use and are employed or recognized by someone in the attempt to articulate or grasp a meaning.[81] This is the psychological side that is "always present." On the other hand, "any device whereby we make an abstraction is a symbolic element, and all abstraction involves symbolization."[82] Langer's famous example is a person's (proper) name—a name borne by a person is at one and the same time a symbol by which we think of the person and a call-name by which we signal the person.[83]

> Through a confusion of these two functions, the proper name is often deemed the bridge from animal semantic, or sign-using, to human language, which is symbol-using. Dogs, we are told, understand names – not only their own, but their masters'. So they do indeed; but they understand them only in the capacity of call-names. If you say "James" to a dog whose master bears that name, the dog will interpret the sound as sign, and look for James. Say it to a person who knows someone called thus, and he will ask: "What about James?" That simple question is forever

---

77. Geertz, *The Interpretation of Culture*, 110.
78. See Langer, *Philosophical Sketches*; and Pierce, *Philosophical Writings of Pierce*.
79. See Langer, *Philosophy in a New Key*, 60–61.
80. Innis, *Susanne Langer in Focus*, 36.
81. Ibid.
82. Langer, *Philosophical Sketches*, 63.
83. Ibid., 62.

> beyond the dog; signification is the only meaning a name can have for him—a meaning which the master's name shares with the master's smell, with his footfall, and his characteristic ring of the door bell.[84]

Thus, a symbol is "anything—an action, a practice, an object, a pattern of sounds, a cremation ceremony, the gathering together of people to share a meal—that is a vehicle of meaning."[85] The particular lives that people live are, for Geertz, "symbols."[86] A symbol, for Geertz, is therefore, "a relational entity in which meaning, understood as a public phenomenon, is suspended. It is suspended in the sense that the symbol is comprised of three elements: the representamen (the tangible side of the symbol), the object (that which the symbol refers to), and the interpretant (which is the relation between the representamen and the object."[87] What this means then is that meaning is not to be seen as something "stored" in symbols as a free-floating phenomenon, but a matter of relations between persons, their natural environment, and their culture.[88]

Although Geertz's privileges the use of the term symbol, he is not opposed to substituting it for "sign," as long as sign is understood in the Peircean way (sign as conceptual, as opposed to a signal), not the Saussurean way. Geertz is very clear that Ferdinand de Saussure and the structuralism that followed in his steps is not the approach he uses.[89] But Geertz is in agreement again with Charles Peirce and Susan Langer for whom sign is not radically different from symbol.

> Signs in the Peircean sense have an *aboutness*. Therefore, when I use the term symbol in my work, it is to be understood as a sign (an index for example), which becomes symbolical via a cultural interpretation. Dogs cannot, in my view, respond to symbols. They can only respond to signs. The famous example is from Langer, where she tells of a person who comes into a room where there is a dog. The person said the master's name—for example, "James"—and

---

84. Ibid., 61–62.
85. Shweder, "The Resolute Irresolution of Clifford Geertz," 193 (see n4).
86. Ibid.
87. Micheelseen, "I Don't Do Systems," 15.
88. Ibid.
89. Ibid., 7.

"Cultural Turn" and the Problematic of Inculturation

the dog responded by looking for James. If you do the same to a human, the person would properly respond with: "What about James"? You see, there is an "aboutness". That is the distinction I want to hold on to.[90]

Geertz also sees cultural patterns as "models" in that "they are sets of symbols whose relations to one another 'model' relations among entities, process or what-have-you in physical, organic, social, or psychological systems by 'paralleling,' 'imitating,' or 'simulating' them."[91] The desire to stress the interpretive function of religion leads him to distinguish two senses of the term model: a "model of" and a "model for" sense. The "of" sense stresses manipulation of symbol structures in order to bring them closely "into parallel with the pre-established nonsymbolic system, as when we grasp how dams work by developing a theory of hydraulics or constructing a flow chart."[92] Steven Caton has suggested that the "model of" is analogous to what Kenneth Burke called "the mapping function" in literary text.[93] The "for" sense, on the other hand, stresses the manipulation of "nonsymbolic systems in terms of the relationship expressed in the symbolic, as when we construct a dam according to the specifications implied in an hydraulic theory or the conclusions drawn from a flow chart."[94] Thus, "model" has an intrinsic double aspect in that it gives objective meaning to social and psychological reality "both by shaping themselves to it and by shaping it to themselves."[95] This double aspect sets true symbols off from other types of significative forms.[96]

Why Geertz's Semiotic Analysis is Best Suited for a Theology of Inculturation

Geertz's work is by no means perfect. His semiotic approach to culture has come under attack, particularly from those who want to replace it with a new approach they call the "ontological turn"—that human differences are

---

90. Ibid., 8.

91. Geertz, *The Interpretation of Cultures*, 93, quoting Craig, *The Nature of Explanation*.

92. Geertz, *The Interpretation of Cultures*, 93.

93. Caton, "What Is an 'Authorizing Discourse?,'" 41.

94. Geertz, *The Interpretation of Cultures*, 93.

95. Ibid.

96. Ibid., 94.

to be conceived as "ontological," not "epistemological."[97] There are also those who criticize Geertz for not paying attention to the power structure, domination, conflict, historical change, and the colonial context of some of the marginalized societies he studied in his field work.[98] "Attacked by the positivists for being too interpretive, by the critical studies scholars as being too politically and ethically neutral, and finally by the interpretivists (themselves products of Geertzian revolution) as being too invested in a certain concept of culture, Geertz has frequently gotten it from all sides."[99] Steven Caton has attempted a refutation of some of the criticisms leveled against Geertz. Caton suggests that some of the criticisms against Geertz are misplaced and that Geertz does have a notion of power, contrary to the argument of critics. One of Geertz's notion of power might be called "rhetorical, in the sense that it is closely tied to the persuasiveness of symbols in communicative action. In this vein, one might interpret the statements on power and symbolic action in his study of the Balinese theater state as a 'spectacle' of power."[100] Continuing on defense of Geertz on the supposed lack of concern for the problem of power raised by Talal Asad in *Genealogies of Religion*, Caton writes:

> Of course, this criticism has been made before by such materialist and Marxist-inspired anthropologists as Eric Wolf and William Roseberry, and while Asad has from time to time been a Marxist theoretician, his criticism of Geertz is more subtle than to say that his definition does not address power. There is, after all, no a priori reason that a definition of culture must take power into account, and the reason that Geertz's definition is found wanting may be a consequence of shifting interests and priorities in anthropology.[101]

The pitfalls of Geertz' work notwithstanding, Geertz is one of the few cultural anthropologists that devoted proper attention to the interface of politics and culture. A country's politics reflects the design of its culture. "Between the stream of events that make up political life and the web of beliefs that comprises a culture it is difficult to find a middle term. On the one hand, everything looks like a clutter of schemes and surprises, on the other,

---

97. See Palecek and Risjord, "Relativism and the Ontological Turn," 3–23. For more criticisms of Geertz's semiotic approach, see Clifford and Marcus, *Writing Culture*.
98. Swidler, "Geertz's Ambiguous Legacy," 301.
99. See Ortner, *The Fate of "Culture*," 1.
100. Caton, "What Is an 'Authorizing Discourse?," 42.
101. Ibid., 41.

"Cultural Turn" and the Problematic of Inculturation

like a vast geometry of settled judgments."[102] Culture is the structure of meaning through which a people give shape to their experience.[103] Geertz's favorite example is the culturally heterogeneous Indonesia, a country with a mixture of Polynesian, Indic, Islamic, Chinese, and European traditions. After about two hundred years of colonization and foreign rule, Indonesia's struggle for political self-determination becomes even more complex.

> A great part of the problem, of course, is that the country is archipelagic in more than geography. Insofar as it displays a pervasive temper, it is one riven with internal contrasts and contradictions. There are the regional differences (the rhetorical combativeness of the Minangkabau and the reflective elusiveness of the Javanese, for example); there are the faith-and-custom "ethnic" divergences among even closely related groups, as in the East Sumantran "boiling pot"; there are the class conflicts reflected in the nativistic movement material and the vocational ones reflected in that of the struggle for a workable legal system. There are racial minorities (Christians and Hindus); local minorities (Djarkata Batak, Surabaja Madurese). The nationalist slogan, "One People, One Country, One Language," is a hope, not a description.[104]

The Indonesia problem is not peculiar, but rather paradigmatic of the problems confronting newly emerging nation-states, like those of Africa, after the end of colonial rule. Indonesia, for example, acts as though it is culturally homogeneous, when in actual fact it is culturally heterogeneous, and by so doing creates "anarchic politics of meaning outside the established structures of civil government."[105] It is particularly this lack of attention to cultural heterogeneity and lack of attention to "differences" that Geertz describes as dangerous and untenable.

Geertz is a self-proclaimed "a cases-and-interpretations type of anthropologist, one concerned above all with the specifics of local cultures."[106] Geertz helped bring to the forefront the idea that cultures are not unitary. Geertz recognition of cultural pluralism and his analysis thereof is well suited for a theology of inculturation—one that accounts for political freedom and theological self-determination. Etched in his work is the idea that

102. Geertz, *The Interpretation of Cultures*, 311.
103. Ibid., 312.
104. Ibid., 315.
105. Ibid., 316.
106. Rosaldo Jr., "A Note on Geertz as a Cultural Essayist," 32.

all attempts to locate universal essence in human nature will ultimately fail. Geertz shows "that across history and culture, human nature is continuously transformed by the never-ending attempt of particular groups of human beings—Balinese, Moroccans, Northern European Calvinists, Satmar Hasidim—to understand themselves and create a social world that manifests their self-understandings."[107]

Geertz's cultural relativity (not a moral relativist) places premium on understanding cultural differences. His "antipathy for general laws and formal principles"[108] is evident in his essay "Anti Anti-Relativism," where he appeals to a quote from Michel de Montaigne to denounce anti relativism prevalent in anthropology: "Each man calls barbarism whatever is not his own practice ... for we have no other criterion of reason than the example and idea of the opinions and customs of the country we live in."[109] For Geertz, there is no such thing as the "mind for all cultures" and there is no fixed kernel to human nature.[110] Rather, he shows that:

> (i) Diversity is inherent in the human condition. (ii) There is no universal essence to human nature that strongly determines human behavior. (iii) Across time and space (history and culture), human nature is continuously transformed by the never-ending attempt of particular groups of people—Balinese, Moroccans, Swedes—to understand themselves and to create a social world that makes manifest their self-understandings. (iv) In science, as in life, securing universal agreement about what is good, tree, beautiful, or efficient is rarely possible. Even more importantly, the ecumenical impulse to value uniformity (convergence in belief) over variety and to overlook, devalue, or eradicate "difference" is not a good thing.[111]

Geertz's strong stance against the functionalist and mechanistic worldviews of Durkheim, Marx, Freud, and their allies challenged and reversed their view of society as a machine or an organism "in which complex human intentions and complex cultural formations are reduced to their effects on that social machine or social organism."[112] This is not to suggest that Geertz

---

107. Shweder, "The Resolute Irresolution of Clifford Geertz," 202.

108. Schweder, "Available Light," 1511

109. Geertz, *Available Light*, 45, quoting Montaigne, *Les Essais de Michel de Montaigne*, 205.

110. Schweder, "Available Light," 1511.

111. Ibid.

112. Ortner, "Thick Resistance," 137.

"Cultural Turn" and the Problematic of Inculturation

abandons the findings of the social and behavioral anthropologists before him. Rather, he uses them as a starting point and widens their scope. Emile Durkheim's analysis of the nature of the sacred, Marx Weber's method of *Vesterhenden*, Freud's insight into personal rituals and collective practices, and Malinowski's distinction between religion and common sense dominated the field of social anthropology before Geertz. Although Geertz saw their dominance of social anthropology as "parochializing,"[113] he adds to their insight the view that culture is not a unified corpus of symbols with a clearly defined meaning, but a contested, temporal, and emergent reality.[114] Geertz understands an anthropological study of religion as a two-stage operation: analysis of system of meanings embodied in symbols which up the religion and relating the systems to socio-cultural and psychological processes. His disaffection with most social anthropologists of his time was because they concentrated on the second stage, ignoring the first stage in the process.[115]

Along these lines, Geertz provides an analysis of culture that helps us to see how different orders of reality (ethos, worldview, and ritual experience) intersect and co-mingle. He shows us that culture, like society, "is a field of play with its borders far less clear than in earlier imaginations, its internal harmonies far less apparent, in which actors and groups contend for position and power, sometimes in institutions, sometimes over control of meaning."[116] Geertz's anthropological understanding of culture, i.e., semiotic approach, which in itself is a cluster of signs or symbols, legitimated the task of giving serious attention to the culture of oppressed and subordinated groups. Geertz's method of unpacking the inherent meaning in symbolic system is through a method he calls "thick description"—the process of spelling out context-dependent meanings. A specific action or activity, for example, a Balinese cockfight, is a context-dependent meaning whose import may be clear to the Balinese but not to the outsider or ethnographer.[117] Because Geertz was weary that no ethnography exists apart from the ethnographer or anthropologist's written version, he insists that "cultures and peoples should speak for themselves." He sees his method of thick description as suited for this:

113. Geertz, *The Interpretation of Culture*, 88.
114. Clifford and Marcus, eds., *Writing Culture*, 19.
115. Geertz, *The Interpretation of Culture*, 125.
116. Suny, "Back and Beyond," 1485–86.
117. See Shweder, "The Resolute Irresolution of Clifford Geertz," 193 (see n4).

> Such an approach is neither introspectionist nor behaviorist; it is semantic. It is concerned with the collectively created patterns of meaning the individual uses to give form to experience and point to action, with conceptions embodied in symbols and clusters of symbols, and with the directive force of such conceptions in public and private life.[118]

He speaks of understanding a people's culture as exposing "their normalness without reducing their particularity. It renders them accessible: setting them in the frame of their own banalities, it dissolves their opacity."[119] Only a native makes first order interpretation. All other interpretations are either second or third order. They are fiction, not in the sense that they are false, but fiction in the original meaning of *fictio* as "something made," "something fashioned."[120]

Geertz is one that recognizes that the end of colonization and the emergence of new nation-states in Asia and Africa calls for a "serious rethinking" of our conceptualization of multi-ethnic, multi-religious, and multi-linguistic society.[121] Colonization has complicated key social science concepts like "culture," "state," and "society," making the "boundaries, coherence, and systematicity of their referents" more difficult to define and conceptualize.[122] Geertz suggests that we re-think what he calls the "totalizing concepts" that we have "long been accustomed to using in organizing our ideas about world politics, and particularly about similarity and difference among peoples, societies, states, and cultures: concepts like [all these terms in the heaviest of shudder quotes] "tradition," "identity," "religion," "ideology," "values," "nation," indeed even "culture," "society," "state," or "people" themselves."[123] He suggests that new or reconditioned general notions that say something useful need to be constructed.

Rather than refer to postcolonial societies as "Third World" or "developing nations," Geertz chooses to use the term "complicated places." As nation-states, "'complicated places' do not lend themselves to normative and systemic representation. They require, instead, careful historical understanding, a particularistic approach that is attentive both to political

---

118. Geertz, *Islam Observed*, 95–96.
119. Geertz, *The Interpretation of Culture*, 14.
120. Ibid., 15.
121. See Geertz, "What Is a State," 577–93.
122. Ibid., 590.
123. Ibid., 578.

resources and to semiotic process."¹²⁴ Regardless of their complexities, these "complicated places," according to Geertz, have their own specific cultural identities and differences. Wittgenstein's notion of family resemblances, which Geertz draws on, explicates this point:

> Wittgenstein's idea is that two cousins, for example, may resemble each other in their hair, eyes, and ears, and two other cousins may resemble each other in their lips, teeth, and noses. As a total group of cousins, they probably do not have any single feature in common; there is no lowest common denominator that unites all family members. Instead, the strength of their connections resides in the significant, if incomplete, overlap of such features.¹²⁵

In a multi-cultural and increasingly pluralistic world, Geertz helps us understand what difference "difference" makes. He provides a way by which we can talk about different conceptions of the self as these conceptions are made manifest by different groups of people in their various ways of life. Even if it is just for the sake of intra and internationality tranquility, differences need to be understood.¹²⁶

Theological Implications of Geertz's Semiotic Work

Clifford Geertz's anthropological notion of culture and the transformation he effected has wide range implications for anthropology and the humanities broadly conceived. Geertz's work on culture complements the parallels one that Bernard Lonergan carried out in theology. In fact, Lonergan does acknowledge the influence of Geertz's type of anthropological work that "has made us aware of the enormous variety of human social arrangements, cultures, mentalities," and how these discoveries put us "in a position to understand the variations that have taken place in the expression of Christian doctrines."¹²⁷ Like Geertz, Lonergan sees culture as a set of meanings and values informing a common way of life, and like Geertz again, acknowledges that there are as many cultures as there are distinct sets of meanings and values informing a people's common way of life.¹²⁸

---

124. Ibid, 590.
125. Rosaldo Jr., "A Note on Geertz as a Cultural Essayist," 33.
126. Shweder, "The Resolute Irresolution of Clifford Geertz," 203.
127. Lonergan, *Method in Theology*, 300.
128. Ibid., 301.

Using an empirical notion of culture, Lonergan suggests that theology is a function, not only of revelation and faith, but also of culture, and as such cultural change also entails a theological change.[129] "A theology," he writes, "mediates between a cultural matrix and the significance and role of religion in that matrix."[130] The mediation is not a one-way street, but a mutual self-mediation.[131] The political independence of many of the African and Asian countries (as well as Latin America) came with some sweeping cultural changes. But the theological change that ought to accompany these cultural changes has, in some cases, been slow, tepid, or nonexistent. The longing for freedom, a political yearning of many of the colonized countries before independence, also has its theological dimension. Theology became a tool for interpreting the divine character of struggle for liberation[132] when the colonized people discovered that their search for political self-determination was in like manner a search for that biblical God who takes sides with the poor and oppressed. The old (colonial) theology could not address with specificity and clarity the problem of identity that plagued the colonized.[133] The old theology was plagued by what Lonergan calls classicism—"the mistaken view of conceiving culture normatively and of concluding that there is just one human culture."[134] The insistence on cultural homogeneity was based on a common sense procedure, which because it was undifferentiated, became a common nonsense. Common nonsense, as Lonergan captures it, because it is common is always pretentious, dangerous, and disastrous.[135]

Before the Second Vatican Council (1962–65), "Post-Reformation Catholic philosophy and theology—leery of change and wary of innovating—waged a 'persistent age-long rearguard action' against those 'pernicious novelties' that challenged classical culture and its correlative worldview."[136]

> The culture of the time was classicist. It was conceived not empirically but normatively, not as the meanings and values inherent

---

129. Lonergan, "The Achievement of Bernard Lonergan," 287.
130. Lonergan, *Method in Theology*, xi.
131. Doran, "Lonergan and Balthasar," 65.
132. Cone, *A Black Theology of Liberation*, v.
133. Erskine, *Decolonizing Theology*, 1.
134. Lonergan, *Method in Theology*, 124.
135. Ibid., 98.
136. Brown, "Classicism."

"Cultural Turn" and the Problematic of Inculturation

> in a given way of life, but as the right set of meanings and values that were to be accepted and respected if one was not to be a plebian, a foreigner, a native, a barbarian. Classicist philosophy was the one perennial philosophy. Classicist art was the set of immortal classics. Classicist laws and structures were the deposit of the wisdom and prudence of mankind. This classicist outlook was a great protector of good manners and a great support of good morals, but it had one enormous drawback. It included a built-in incapacity to grasp the need for change and to effect the necessary adaptations.[137]

At the height of their power, the glory of Greece and the grandeur of Rome provided, for centuries, "the intellectual foundation and cultural matrix within which the western humankind understood itself and took its bearings in the cosmos."[138] No one in their right mind will dismiss the achievements of the Greeks (Plato and Aristotle, for example) and the great Latin classics (Thomas Aquinas and Bonaventure, for example) as classicists. The great philosophers who worked out the Greek achievement and the great Latin theologians who assimilated and adapted Greek philosophy in fact stood against all that classicism represented. "There could have been no Aquinas without the preceding development of Scholasticism."[139] The problem of classicism rather stems from those who would later use these Greek and Latin achievements, standardized and viewed them, not as a particular viewpoint, but as "a genus of viewpoints, a comprehensive view, a 'total mentality.'"[140] They thought "not in terms of evolution and development, but of universality and permanence."[141] While Christians are right to be proud of the achievements of their predecessors, they also need to be mindful that their predecessors "took on the coloring of their age and shared its limitations."[142]

Writing about the concrete realities of classicist mentality on his own experience as a pastor in Jamaica, for example, the Caribbean theologian, Noel Erskine, recounts how the theology did not address the identity problem that slavery created among Caribbean peoples and how the God that was presented within the Caribbean church was often not the symbol

---

137. Lonergan, "The Response of the Jesuit," 182.
138. Brown, "Classicism."
139. Lonergan, "Belief: Today's Issue," 99.
140. Brown, "Classicism."
141. Lonergan, "Theology in Its New Context," 59.
142. Lonergan, "The Response of the Jesuit," 182.

of freedom that the Caribbean people yearned for. Church experience seemed rather like an extension of the European and the North American Church.[143] According to Erskine, in the Caribbean liturgy the hymns were imported from Europe. The lyric of one of such hymns "Lord, wash me until I am whiter than snow" does not make any theological sense for a black Caribbean who had no idea of the meaning or symbolism of snow. The point here, as Erskine himself correctly pointed out, is not that imports may not have their place in liturgies of indigenous peoples, "but that God, when understood through the medium of other people's experience, is in danger of losing identity [and meaning]."[144] What often goes by the name classicism therefore, is not a repudiation of the achievements of the past, but a calling to mind of "a whole set of conclusions concerning the defects our theological inheritance and the remedies that can be brought to bear."[145]

The problem posed by classicism, theologically, is akin to the problem of grand narratives. According to Miroslav Volf, the grand idea of universal emancipation "sets up freedom as the single goal of universal history and then forces the multiple streams of history into the great river that flows toward that goal."[146] The irony is that grand narratives speak of universal liberation but their so called universal liberation is formulated from a particular standpoint. It is like the classicist who conceives culture normatively using his or her own particular culture as the norm and ideal to be pursued. The problem with grand narratives is that it can lead to *systematic totalization*—the mistaken notion that final reconciliation of all things (and all cultures) is possible and desirable.[147] The classicist notion of culture derives from the same *Aufklarer* narrative—that people of other cultures can be brought to true freedom through emancipation from ignorance and servitude of their culture. The classicist assumptions that there is *de jure* one fixed and immutable culture that is normative for all, irrespective of time and place, stands in sharp contrast to the semiotic empirical approach of Clifford Geertz that recognizes several human cultures and that these cultures, without exemption, are all subject to development and corruption. The final reconciliation that grand narratives seek is not the God project we read in Colossians 1:20, i.e., the final reconciliation of all things in Christ,

---

143. Erskine, *Decolonizing Theology*, 1.
144. Ibid.
145. Lonergan, "Belief," 98.
146. Volf, *Exclusion and Embrace*, 106.
147. Ibid., 109.

"Cultural Turn" and the Problematic of Inculturation

but the mistaken notion that cultures can be reconciled and reduced to one. The universality of grand narratives is the main reason for their failure, for cultures and subcultures are intrinsically plural.[148] Grand narratives do violence to small narratives thereby perpetuating violence on "other" cultures. In its attempt to totalize, grand narratives suppress the riches of other cultures, coercing them to fit into a single mold, a unity.[149] According to Miroslav Volf, to guard against the tyranny of "the whole and the one," which grand narratives suggest, we should keep reminding ourselves that cultures are "fluid, never final and universal, always temporal and local."[150]

The Second Vatican Council, however, recognized that if the Christian church is to be meaningful in a world of multiple cultures it must disengage itself from classicist thought-forms and viewpoints and appropriate the social order and cultural achievements of different times and places.[151] To make Christianity meaningful to multiplicity of cultures demands that the faith be explained with new imagery, new concepts, and new thought-forms. "The Aristotelian analyses, concepts, words, that in the Middle Ages that became part of the Catholic patrimony to resist both Renaissance scoffing and Protestant condemnation" are no longer entirely adequate.[152] "Under the cumulative onslaught of the scientific, historical, and philosophical revolutions of the last three centuries, classical culture has vanished, and the thought-forms built on its foundations have collapsed."[153]

Not only was Vatican II's concept of culture modern and progressive—along the line of Geertz's conception of culture, it also contains safeguards against favoring diverse cultures to the detriment of the integrity of the Gospel.[154] As Denis Doyle explains:

> The unfinished Vatican I (1869–70) had placed an imbalanced emphasis upon the papacy and the church universal in relation to the episcopacy and local churches. A strong papacy held several advantages for the Church in its struggles with an often hostile nineteenth- and early twentieth century world, but the stress on the "universal" was not conducive to a focus on diverse cultures.

---

148. Ibid., 106.
149. Ibid., 107.
150. Ibid.
151. Lonergan, "Belief," 98.
152. Lonergan, "Theology in Its New Context," 60.
153. Brown, "Classicism."
154. Doyle, "The Concept of Inculturation in Roman Catholicism," 1.

> There was a need to redress the balance by giving due attention to bishops and to particular churches. There was a significant connection between valuing the role of particular churches and valuing the contributions of diverse cultures.[155]

Here Geertz's cultural relativity becomes vital. His notion of cultural relativism is the modest view "that, simply because a culture is different from one's own, or because some foreigner differs from oneself, it does not follow that they are demented, dangerous, stupid, or pathological. They could simply be different, living with distinctive assumptions that may be rendered intelligible in their own context."[156] To be clear, when Geertz speaks of cultural relativism he does not mean or imply ethical relativism. "Quite the contrary. When different peoples, however defined, bump up against one another, they tend, he thought, to maintain not only their cultural, but also their ethical, assumptions. Engaging with other cultural worlds does not mean losing one's own ethical bearings."[157] Thus, Geertz takes cultural relativity seriously in the same way Lonergan "takes relativity seriously without being relativistic," i.e., the way he takes "the absurdity of and apparently random and chaotic dimensions of our world experience fully seriously without capitulating to nihilism in any form."[158]

Conclusion

The cultural turn effected by Clifford Geertz is sometimes referred to as the "literary turn" in anthropology—a text centered and text-oriented approach by which cultures are to be "read" or interpreted either as texts or a collections of texts.[159] This approach that views the culture of a people as an ensemble of texts to be read has its roots in the early 20th century German tradition of *Vestehen* (associated primarily with Wilhelm Dilthey and Max Weber). Whereas earlier approaches to the study of culture were concerned with the question of what constitutes "true" meanings, Geertz's literary turn and semiotic approach abandons the notion of "true" meanings, recognizing instead "differences." One of the goals of the semiotic tradition is "to aid us in gaining access to the conceptual world in which our subjects live

---

155. Ibid., 2.
156. Rosaldo, "Geertz's Gifts," 210.
157. Ibid.
158. Lawrence, "The Fragility of Consciousness," 56.
159. Aleksandar, "Clifford Geertz," 43.

so that we can, in some extended sense of the term, converse with them."[160] Geertz's conversational or dialogical approach shows that it is "by rendering intelligible the actual variations, historical and cultural, in human forms of life, each in its full singularity, that one can expand... the awareness of human beings of the range and character of human possibility."[161] Geertz in fact understands culture almost the way Lonergan does. Lonergan sees culture as the "complex web of meanings and values which make a way of life worth living, and a society worth belonging to."[162] The difference, which needs to be pointed out, is that Lonergan provides a nuance that is missing in Geertz's own work. For example, although not explicitly stated, from Lonergan's work one can differentiate between two forms of culture: traditional or pre-critical and classical or higher cultures,[163] a distinction almost impossible to see in Geertz's work. Traditional or pre-critical cultures" are structured by an 'everyday' or 'common-sense' level of 'values and meanings' constituted primarily by those spontaneous 'affective responses' shaped via the appropriation of a particular group's formative 'rituals, stories, legends, [and] myths.'"[164] The classical culture, on the other hand, is "a 'higher' or 'superstructural' level of culture through which 'meanings are elaborated and values are discerned in a far more reflective, deliberate [and] critical fashion.'"[165] The transition from traditional or pre-critical form of culture, according to Lonergan, can be associated with what Karl Jaspers (1883–1969) calls the Axial Period (800–500 BCE).[166] Lonergan usually associates the classical culture "with a series of interrelated features: (1) control of meaning and expression by a logic; (2) scientific inquiry of the Aristotelian type; (3) the metaphysical soul; ... (4) a fixed and unchanging human nature; and (5) ... a foundation consisting of propositions that are to be regarded as self-evident, necessary first principles."[167] It is these

160. Geertz, *The Interpretation of Culture*, 24.

161. Rosaldo, "Geertz's Gifts," 210.

162. Lonergan, "Belief," 90–91.

163. Olkovich, "Conceptualism, Classicism and Bernard Lonergan's Retrieval of Aquinas," 39.

164. Ibid., quoting Bernard Lonergan, "Belief," 91. See also Byrne, "The Fabric of Lonergan's Thought," 7–8.

165. Olkovich, "Conceptualism, Classicism and Bernard Lonergan's Retrieval of Aquinas," 39, quoting Lonergan, "The "Absence of God in Modern Culture," 102–3.

166. Olkovich, "Conceptualism, Classicism and Bernard Lonergan's Retrieval of Aquinas," 39.

167. Ibid. See also Lonergan, "The Future of Thomism," 50.

series of interrelated features culminating in the "Greek discovery of the mind" that Lonergan spoke glowing of as a genuine achievement and as an instance of progress in human in thought, as against the 'haute vulgarization' of theory, a degeneration of the classical ideal" the he would later describe pejoratively as classicism.[168]

Lonergan identifies three connected and interrelated developments that culminated in the breakdown of classical control of meaning and classical culture: (*a*) the rise of modern science, (*b*) the shift to modern historical scholarship, and (*c*) the critical turn to the subject in philosophy and the history of ideas.[169]

> First, modern science replaced the classical fixation on necessity, permanence and universality with the quest for 'probability' or 'de facto intelligibility' centered on a concern for knowledge or 'particular and concrete facts.' The shift from the static workings of deductive logic to method of 'observation, experimentation and . . . empirical verification' allowed modern science to remain 'intrinsically open to ever new discoveries that,' as Lonergan argues, 'in turn generate new definitions and formulations to make science not an unchanging system but an ever-ongoing process.' The second and intimately related shift in horizon implicated in the breakdown of the classical mindset is the rise of 'historical consciousness' typically linked to the 19th century birth of 'critical history.' From the perspective of 'historical scholarship' culture ceases to be conceived as 'normative' or absolute and instead comes to be viewed in 'empirical' terms as 'a particular manifestation of the creative self-constitution achieved by a particular people at a particular point in their history. The third and similarly related change in horizon is typically linked with Immanuel Kant's 'Copernican Revolution' in the study of philosophy.[170]

Nevertheless, Both Lonergan and Geertz see the modern scientific method as crucial for a good understanding of culture. Geertz works this out through his "thick description," while Lonergan works this out using his generalized empirical method. Through his various ethnographical studies, Geertz, like Lonergan, came to the realization that "knowing" cannot be conceived on the analogy of ocular vision but that knowledge is mediated

---

168. Olkovich, "Conceptualism, Classicism and Bernard Lonergan's Retrieval of Aquinas," 39.

169. Ibid., 47.

170. Ibid., 48.

"Cultural Turn" and the Problematic of Inculturation

by experiencing, understanding, judging, and deciding. Geertz's idea of culture is at what Lonergan calls the third stage of meaning—where "meaning not merely differentiates into the realms of common sense, theory, and interiority, but also acquires the universal immediacy... and the molding power of universal education."[171] What Geertz calls cultural relativity is, as it were, a way of calling attention to practical insights to be derived when one acknowledges cultural shift—that "culture is then a creative, contingent, indeed artistic expression of the human spirit."[172] Our next task, hence, is to do what Lonergan calls systematic exigence, as a way of arriving at the meaning of inculturation. "The systematic exigence not merely raises questions that common sense cannot answer but also demands a context for its answers, a context that common sense cannot supply or comprehend."[173]

---

171. Lonergan, *Method in Theology*, 99.
172. Ormerod, "The Times They Are a-Changin'," 840.
173. Lonergan, *Method in Theology*, 82.

5

Inculturation Reconsidered in Light of New Studies in Semiotics

From a semiotic point of view, the classicist ideal and its education that was normative and was the accepted practice of Western Christianity derives from a common sense or common nonsense notion that is resistant to change, dialogue, openness to the other, and the mediation and plurality of human existence. This antiquated relic of pre-scientific age,[1] like all brands of common sense, feeds the fragmentation of knowledge, increases the potential for ideological stalemates, leads to recriminations against peoples or cultures that are other than one's own, and denies the symbols and values that make up the very heart of (indigenous) peoples' existence. In stifling dialogue and precluding communication with cultures, classicism sows seeds of totalitarianism, failing to recognize that even within cultures some variants of sub-cultures might be distinguished.[2] As the "center of ecclesial gravity shifts inexorably from the North Atlantic to the Third World,"[3] the science of semiotics helps our quest to work out a critical realism that serves as a "common ground on which people of intelligence might meet."[4] This critical realism, deriving from the American philosopher and semiotician, Charles Sanders Peirce, the American Cultural anthropologist, Clifford Geertz, and the Canadian Jesuit theologian and philosopher, Bernard Lonergan, is an anti-dote to the to the counterpositions that developed out of the Anglo-American stream of thought about the nature of human knowing and the naïve realism and reductionism that developed out of the

---

1. Lonergan, *Method in Theology*, 84.
2. See Doran, "Common Ground," ix.
3. Shorter, *Toward a Theology of Inculturation*, xi.
4. Doran, "Common Ground," xi.

Greco-Roman world and the classical culture deriving from it.[5] Classical culture thrived on a distortion of a metaphysical frame for addressing reality, a distortion or collapse that both Peirce-Geertz and Lonergan adequately addressed. Lonergan thinks this distortion is the product of the myth that reality can be conceived on the analogy of ocular vision—the myth that reality is "already-out-there-now" waiting to be seen and apprehended. Because Peirce-Geertz and Lonergan ground metaphysics in the practices of the sciences and common sense, a synthesis of their thought specifies the depth and breadth of the dialogue that should take place between science and theology as theology moves from the ghetto of Western civilization to a world church.[6]

At issue here is "the surprising scale and depth of the worldwide Christian resurgence, a resurgence that seems to proceed without Western organizational structures."[7] In those parts of the world hit by this tidal wave of Christian resurgence, "even church leaders have been unable to comprehend fully, still less to respond effectively to, the magnitude of the resurgence."[8] Before the Catholic Church officially came up with institutional organization to cope with the momentum of this resurgence, Lonergan was one of the leading voices to recognize how the faith must be steeped in culture, if it is to become meaningful in a rapidly changing world. Following the reforms of the Second Vatican Council (1962–65), Lonergan again pointed out how Catholic thought must be re-thought, if the *aggionarmento* program of Saint John XXIII is to be successful. Lonergan was devoted to a complete overall and restructuring of theology as the answer to the most important need of our time.[9] He saw the Leonine project of increasing and perfecting *vetera* with the *nova* as demanding a far greater challenge than was ordinarily assumed, i.e., that of knowing, understanding, assimilating and transforming the contemporary cultural situation.[10] More importantly, more than most of his contemporaries, he saw the Leonine program as demanding a radical shift from the "first

---

5. See Forest, "Lonergan and the Classical American Tradition," 17–44.

6. See Peirce, *Collected Papers of Charles Sanders Peirce*; *Semiotic and Significs*; *The Essential Peirce*.

7. Sanneh, *Whose Religion is Christianity?*, 3.

8. Ibid.

9. Crowe, *Method in Theology*, 7.

10. Lawrence, "Lonergan as Political Theologian," 14.

principles" of scholasticism and classical culture to a transcendental method.[11] What he labelled transcendental method, like the semiotic work of Peirce, brings to light the conditions of the possibility of knowing something in its totality.[12] Whereas the scholastics sought a secure foundation for knowledge, Lonergan, like Peirce, shows that human knowledge is not intuitive but discursive and open to development and purification. Since we have no immediate knowledge of anything, the "foundations" of human knowledge and the "first principles" on which classical culture thrived also have to be re-thought in a radical way.[13] We come to knowledge, not by some first principles "but by a self-correcting process of learning, in which insights gradually accumulate, coalesce, qualify, and correct one another, until a point is reached where we are able to meet situations as they arise, size them up by adding a few more insights to the acquired store, and so deal with them in an appropriate fashion."[14]

If Lonergan and Peirce are correct "that all human cognition is discursive and that judgment is the base unit of such cognition, then there are no judgments such that are self-evident and self-justifying."[15] Knowledge consists rather in judgments reasonably affirmed as a result of questions intelligently put to the data of experience.[16] As regards the Jesus mandate to proclaim the Good News and make disciples of all nations (Matt.28:19), the implication here is that the "foundation" on which classicism built its earlier understanding of this message is passé. Insights from Peirce and Lonergan's critical realism, supported by Post-modern scientific views of culture—linguistics, as well as structuralist and interpretive traditions of cultural analysis, put us in a better position to construct a theology, i.e., inculturation, that adequately meets the Jesus mandate of Matthew 28:19. Reflections on culture is not just about thematizing the meanings and values embodied in the way of life of a people, but with "control of meaning," i.e., attunement with the deepest exigencies of human liberty.[17] The task

---

11. See Potter, "Foundations: Lonergan and Peirce," 181. See also Lonergan, "The Future of Thomism," 50–52.

12. Lonergan, *Method in Theology*, 13–14, esp. n4.

13. Potter, "Lonergan and Peirce," 182.

14. Lonergan, *Method in Theology*, 81.

15. Potter, "Lonergan and Peirce," 183.

16. Meynell, *The Theology of Bernard Lonergan*, 4.

17. Lawrence, "Lonergan As political Theologian," 12. See also Lonergan, "Dimensions of Meaning," 252–67.

of this chapter, in essence, is the systematic exigence of doing theology that Lonergan suggests is the pathway for moving Catholic theology forward—one that separates the realm of common sense from the realm of theory.[18] The goal of this critical exigence is to reach an understanding of inculturation—the the theology of a multicultural society.[19]

Restating the Problem

Hillaire Belloc (1870–1953) captured the allure of European culture and its ties to Christianity with his famous 1924 quip: "the faith is Europe and Europe is the faith."[20] The Christianity of which Belloc spoke is more properly Christendom—the political and religious coming together of Roman Empire and the Christian religion that began in the Fourth century when Constantine made Christianity the official state religion in Roman Empire. Christianity in its flirtations with the state, in turn adopted imperial Roman view of culture that divided the world into camps: the civilized (cultured) and the barbarian (uncultured).[21] This was "strongly reinforced when the Pope, in the Fifth century, effectively became heir to the extinct line of western emperors, and the eastern, Byzantine branch of the Empire was increasingly isolated from its Western tradition of origin."[22] According to Aylward Shorter, the Church's monoculturalism received a powerful reinforcement when the Roman Empire and Christianity aligned together to become the politico-religious system known as Christendom.[23] The immutability of the Christian cultural ideal was officially stamped and sealed in the high middle Ages when classical Greco-Roman philosophy was applied to the truths of revelation.[24] It is no surprising, therefore, that Western writers like Christopher Dawson (1889–1970) and Arnold Toynbee (1889–1975), very much in the tradition of Belloc, "saw the hand of Providence in the historical conjunction of Christianity and Western culture."[25] Toynbee saw the

18. Lonergan, *Method in Theology*, 81.
19. Shorter, *Toward a Theology of Inculturation*, xi.
20. See Schall, "Belloc's Infamous Phrase."
21. Shorter, *Toward a Theology of Inculturation*, 18.
22. Ibid.
23. Ibid.
24. Ibid.
25. Ibid., 9.

world as "being unified under the aegis of Western culture, the origins of which are to be found—after a Greco-Roman 'overture'—in Christianity."[26]

Reeling over the pride of being identified with the superior Greco-Roman imperial culture, Christendom "assumed that the Gospel must be proclaimed everywhere in a single, 'perfect,' cultural form. Any variation was deemed to be either a deviation or a stage of development towards the, as yet, unrealized ideal."[27] But Christianity is no longer Christendom, a religion of one cultural mandate.[28] Today "Christianity is the religion of over two thousand different language groups in the world. More people pray and worship in more languages in Christianity than in any other religion in the world."[29] Inculturation stands in contrast to the worldview perpetuated by Christendom. While it celebrates the achievement of Europe and the grandeur of its civilization, inculturation rejects the notion that the faith is tied to Europe or any one particular civilization. Inculturation also rejects that theology as conceived in the European world is an immutable and permanent achievement. In fact, in seeking a fresh understanding of the gospel in a new world order, inculturation helps Christianity get over its "Christendom guilt complex."[30]

For all the centuries of the Church's life up to the period leading up to the Second Vatican Council, a monocultural view of the world was undoubtedly propagated by bishops, priests, Church theologians. In fact, it was not until Pius XII's address to the Pontifical Mission Aid Societies (1944) that the Church began to move toward a pluralistic view of culture.[31] It was at this time that Karl Rahner observed that before Vatican II "the actual concrete activity of the Church in its relation to the world outside of Europe was . . . the activity of an export firm which exported a European religion as a commodity it did not really want to change but sent throughout the world together with the rest of the culture and civilization it considered superior."[32] Official Catholicism, according to Rahner, operated with the "mentality of a centralized bureaucracy which thinks it knows

26. Ibid., 20.

27. Ibid., 18.

28. Sanneh, *Whose Religion is Christianity?*, 69.

29. Ibid.

30. Ibid.

31. Shorter, *Toward a Theology of Inculturation*, 18. See also Pius XII, "Allocution to the *Pontifical* Mission Aid Societies," 210; and Pius XII, Evangelii *Praeconis*.

32. Rahner, "Towards a Fundamental Theological Interpretation of Vatican II," 717.

best what serves the kingdom of God and the salvation of souls throughout the world and in such decisions takes the mentality of Rome or Italy in a frighteningly naive way as a self evident standard."[33] Lamin Sanneh has amplified this by suggesting that the West "should get over its Christendom guilt complex about Christianity as colonialism by accepting that Christianity has survived its European political habits and is thriving today in its post-Western phase among non-Western populations, sometimes because of, and often in spite of, Western missionaries."[34]

Case Study: The Mayas of the Guatemalan Highlands

Vatican II gave impetus to uprooting classicism in Roman Catholicism, and rightly too, because classicism, in spite of its benefits, has its own seed of self-destruction. Classicism lacks balance and depth in its values and destructive of human progress.[35] In his well-researched work on Guatemalan Catholics and the Mayas, Michael Duffey highlights why the first evangelization of the native peoples of the Americas was unfortunate in many respects. Spanish missionaries to the Mayas adopted a policy of "forced conversion." Pedro de Alvarado, a man that in many ways embodied the abuse of forced conversion, issued an ultimatum to the Mayas of Guatemala highlands in 1525, which led to death and destruction of both the Mayas and their cultural traditions. Alvarado was convinced that the coming of the Spanish missionary to the Mayan territory was of utmost benefit to the Mayas mainly because they (the Spanish missionaries) were bringing tidings of the true religion and culture to the Mayas. He warned that should the Mayas refuse to accept peacefully then "death and destruction" will follow. "The Mayas refused, and death and destruction did follow, as it had for the Mixtecs, the Zapotecs, the Tzotzil Mayans of southern Mexico, and the neighboring Guatemalan kingdom of the K'iche' Mayas (the Guatemalan department in which they live is often Latinized as "Quiché")."[36] Coerced conversion always produces, as it did for the Mayas, mixed results. It makes Christianity seem like an alien patch superimposed on culture. In the case of the Mayas, "despite centuries of efforts by missionaries to uproot Mayan religious beliefs and practices, the Mayan cosmological vision continues to

---

33. Ibid., 717–78.
34. Sanneh, *Whose Religion is Christianity?*, 74–75.
35. Lonergan, "Belief: Today's Issue," 99.
36. Duffey, "Guatemalan Catholics and Mayas," 87.

provide the center of Mayan life."[37] The failure to properly integrate Mayan religious system and cultural values into Christianity has led to various Mayan responses to Christianity in the twenty first century. Two of these different responses warrant our attention.

The first response seeks a "return to an older Mayan culture shorn of Christianity."[38] Mayas who hold this view complain that in spite of the Church's rhetoric of championing cultural rights of the native peoples that the Church's "support of Mayan religious views and ritual practices is less clear."[39] Many who have since left the Catholic Church to return to their indigenous roots complain that the "Catholic Church has yet to engage in a dialogue among equals" and that the "conflation of cultural rights and religion demanded an outright repudiation of Christianity."[40] The second response, a quest for "Mayanized theology," seeks to "fully universalize Christianity by consciously framing Christian beliefs within the conceptual structures of Mayan cosmovision."[41] This second response affirms how the Mayas have been deprived of their lands, and ignored and pushed to the margins in the juridical and political reordering of colonial society and chides the Church's hierarchy for failing to realize "that the practices of the conquest continue today: we are being robbed of our unique identity. We are asked to desist from being ourselves."[42] Thus, they call for a space not only in which the Mayas can develop and express themselves fully in their music, art, spirituality, and family relations, but also "demands a reexamination of fundamental Christian images, symbols, and archetypes through the lens of traditional Mayan cosmovision(s)" in order to "identify points of potential conjuncture" between European and indigenous systems of organizing all realities that make up the world."[43]

The Mayan example is an instance of the cry for freedom that resounds from the oppressed people in Africa, the Caribbean, Latin America, Asia, the South Pacific, and North America—the recognition that theology "as it

---

37. Ibid., 88.
38. Ibid.
39. Ibid.
40. Ibid.
41. Ibid.
42. Ibid.
43. Ibid.

was handed to them by their colonial overlords, was unable to address with specificity and clarity the problem of identity that plagued them."[44]

Emergence of historical consciousness (i.e., advance and dissemination of meaning) ushered in by post-modern understanding of culture came with the realization that the Christendom era theology cannot adequately answer the new questions of the emerging churches of Latin America, Africa, Asia, and Oceana, necessitated a call for "shift in perspective."[45] The particularities of their time and culture have made these churches to realize that they can no longer be content "to repeat the tradition as it has come down to them in rote fashion."[46] The idea has come to be accepted "that each society has its own culture, functioning as an integrated system of assumptions, practices, and symbols."[47] The crucial problem is not that imports or any foreign may not have a place in the spiritual life of a people "but that God, when understood through the medium of other people's experience is in danger of losing identity for oppressed people."[48] The Mayan example shows us that what the Church needs to move forward is not a juxtaposition of two differing world views (i.e., indigenous culture and Christian faith), but a creative blending of indigenous culture and Christian faith.

Lonergan sees the dilemma facing the Church as analogous to the one Christians faced in the thirteenth century, a dilemma that was met by the genius of Aquinas: "Then Greek and Arabic culture was pouring into Western Europe and, if it was not to destroy Christendom, it had to be known, assimilated, transformed. Today modern culture, in many ways more stupendous than any that ever existed, is surging round us. It too has to be known, assimilated, transformed."[49] Contemporary Guatemalan bishops are now beginning to meet their own dilemma by moving in the direction of assimilation and transformation in order not to make God foreign to the consciousness of the Mayas. One such bishop is Bishop Julio Cabrera of K'iche, who in 1999 recognized how the Mayan cosmovision enriches the Catholic faith:

> He acknowledged the wisdom and vitality of Mayan cultures, noting the values of harmony and equilibrium in the Mayan

44. Erskine, *Decolonizing Theology*, 1.
45. Schreiter, *Constructing Local Theologies*, 5.
46. Ibid., xi.
47. Stanley, "Inculturation," 22.
48. Erskine, *Decolonizing Theology*, 1.
49. Lonergan, "Belief," 99.

cosmovision, which manifest a deep respect for the Creator, for mother earth, and for all human beings. Cabrera recognized the Mayas' care for land and nature, their strong sense of community and family, their respect for elders and ancestors, and their preservation of customs and traditions. He laid out a pastoral plan intended to bridge cultures by committing the church to supporting Mayan communities "in conserving, renewing, and enlivening their cultural identity" and continuing the process of becoming an "autochthonous church"—that is, a church springing from the Mayan culture itself.[50]

Vatican II was a watershed moment in the shift in attitude towards cultures that are non-European, at least in Catholic circles. Vatican II was, in some sense, the Catholic Church's first official self-actualization as a world Church.[51] The effect of the Council on the world was "paradigmatic and unprecedented in the history of the Church."[52] Although the Council spoke more of adaptation, not inculturation, "it nevertheless recognized the need for a new interpretation of its meaning."[53] *Evangelii Nuntiandi* (1975), issued on the tenth anniversary of the closing of the Second Vatican Council, addresses the "the split between the Gospel and culture," characterizing it as "the drama of our time" (*EN*, no. 20). In this encyclical Paul VI pointed out that though the Gospel and evangelization are independent of cultures, they "are not necessarily incompatible with them; rather they are capable of permeating them all without becoming subject to any one of them" (*EN*, no. 20). The question of "how to evangelize," according to Paul VI, is always and "permanently relevant, because the methods of evangelizing vary according to the different circumstances of time, place, and culture" (*EN*, no. 40). He therefore, admonished those who evangelize to "give the maximum attention to the dignity, precision and adaptation of their language" (*EN*, no. 73).

The Pope used the word "adaptation" which, though it may be thought to be related, is not the same as inculturation. He did not use the term *inculturation*. Only later papal documents would elaborate on the realities of inculturation or adaptation, including John Paul II's *Catechesi Tradendae* (1979), *Slavorum Apostoli* (1985), *Redemptoris Missio* (1993), and *Fides et*

50. Duffey, "Guatemalan Catholics and Mayas," 90.
51. Rahner, "Towards a Fundamental Theological Interpretation of Vatican II," 717.
52. Dadosky, "Towards a Fundamental Theological Re-Interpretation of Vatican II," 742.
53. Grenham, *The Unknown God*, 49.

Ratio (1998). There are also references in the final document of the Latin American Episcopal Conference (Medellin, 1968; Puebla, 1979; Santo Domingo, 1992), the International Theological Commission's "Faith and Inculturation" (1988), the Congregation for the Clergy's "General Directory for Catechesis" (1997), and post-Synodal Apostolic Exhortations of the following synods: African Bishop's synod (1994), Asian Bishops synod (1998), and the Oceania Bishops synod (1999).[54]

Among Protestants it is more much difficult to pin point a particular standard watershed moment, like Vatican II was for Roman Catholicism.[55] But what is clear was that by the 1970s there were loud calls for "accommodation," "localization," "indigenization," "adaptation," and "inculturation" in Protestant evangelical missions.[56] The need for inculturation or adaptation began to feature prominently in the statements of the Lutheran World Federation (Nairobi, 1996), The World Council of Churches (Jerusalem, 1995), and the World Council of Churches Commission on World Mission and Evangelization (WCC-WCME) Ecumenical Conference in Salvador de Bahia (Brazil, 1996).[57] One of the significant attempts to address the issue of the gospel engagement with culture was undertaken by the American Lutheran theologian, H. Richard Niebuhr (1894–1962) whose influential work, *Christ and Culture*, advances a fivefold typology for Christian relationships with culture: (1) Christ against culture; (2) Christ of culture; (3) Christ above culture; (4) Christ and culture in paradox; and (5) Christ transformer of culture.[58] Niebuhr's preference for the latter, i.e., Christ transformer of culture, poses a further problem to be investigated by a theology of inculturation.

Some Helpful but Insufficient Terms

The notion of inculturation rests on the distinction and interaction between faith and culture.[59] Inability to make a proper distinction has sometimes

54. Phan, *In Our Own Tongues*, 4

55. Grenham, *The Unknown God*, 47. See also Comby, *How to Understand the History of Christian Mission*.

56. Schreiter, *Constructing Local Theologies*, 2. See also Haleblian, "The Problem of Contextualization," 95–111.

57. Phan, *In Our Own Tongues*, 5.

58. See Niebuhr, *Christ and Culture*.

59. Shorter, *Toward a Theology of Inculturation*, 3.

led to the term being treated as "a dilettantish kind of neologism."[60] The term is also susceptible to oversimplification and misinterpretation because of the relative newness of the human sciences out of which the term emerged and the fluidity of their vocabulary.[61] This fluidity has led some to raise concern that inculturation risks being "consigned to the dustbin of faded 'buzz words.'"[62] While such concern is not entertained here for the simple fact that the theological and historical problem represented by the word is too critical for this to happen,[63] still there is need to clarify the meaning of the term and distinguish it from similar and related terms that are too often confused with inculturation. That said, inculturation is difficult and the meaning of the term can be rather obscure. In fact it is easy to determine what inculturation is not than what it actually is. Not even the popularity of the word in recent papal encyclicals has helped to clarify the meaning of the term. There are those, for example, who think "inculturation" is "an ugly and uninspiring word."[64] These people want to augment the word and make it more appealing and intelligible. They too have come up with their own terms that they think can serve as a substitute. But these terms in turn create more difficulties. Here are some of those terms with their strengths and weaknesses outlined.

a. **Localization**

Localization suggests a connection with the local Church. Localization is based on two main assumptions: that there is something that can be recognized as "true Christianity" and that there is something that can be recognized as "true local culture." For this reason localization is often viewed with suspicion because "the models underlying this assumption tend to be static and in practice can be seen as an attempt by the mainstream church authorities to maintain definitional control over the faith of the mission or the former mission churches."[65] There are many issues that localization leaves unresolved: What is meant by culture? Who constitutes the local culture? Who constitutes the local church?

---

60. Schreiter, *Constructing Local Theologies*, 6.
61. Shorter, *Toward a Theology of Inculturation*, 4.
62. Starkloff, "Inculturation and Cultural Systems," 66.
63. Ibid.
64. Shorter, *Toward a Theology of Inculturation*, 10.
65. Bowie, "The Inculturation Debate in Africa," 67–68.

Inculturation Reconsidered

By what criteria does one determine what are valid indigenous practices and customs? Who adjudicates? And whose culture and whose definition is to be regarded as normative?[66]

The idea of localization stems from the mistaken notion that culture is a one big idea—a conception that defines it in terms of essence-and-accident and a natural-kind of way, and society like a giant machine or a quasi-organism. Thus, equating localization with inculturation, to use Geertz's own analogy, does not steer clear of "what statisticians call type-one and type-two errors—accepting hypothesis one would be better advised to reject and rejecting ones one would be wiser to accept."[67] The error here, as it pertains to localization, is the problem of "over interpretation and under interpretation," i.e., reading more into a cultural situation than reason permits and at other times less into it than it demands.[68] Much as localization tries to recognize the way a given society constructs its ways of life, it fails to see social life "as organized in terms of symbols (signs, representations, signifiants, *Darstellungen* . . .) whose meaning (sense, import, signification, *Bedeutung* . . .) we must grasp" to properly understand the culture or society.[69]

Culture, as we pointed out in the last chapter, is like a (behavioral) text to be read and interpreted. To see culture as "readable," as Geertz points out, "is to alter our whole sense of what such interpretation is and shift it toward modes of thought rather more familiar to the translator, the exegete, or the iconographer than to the test giver, the factor analyst, or the pollster."[70] Let's take the example of naming ceremony in Bali that Geertz cites:

> All Balinese receive what might be called birth-order names. There are four of these, "first-born," "second-born," "third-born," "fourth-born," after which they recycle, so that the fifth-born child is called again "first-born," the sixth "second-born," and so on. Further, these names are bestowed independently of the fates of the children. Dead children, even stillborn ones,

---

66. Ibid., 68.
67. Geertz, *Local Knowledge*, 16.
68. Ibid., 16.
69. Ibid., 21.
70. Ibid., 31.

count, so that in fact, in this still high-birthrate, high-mortality society, the names do not really tell you anything very reliable about the birth-order relations of concrete individuals. Within a set of living siblings, someone called "first-born" may actually be first, fifth, or ninth-born, or if somebody is missing, almost anything in between, and someone called "second-born" may in fact be older. The birth-order naming system does not identify individuals as individuals, nor is it intended to; what it does is to suggest that, for all procreating couples, births form a circular succession of "firsts," "seconds," "thirds," and "fourths," an endless four-stage replication of an imperishable form.[71]

How do you "localize" this mode of expression of the Balinese conception of personhood? Wouldn't it be more meaningful to attempt to understand the vehicle of expression (signs and symbols) that embodies their concept of personhood?

b. **Accommodation**

The names of Jesuit missionaries Matteo Ricci (1552–1610) and Francis Xavier (1506–52) are often invoked in contemporary discussion of inculturation. It is safe to say that the origins of early Christian experiment with accommodation is traceable to them. Francis Xavier arrived in Japan in 1543 while Ricci arrived in China in 1583, in the backdrop of the Catholic counter-reformation, when the Society of Jesus was eager to spread the Gospel in the Far East, particularly in the regions of China and Japan. These Jesuit missionaries encountered Confucianism, Buddhism, Taoism, and various Eastern philosophies and attempted to adapt and integrate them into Christian worldviews and values. They learned Chinese and Japanese cultures and recognized their positive values for Christianity. With the help of his Chinese friends, for example, Ricci translated the four classical works of Confucianism (The Analects, the Book of Mencius, the Doctrine of the Mean, and the Great Learning) into Latin and transliterated the Chinese name Kong Fuzi in English as Confucius.[72] Ricci and his companions adopted the missionary method of accommodation in their various encounters with Eastern religions. They saw parallels between Christianity and

---

71. Ibid., 63.

72. Chung, "Inculturation and Recognition of the Other," 80.

Inculturation Reconsidered

Buddhism: the robes that Buddhist monks wore, their method of chanting, and their espousal of vowed life—celibacy and poverty, etc.[73] Ricci also thought that Confucius taught human ethical morality that was congruous to Christian teachings. Ricci's overall method has been summarized thus:

> He utilizes Catholic doctrines as a complement to Confucianism; in some respects he elevates the Catholic doctrines above and against Confucian teaching by transcending and transforming the Confucian one. But he does not hesitate to undertake some revisions of the Catholic teaching in seeking agreement with Confucian instruction. His dialogical principle is based on a critical complement to Confucian instruction and the self-renewal of Catholic teaching in harmonious co-existence with Confucian philosophy so that mutual respect and harmonious life are underscored.[74]

As ingenious as the Ricci policy of accommodation was, it was not without controversy. It eventually led to the so called "Rites controversy" that involved eight popes and lasted over seventy years.[75] "Those who were tolerant of Chinese rites favored greater cultural adaptation, declaring the rites to be non-religious. Others who opposed [them] denounced these rites as superstitious paganism."[76] Accommodation policy is still ambiguous today as it was at the time of Ricci.

What Ricci and his Jesuit companions did may have been valuable for the time and needs to be commended. Working out of a cultural matrix of classicism, they employed the principle of accommodation to solve a particular problem. But of all the terms that have been substituted for inculturation accommodation is the weakest. Accommodation "is externalized in the sense that it is seen as a method of accommodating or adapting Christian faith to the context whereas true inculturation is the hermeneutics of interpreting faith through the given cultural context."[77] It does not address the point that culture is always already a sym-

---

73. Ibid., 81.
74. Ibid., 83.
75. Ibid., 92.
76. Ibid.
77. Kavunkal, "Inculturation and Future Scanning," 95.

bolic act. When Geertz speaks of culture "as a system of symbols which acts," it does not mean that there is a bifurcation in the sense that one has culture as a self-contained system on one side and action on the other but that culture is always already a symbolic act "never reducible to the wider ground of social institutions and material realities that influence it (and vice versa)."[78] In the eighteenth century, when people spoke only of culture (not cultures) and in ways synonymous with "civilization," i.e., as opposed to barbarism, culture was conceived, not empirically, but normatively. It connoted an evolutionary process of becoming "civilized" and the pinnacle of this evolutionary process of becoming civilized was the eighteenth-century European culture.[79] As Lonergan describes it:

> It was a matter of acquiring and assimilating the tastes and skills, the ideals, virtues, and ideas, that were pressed upon one in a good home and through a curriculum in the liberal arts. It stressed not facts but values. It could not but claim to be universalist. Its classics were immortal works of art, its philosophy, was the perennial philosophy, its laws and structures were the deposit of the wisdom and the prudence of mankind. Classicist education was a matter of models to be imitated, of ideal characters to be emulated, of eternal verities and universally valid laws.[80]

The first to attack this unitary and parochial view of culture was the German philosopher Johann Gottfried von Herder (1744–1803) who broke accepted conventions by being the first to speak of cultures in the plural and suggested that "the very thought of a superior European culture is a blatant insult to the majesty of Nature."[81] Clifford Geertz, following in the steps of Herder, also denounced ethnographers and anthropologist like Edward Burnett Tylor (1832–1917) and the contemporary interpretive anthropologist Stephen Tyler for subscribing to the view that culture consists in "mental phenomena which can be analyzed by formal methods similar to those of mathematics and

---

78. Caton, "What Is an 'Authorizing Discourse'?," 41.
79. Mukerji and Schudson, "Rethinking Popular Culture," 2.
80. Lonergan, *Method in Theology*, 301.
81. Mukerji and Schudson, "Rethinking Popular Culture," 2.

logic," a view Geertz suggests amounts to cognitivist fallacy.[82] The world of everyday life in which people live, Geertz points out, is a cultural product that is framed in symbolic conceptions of "stubborn fact" that is handed down from one generation to another. The "stubborn fact," to use Geertz's own analogy, is like Mount Everest in the sense that it is just there. "The thing to do with it, if one feels the need to do anything with it at all, is to climb it."[83]

Jean Marc Ela's criticism of accommodation model that was practiced in liturgical services in Cameroon buttresses Geertz's point. Ela writes that in spite of the introduction of native songs and indigenous musical instruments liturgical reforms have yet to succeed because the "reform" is merely a translation of "the Roman Rite." The abiding questions for Ela, therefore are these: "Is liturgical pluralism consonant with catholicity? Is it enough to translate into the vernacular prayers composed elsewhere and in another spirit? Or should we encourage a genuinely African style of Christian prayer?"[84] The idea of "accommodation" suggests, real or imagined, an elitism of some sort, i.e., that there is somebody from a "superior" culture who stands in a position to adjudicate what is or not to be accommodated. It considers cultures, not in their concrete individualities and totality of their aspects, but from an abstract viewpoint.[85] Rather than grasp the unity-identity whole and the intelligible unities in the multitudes of cultures, accommodation assumes that there is an "already out there now real" proto culture that is unquestionable.

c. Adaptation

Adaptation, like accommodation, was popularly used before Vatican II.[86] "As early as 1938, Henri de Lubac, citing John Henry Newman, identified cultural adaptation as a key element of Catholicism. De Lubac argued that Christian salvation cannot be segmented off to another realm but is truly linked with

---

82. Geertz, *The Interpretation of Cultures*, 12.
83. Ibid., 111.
84. Ela, *African Cry*, 113.
85. See "the general notion of the thing" in chapter 8 of Lonergan, *Insight*, 270–95.
86. Shorter, *Toward a Theology of Inculturation*, 11.

human destiny and connected with human societies in a real way."[87] Adaptation had its place and was helpful in the climate in which it was developed. Adaptation was a method often associated with the Jesuit missionary to South India, Roberto de Nobili (1577–1656). De Nobili arrived in India in 1605 and worked in the Tamul city of Mandurai. His greatest challenge was how to meet the Indian caste system and custom in light of Christian teachings. But to his credit, de Nobili showed an ample amount of respect to local customs and valued the culture and people of India. De Nobili adopted a method of adaptation, similar to the accommodation method of Matheo Ricci in China. At a time when most European missionaries found it near impossible to consider anything other than their own perceptions and attitudes as worthy of value, de Nobili transcended such parochial attitudes and made fundamental adaptations, securing in the process the approval of the Holy See. His method became the official Catholic policy in 1659, barely three years after his death.[88]

In the post-colonial era, shortly after many of the missionaries left Africa and Asia, adaptation was seen was an alternative to the failed acculturation experiment used by some missionaries. It was a method that many who wanted to uphold cultural sensitivity saw at the time as a viable alternative. The logic behind adaptation is simply "that the kernel of the Gospel or Christianity is wrapped within a Western cultural husk, which is seen as unavoidable when Western missionaries initially entered non-Western territories to proclaim the Gospel. Adaptation therefore implies 'undressing' the kernel of the Gospel from its Western cultural outfit, and re-clothing it with a 'cultural attire' of the people to whom Jesus' message of salvation is brought."[89] Adaptation also implies that for Christianity to be permanently and fruitfully embedded in non-Western cultures it must ipso facto be translated into the cultural categories of the people to whom the gospel is proclaimed. Since this must be done without losing the essentials of the faith, what this means is that the

---

87. Doyle, "The Concept of Inculturation in Roman Catholicism," 2. See also Lubac, *Catholicism*.

88. See Collins, "The Praxis of Inculturation for Mission," 324.

89. Wielzen, "Popular Religiosity and Roman Liturgy," 177.

Christian faith is made to adapt to the cultural milieu only by "appropriating an indigenous color that will enable it to root itself in the culture of the people."[90]

The problem with adaptation, which surfaced even as far back as the time of de Nobili, was that adaptation, like its closely related term accommodation, stands to be "misinterpreted as implying compromise or concession or even adulteration."[91] It is no wonder that at the end of the 1974 synod, the bishops of Africa and Madagascar proclaimed that the theology of adaptation was passé.[92]

d. Interculturation

There are scholars who show preference for the term *interculturation*. Bishop Joseph Blomjous (1908–92) who was credited with the term in 1980 was said to have coined it as a corrective to what he saw as the deficiencies in the word *inculturation*.[93] We are not clear what Blomjous thought these "deficiencies" were, but Aylward Shorter suggests that it might not be unrelated to the missionary practice or view of inculturation that misses the reciprocal character of mission. This mistaken view suggests that evangelization is a one-way process in which only the recipient of Christian faith benefits from the operation.[94] The concept of inculturation in their view, also does not fully take into account "the complicated reality of the interaction between the accumulated Christian culture in which the Gospel is carried and the various levels of meaning that other cultures and other religions manifests."[95] Their preferred term interculturation, is intended, therefore, to preserve both the mutuality and partnership that inculturation entails.[96]

First of all, the suggestion that inculturation is a one-way stream whereby only the recipient of the faith benefits from the

---

90. Ibid.

91. Doyle, "The Concept of Inculturation in Roman Catholicism," 7.

92. Ela, *African Cry*, 135.

93. See Blomjous, "Development in Mission Thinking and Practice 1959–1980," 393–98.

94. Shorter, *Toward a Theology of Inculturation*, 13.

95. Grenham, *The Unknown God*, 64.

96. Ibid., 65.

process is short-sighted. "Inculturation implies that the Christian message transforms a culture. It is also the case that Christianity is transformed by culture, not a way that falsifies the message, but in the way in which the message is formulated and interpreted anew."[97] Second, many of the advocates of interculturation seem to be working out of a particular notion of cultural model that is no longer tenable in light of semiotic understanding of culture. For the sake of simplicity, let us take the distinctions made by the Indian writer Ram Adhar Mall as an example. Mall distinguishes three types of models in the meeting of cultures: identity model, alterity model, and analogy model.[98] Some cultural anthropologists have equated the identity model with mono-culturation—"the assumption that we and the others are basically the same," the alterity model with multi-culturation—"the assumption that we and others are essentially different," and the analogy model with inter-culturation, "the assumption that there are cultural overlaps between us and others."[99] Advocates of interculturation, to their credit, are trying to bring a balance between identity model and alterity model.[100] Still they leave many questions unanswered. While interculturation abhors the uncritical acceptance of classicist cultures and values, it does not, address the issue of inclusiveness and universal acceptance of indigenous cultures at the heart of this rejection of classical values.

Advocates of interculturation got a boost in the 1990s when then Cardinal Joseph Ratzinger (who later became Pope Benedict XVI) favored the word "interculturality" in an address to Asian bishops and later in his reflections on John Paul II's encyclical *Fides et Ratio* (Faith and Reason).[101] Cardinal Ratzinger used the term "interculturality" to designate the "meeting of cultures." Cardinal Ratzinger's preference for "interculturality" over "inculturation" hinged on the idea that there is no such thing as faith devoid of culture or culture devoid of faith and that if all cultures are potentially universal and open to each other then

---

97. Shorter, *Towards a Theology of Inculturation*, 14.
98. See Mall, *Intercultural Philosophy*.
99. Wijsen, "Global Christianity," 158.
100. Ibid., 159.
101. See Arbuckle, *Culture, Inculturation, and Theologians*, 177.

INCULTURATION RECONSIDERED

interculturality can lead to "new forms" of flourishing.[102] What Cardinal Ratzinger describes as "interculturation" is a little different from the original meaning of interculturality as used by Blomjous. Second, interculturality may be applicable in some cultural settings, but not all. It meets, for example, the United States of America situation where immigrants from distant places like Africa, Europe, Mexico, the Philippines, and a whole host of Asian countries come with their own cultures and confront at one and the same time both the gospel and the existing American culture. The American Catholic culture, according to David O'Brien, is marked by three distinctive styles: the republican style with its dualism of citizenship and discipleship, the immigrant style with its rich history and relatively clear pastoral and political strategy, and the evangelical style which reflects the dynamics of American democratic religious and cultural pluralism.[103] Catholics coming to the United States, say from an African or Asian country, will have to negotiate between their own native or indigenous cultures (and even sub-cultures), the gospel, and the dominant American culture with its distinctive styles. How they navigate this complex process is beyond the scope of this work.

The problematic of Cardinal Ratzinger's preference for "interculturality" over "inculturation" has yet to be resolved. The difficulty is not unrelated to the fact that "interculturality" is a cultural anthropological term, while inculturation is strictly speaking a theological term. Second, "interculturality," which is the initial contact in the meeting of two or more cultures, is a first but nonetheless significant step in the process of inculturation.[104] Interculturality opens up dialogue and initiates parameters of fruitful conversation between two or more parties who are aware that their cultures are different.[105] Inculturation, on the other hand, is a critical development that follows this first initial contact.

---

102. See Ratzinger, "Christ, Faith and the Challenge of Cultures," 681.
103. O'Brien, *Public Catholicism*, xi.
104. Arbuckle, *Culture, Inculturation, and Theologians*, 177.
105. Ibid., 180.

e. Contextualization

As Christian Churches increasingly come to terms with the fact that no one cultural expression of Christianity holds a monopoly of expressing the fullness of the gospel,[106] more and more terms are being invoked to express this dynamic relationship between the gospel and culture. Steven Bevans who is a leading figure in development and use of the term "contextualization" has identified different variants or models of contextualization.[107] Lamin Sanneh, another leading proponent of contextual theology, has argued that Christianity is "unique in being the only world religion that is transmitted without the language or originating culture of its founder."[108] He argues that not only do people have the right to understand what they were being taught, but also "that there was nothing God wanted to say that could not be said in simple everyday language."[109]

Contextual theology, generally speaking, is "theology from below." It addresses the concerns of the poor and culturally marginalized. It is a theology "from the underside of history."[110] In countries like South Africa and the United States of America where black people are less privileged, contextual theology usually takes the form of protest against white theology. In the words of James Cone, contextual theology "takes on the character of rebellion against things as they are."[111] Contextualization is the preferred term of the World Council of Churches (WCC).[112] In 1996 the WCC held a conference in Salvador on World Mission and Evangelism to discuss far ranging implications of the movement of the gospel from Western cultures to indigenous cultures. Similar conferences on contextualization were also held by Evangelicals in Willowbank (1978) and Haslev (1997). Contextualization suggests that theology is, first and foremost, context based. The argument that there is no such thing as a universal theology

---

106. See Sanneh, *Translating the Message*, 74.
107. See Bevans, *Models of Contextual Theology*.
108. See Sanneh, *Whose Religion is Christianity?*, 98.
109. Ibid.
110. See Bosch, *Transforming Mission*, 423.
111. Cone, *A Black Theology of Liberation*, 17.
112. Shorter, *Toward a Theology of Inculturation*, 11.

is fast gaining currency in contemporary systematic theology. There is a broad recognition in theology, missiology especially, that all theologies are, by their nature, context based. Interpreting a text, for example, is not only a literary, but also a social, economic, cultural, and political exercise.[113] In the last decade or more there has been a call for "a new round of contextual theologies" that adequately accounts for the difference between broad notion of contextualization and specific quest for contextualization. The suggestion here is that although all theology is context based, broad notions of contextualization is, as the term indicates, often too broad. But specific notions of contextualization is a "conscious and deliberate attempt at bringing context and the text of the Bible into discourse with one another."[114] Although contextualization "has the advantage of not having many previous associations and of being readily used in translation into a wide variety of languages,"[115] the problem with it however, is that it has "a more extended and less precise meaning."[116] Another pitfall of contextual theology is that context often determines what are valued and what are not valued in religion. Contexts are "constructed strategies" and are often preloaded with their own biases and prejudices.[117]

f. Indigenization

Indigenization was one of the terms that was used initially for the newly emerging theologies of Africa and Asia. As the term itself suggests, indigenization is an imperative "to go native."[118] It also "emphasizes the fact that theology is done by and for a given geographical area—by local people for their area, rather than by outsiders."[119] One of its benefits is that it fosters and develops local cultures. But the problem with the indigenization is contained

---

113. See Bosch, *Transforming Mission*, 423.
114. Botha, "If Everything is Contextualization, Nothing is Contextualization," 186.
115. Shorter, *Toward a Theology of Inculturation*, 6.
116. Ibid., 11.
117. Sanneh, *Whose Religion is Christianity?*, 5.
118. Wielzen, "Popular Religiosity and Roman Liturgy," 180.
119. Schreiter, *Constructing Local Theologies*, 5.

in the history of the term itself.[120] The term "indigenous," for people in colonized regions of the world, has a ring of replacing the personnel of the colonizers with local personnel and can be unsuited for the new shift that is required in theology.[121] Indigenization also carries the danger of "cultural romanticism (i.e., dreaming of a glorious past) and culturalism (i.e., considering indigenous culture as the determining norm of the process of the encounter between the Gospel and culture)."[122]

Indigenization does not achieve the goal of inculturation in the sense that it does not root the gospel in the local culture. Jean Marc Ela rejected any thing that goes under the rubric of indigenization because "the rhetoric of indigenization serves only to disguise a truly serious theological problem."[123] Since Africa was essentially evangelized my missionary institutes who came from Europe, their evangelization method was one of "implantation" or indigenization, which unfortunately has become an integral part of church life in Africa to this day. "If we continue to insist on defending and maintaining traditions that owe their origin to Christendom, the African churches will continue to seem a by-product of the Christian West."[124] The concerns surrounding both the understanding and application of indigenization led Ela to seek an alternative:

> Clearly, the so-called young churches are born with the symptoms of early senility. To rediscover themselves, they will have to search along the pathways of their liberation. They will have to emerge from the situations of captivity that weigh upon them and prevent their birth. If they mean to have done, then, with the alienating, paralyzing confusions, they will have to undertake an enormous decoding project, one that will liberate the novelty of the gospel from the sociocultural dross that marks the historicity of any human work. Ultimately, this project will necessarily imply a radical re-examination of the type of ecclesial implantation signaled by works that cost too much. The church will have to be destroyed as a structure

120. Ibid.
121. Ibid.
122. Wielzen, "Popular Religiosity and Roman Liturgy," 180.
123. Ela, *African Cry*, 107.
124. Ibid., 108.

of Christendom in order to rediscover a creativity adequate to the problems posed by the shock of the gospel in an African climate.[125]

g. **Enculturation**

Enculturation is a sociological term that is sometimes confused with inculturation. Cultural anthropologists employ enculturation to describe a process by which a person learns and/or is inserted into his or her own society.[126] It is akin to what social scientists call socialization—the process by which an individual is educated by his or her society.[127] At some point in the learning process, perhaps later in one's life, the one who is being inserted into the culture is expected to attain mastery of the culture into which he or she has been inserted. This competency, i.e., a person's mastery of his or her culture, is what cultural anthropologists call enculturation.[128]

Enculturation differs significantly from inculturation because enculturation assumes that the individual who is being enculturated does not already have a culture. But inculturation takes for granted that the individual already has a prior culture in the process of his or her encounter with the Church.[129] If ever there is a parallel between enculturation and inculturation it will be "in the parallel between the insertion of an individual into his or her own culture and the insertion of the Christian faith into a culture where Christians were not previously present."[130] The benefit then, if any, of associating the anthropological term enculturation with the missiological term inculturation, is that their contrast helps specify the scope of inculturation—that inculturation is conceived as a process by which the Church firmly establishes itself in a particular culture, integrating the cultural elements of the said culture; inculturation purifies the culture that the gospel message encounters and re-orients that culture

---

125. Ibid., 108–9.
126. Shorter, *Toward a Theology of Inculturation*, 5.
127. Ibid.
128. See Herskovits, *Man and His Works*, 39.
129. See Crollius, "What Is So New About Inculturation?," 725.
130. Shorter, *Toward a Theology of Inculturation*, 6.

to the gospel; and that by adopting elements of the culture it encounters, inculturation enriches the universal church.[131]

h. Acculturation

Acculturation is another sociological term that people sometimes confuse with inculturation. Acculturation takes place when two cultures come in contact. It is what some British anthropologists specifically refer to as "culture-contact."[132] According to a working definition provided by a Committee of the Social Science Research Council, "acculturation comprehends those phenomena which result when groups of individuals having different cultures come into continuous first-hand contact, with subsequent changes in the original cultural patterns of either or both groups."[133] Acculturation can either be the result of forceful encounter between two cultures, as in one nation annexing the other, say as a result of victory from war or as a result of respectful encounter between two cultures by way of trade or collaboration. Take the example of the cultural intermingling of African cultures during early European contact with Africa:

> Although Africans very often put up armed resistance against the annexation of their homelands by the colonial powers of Europe, they were initially fascinated by Western culture and technology. When modern states were carved out of the continent and Western education and Western institutions were imposed on them without any alternative, Africans were at first docile. It was only later that they began to rediscover their original culture and to realize the extent to which they had become culturally alienated.[134]

Acculturation, in essence, "is the most important agent of social (cultural) change. Cultures are strictly incommensurable and never absolutely equal or counterbalanced; one will be more assertive, and the least one will be significantly affected by the

---

131. Wielzen, "Popular Religiosity and Roman Liturgy," 173.
132. Dhavamony, *Christian Theology of Inculturation*, 28.
133. Ibid.
134. Shorter, *Toward a Theology of Inculturation*, 9.

contact."¹³⁵ Thus, acculturation is a distinct sociological concept, but still a necessary condition for inculturation.¹³⁶

As a phenomenon that depicts what takes place when two different cultures come in contact with each other and the subsequent changes that take place in the cultural pattern of either or both cultures, acculturation does not specify which of the cultures hold a dominant position and which holds a subservient position. It leaves the various possibilities open.¹³⁷ But under the onslaught of colonial ideology, the reciprocal power relations of the two cultures that encounter each other changed in the missionary era due in large part "to the self-understanding of Western people, including European missionaries who were convinced of their own cultural superiority."¹³⁸ Acculturation in this perverted version not only became synonymous with westernization in the missionary era, it also fed the perception that the culture to which the gospel is preached, i.e., non-Western cultures, need accept "Western cultural patterns without creative assimilation."¹³⁹

In its pure and unadulterated sense, however, acculturation rests on mutual respect and tolerance. It could serve as a preliminary step in the process of inculturation—a necessary condition for a Church that claims to be universal.¹⁴⁰ Inculturation, as we shall see later, takes many forms (liturgical, ecclesial, sacramental, etc.). In matters pertaining to liturgical inculturation, acculturation is indeed a necessary first step. It seems unrealistic to assume that one can embark on liturgical inculturation without first going through the process of acculturation. "A preliminary comparative study between [European] Christian liturgical forms and corresponding cultural elements has to be instituted before moving to the area of inculturation."¹⁴¹ Theologically, when acculturation takes place practical insights and new mean-

135. Gittins, "Beyond Liturgical Inculturation," 48.
136. Shorter, *Toward a Theology of Inculturation*, 7.
137. Wielzen, "Popular Religiosity and Roman Liturgy," 174.
138. Ibid.
139. Ibid.
140. Shorter, *Toward a Theology of Inculturation*, 8.
141. Wielzen, "Popular Religiosity and Roman Liturgy," 174.

ings that can spur inculturation on emerge. This was the case when European culture came in contact with Eastern cultures and developed new art forms; it was also the case when Arabic philosophers introduced Aristotle to the Christian West.[142] Practical insights can occur in different ways. It can take place when creative persons develop a new philosophy or when God communicates new meanings and values into human history.[143] "Whatever their source, new meanings and values may be incompatible with the present social ordering. New insights into the meaning of human dignity may be incompatible with slavery, the denial of women's voting rights, and child labor. These insights grow among people through debate, discussion, and art."[144] These practical insights are helpful, but by no means constitute inculturation. What inculturation does then is "promote a certain vision of life around these new meanings and values" that have been formed.[145]

Thus, in and of itself, the Church's contact with Greek or European culture cannot be called inculturation because inculturation is a term reserved for the "insertion of Christianity into a culture, generally outside the Western Judeo-Christian context, and that culture's response to the Christian message."[146] Inculturation is a phenomenon that transcends acculturation. "It is a stage when a human culture is enlivened by the Gospel from within, a stage which presupposes a measure of reformulation or, more accurately, reinterpretation."[147] In a nutshell, what missionaries do in the process of acculturation is merely "accommodate" or "adapt" the Christian message using cultural expressions that can make the message easily understandable. "They use elements from the local culture simply in order to communicate meaning and to enable their hearers to grasp that meaning according to

---

142. Ormerod, "The Times They Are A-Changin'," 841.
143. Ibid.
144. Ibid.
145. Ibid.
146. Bowie, "The Inculturation Debate in Africa," 70.
147. Shorter, *Toward a Theology of Inculturation*, 12.

their own cultural categories. In itself this facilitates the process of inculturation carried out by the local people."[148]

The Matter of Inculturation Revisited

In earlier chapters, following the C. S. Peirce-Clifford Geertz semiotics, we spoke of culture in empirical terms. Following the same semiotic interpretation we reinforced the idea that cultures, metaphorically, are to be read as a sign (Icon-index-symbol) in need of interpretation. Semiotics (the science of sign theory) has had various applications in the history of ideas. The semiotic understanding of culture developed independently by Peirce and Lonergan is well suited for a theology of inculturation. One of the difficulties of inculturation that have been pointed out time and time again is that there seem to be no adequate methodology to address "some of the conceptual logjams" one encounters in the inculturation process.[149] The breadth and depth of the signification, representation, and meaning of the Peircean-Lonergan theory of sign/symbol overcomes these conceptual logjams. The Peircean theory of sign is built on a metaphysical view of reality that views knowledge, not as intuitive, but as discursive. Its various application in the work of Bernard Lonergan (who though does not know or draw from Peirce holds a view similar to that of Peirce) shows how this semiotic understanding can come together theologically. Together they show how semiotics is adequate for this kind of theology that seeks a move away from a classicist mentality that thought of itself as producing perennial philosophy, "immortal works of art," models to be imitated, ideal characters to be emulated, and "eternal verities and universally valid laws."[150] Sign, as conceived by Peirce, is triadic in that it in turn indexes a three mutually related parts: a sign, an object, and an interpretant. The Christian gospel, as the word of God, can be understood as a sign in the Peircean sense. Take, for example, Luke 4:18: "The Spirit of the Lord is upon me" (a sign); "He has sent me to proclaim the good news to the poor" (object); "He has sent me to proclaim that captives will be released" (interpretant). This good news has its signifier or object—it is directed to a Christian community. It also has its interpretant—it has been understood in a particular way by the Christian community. The object, in other words, is the people to whom the message

---

148. Ibid., 14.
149. See Schreiter, "Inculturation of Faith or Identification with Culture," 17.
150. Lonergan, *Method in Theology*, 301.

is addressed. The interpretant is the mode or manner in which the message has been understood and proclaimed in particularities of history. One facet of biblical revelation that can no longer be neglected is the question surrounding how the teachings of the Bible are being mediated to us. It is no longer sufficient to study the Bible with the sole aim of discovering the truth of God. Here an appeal to Lonergan's functional specialty *systematics* helps to elucidate this point. Lonergan distinguishes *systematics* from *doctrines*, making it clear that the former anticipates the latter. *Doctrines* aim at establishing facts and increasing certitude. But *systematics* aim, not at increasing certitude, but at promoting understanding. *Systematics* "strives for some inkling of how it could possibly be that the facts are what they are. Its task is to take over the facts, established in doctrines, and to attempt to work them into an assimilable whole."[151] The problem with the old way of doing theology is that it confuses the mystery of God with the linguistic expression of that mystery. It assumed that the linguistic expression of Church dogmas were permanent and unchangeable achievement. It thought only in terms of universality and permanence, rather than evolution and development. What Peirce is saying philosophically—that knowledge of a situation cannot be predicated on intuition but by a careful analysis of the sign-object-interpretant, Lonergan expresses theologically—that the meaning of words are transient and can be culturally conditioned. Human concepts and actions are products and expressions of acts of understanding that develop over time cumulatively and progressively,[152] a fact that takes front and center of inculturation theology.

Semiotics (understanding sign-object-relations) is to inculturation what the functional specialty *Systematics* specifically is to theology—they both seek increase in understanding—"what church doctrines could possibly mean"[153] when applied to a new context and in a new world order. The disciples on the road to Emmaus understood Jesus only through the breaking of the bread (Luke 24:13–35). How is this to be understood or interpreted in cultures where bread is not a common food staple? Can they understand Jesus too in their own common staple, whatever that may be? Would functional substitution (use of non-European ritual, myth, or symbol) not be more effective in proclaiming Jesus' message in such instance? This is why Jean Marc-Ela insists that the evangelization of Africa presup-

---

151. Ibid., 336.
152. Ibid., 302.
153. Ibid., 345.

poses a language of African mode of thought and African ways of life and that this quest for a language of African conceptual thought be undertaken only by Africans that are close to the masses in the small and rural communities where all the problems of faith and pastoral life ultimately arise. Even if one disagrees with Ela that only Africans can come up with such acceptable linguistic expression, one cannot deny that until such an African expression of the Christian message is located, "all of our undertakings in Africa will continue to be foreign to the black."[154] Inculturation, therefore, seeks to bring together two essential strands of the Christian religion: the Christian message and communication (transformation) of that message. The Christian message of which we speak is the Jesus event—the son of Mary who was nailed to the cross, crucified, died, and rose from the dead.

Inculturation, to be clear, does not compromise the revealed truth or dogma of the Church, the incarnation, the virgin birth, death, and resurrection of Jesus, etc. Dogmas remain ever true, but their meaning and understanding are always in need of improvement. The three irreducible symbols of the Jesus-event are the incarnation, the cross, and the resurrection.[155] These symbols, which are always in tension with one another, are at the same time "always-already inculturated and need to be critically mediated," i.e., critically understood and interpreted.[156] This is what Lonergan was referencing when he writes that "meaning is embodied or carried out in human intersubjectivity, in art, in symbols, in language, and in the lives and deeds of persons."[157] The crucial question to be addressed in inculturation theology is "how to be faithful both to the contemporary experience of the gospel and to the tradition life that has been received."[158] Semiotics helps to accomplish this task by becoming a medium of inquiry—a process of discovery, since the process of inculturation "always involves a conversation between two partners—the universal gospel or fundamental "good news" and the cultural uniqueness of each context in which that message is heard."[159] Semiotics helps inculturation in its dialogue and mediates between the "Christianized culture of the missionary and the hitherto

---

154. Ela, *African Cry*, 132.
155. Mueller, "The Role of Theological Symbols in Mediating Cultural Change," 305.
156. Ibid.
157. Lonergan, *Method in Theology*, 57.
158. Schreiter, *Constructing Local Theologies*, xi.
159. Starkloff, "Inculturation and Cultural System," 69.

un-Christianized culture to which he comes,"[160] understanding that human individuals "differ from one another not only through individuation by matter but also in their mentalities, their characters, their ways of life."[161] Thus, semiotics serves inculturation is all aspects of the two-way process of dialogue—the transformation of the culture which has been nourished by the gospel and enhancement or enrichment of the gospel which has encountered the culture through a new way of understanding and living out the gospel values.[162]

This enterprise, i.e., transformation of culture and enhancement of the gospel by culture, was the motivation behind the development or primitive understanding of the term "inculturation," which the Jesuits claim to have introduced to modern theological discourse, even before the reforms of the Second Vatican Council. Shorter supports this claim, citing Joseph Masson, a Jesuit professor of theology at the Gregorian University in Rome, as speaking about the "urgent need for a Catholicism that is inculturated in a variety of forms."[163] The Jesuits themselves specifically trace the origin of the word to Pedro Arrupe, the general superior of the Society of Jesus in the 1970s, as well as to the decrees of the Thirty-Second General Congregation (1974–75) of their Society. Decree no. 5, titled "The Work of Inculturation of the Faith and the Promotion of Christian Life," spoke of the Society of Jesus as a Society with "a long and venerable missionary tradition of promoting inculturation."[164] The decree, which did not clarify what was meant by "inculturation," recommended that the general (Pedro Arrupe) "obtain 'expert assistance' and write a letter of instruction on the topic, in order 'to clarify for all of us the true meaning and theological understanding of the task and process of inculturation as well as its importance for the apostolic mission of the society today.'"[165] After seeking "expert advice," Arrupe defined inculturation as "the incarnation of Christian life and the Christian message in a particular local cultural context, in such a way that the experience not only finds expression through elements proper to the culture in question (this alone would be no more than a superficial adaptation) but

---

160. Shorter, *Toward a Theology of Inculturation*, 12.
161. Lonergan, *Method in Theology*, 302.
162. Phan, "Cultures, Religions, and Power," 726.
163. Shorter, *Toward a Theology of Inculturation*, 10.
164. Starkloff, "Inculturation and Cultural Systems," 68.
165. Ibid.

Inculturation Reconsidered

becomes a principle that animates, directs, and unifies a culture, transforming and remaking it so as to bring about 'a new creation.'"[166]

Following the Jesuit lead, the first assembly of Federation of Asian Episcopal Conferences (1974) spoke of the need for an indigenous and "inculturated Church."[167] As if to heed this call, the Federation of Asian Bishops' Conferences (FABC) and theologians of Asian background have since been exploring "a new way of being church in Asia, so that the church will be not only in Asia but also of Asia."[168] Peter Schineller today describes the process of inculturation as the "naturalizing of the church in every culture."[169] In 1987 the International Theological Commission of the Roman Catholic Church also attempted a definition of inculturation as "the Church's efforts to make the message of Christ penetrate a given socio-cultural milieu, calling the latter to grow according to all its particular values, as long as these are compatible with the Gospel. The term 'inculturation' includes the notion of growth, of the mutual enrichment of persons and groups, rendered possible by the encounter of the gospel with a social milieu."[170]

It is this same process of inculturation inaugurated by Pedro Arrupe and his Jesuit companions that that we have been attempting to sort out semiotically. The Jesuits who understood the magnitude of the problem facing the Church provided a diagnosis without a proper prognosis. They knew that the realm of common sense on which classical culture operated had to be surpassed and brought to a new level of meaning (realm of theory, interiority, and even transcendence). Where they provided the basis for incarnating the gospel in indigenous cultures, the Peirce-Geertz tradition of semiotics, together with Lonergan's critical exigence, provided the operational procedures for realizing it. These operational procedures, which gave relevance to an empirical understanding of culture, has fed the theological understanding that "no culture is so advanced and so superior that it can claim exclusive access or advantage to the truth of God, and none so marginal or inferior that it can be excluded."[171]

---

166. Ibid., 69, citing Arrupe, "Letter to the Whole Society on Inculturation," 2.
167. Starkloff, "Inculturation and Cultural System," 69.
168. Peter Phan, *In Our Own Tongues*, xi.
169. Schineller, "Inculturation," 109.
170. See Scherer and Bevans, *New Directions on Mission and Evangelization 1*, 156.
171. Sanneh, *Whose Religion is Christianity?*, 106.

6

Ten Habits of Highly Effective Work in African Theology of Inculturation

CHRISTIAN EXPANSION WAS POSSIBLE, at least as far as Africa was concerned, because Christianity resonated well with African traditions and cultures. Christianity provided the litmus test that re-oriented the worldview of the African and with it came the realization that there is no valid alternative to the gospel message. African Traditional Religions (ATRs) provided ethical rules of conduct in small scale African societies that guided people's behaviors within particularities of the family, village, clan, and tribe. But the moral framework was limited in so far as "small-scale societies insulated people from historical pressures and thus removed the need for adjustments in people's worldview."[1] In socio-political parlance, Christianity helped Africans meet the challenges that come with transitioning from small-scale societies to postcolonial nation-states by reconfiguring the old moral framework provided by ATRs, albeit without subverting it.[2] As Christianity becomes more and more entrenched in African societies and these societies move increasingly away from the old configuration in which one's loyalty was essentially to one's tribe, village, or clan, the challenge now is how to move away from such parochial allegiance to a wider and more inclusive one and in a network of human relationships implement the radical and inescapable solidarity with the poor and afflicted that the Christian gospel demands.

Since Africans have discovered that there is no valid alternative to Jesus Christ, should not the question then change from WHY should we relate to Jesus to HOW may we understand more fully this Jesus Christ who relates to us more meaningfully and most profoundly beyond the

1. Sanneh, *Whose Religion is Christianity?*, 43.
2. Ibid.

particularities of our clan, family, tribe and nation?[3] Thus, if in earlier chapters we employed a critical hermeneutic to diagnose failures of human understanding that have made the gospel seem alien to African cultures, in this chapter we combine both academic and popular style because of our need for hermeneutic of recovery. This "recovery" is geared towards helping us construct an African theology of inculturation, one that is not only grounded in systematics of history, but that is also empirical, critical, normative, dialectic, and practical in the Lonergan sense of the term.[4] If an African Christian theology of inculturation is to avoid the errors of the old style theology, which substituted (to borrow a phrase from Doran) "one set of alienations for another," then it must not only "ground a differentiation of praxis from technique,"[5] it must also draw from Lonergan to show how genuine development can and do occur.[6] Development, as an instance of human progress, is the intelligent emergent probability that arises in the measure that one understands oneself and one's environment and is able to implement that understanding.[7]

Difficulties of Inculturation

Unlike the worldview of the Europeans who brought the good news of the Christian message to Africa, community is the focal point of African society, not the individual. The individual exists for the community and community for the individual. The question, as Africans continue to embrace Christianity in droves, has been how might Christianity help Africans become renewed Africans, not re-made Europeans?[8] Long ago Eugene Hillman posed the question as to whether the unprecedented church growth in Africa was really a consequence of the gospel received and understood and not merely an element in the colonial process of westernization that promotes a foreign religion together with its other foreign exports, like western-style clothing, schooling, music, languages, technologies, weap-

3. See Bediako, *Jesus and the Gospel in Africa*, 32.
4. See Ormerod, "System, History, and a Theology of Ministry," 432–46; Ormerod, "The Structure of a Systematic Ecclesiology," 3–30; and Ormerod, "The Times They Are A-Changin'," 834–55.
5. Doran, "Lonergan and Balthasar," 83.
6. See Lonergan, "Theology and Praxis," 185.
7. Lonergan, *Insight*, 261.
8. Sanneh, *Whose Religion is Christianity?*, 43.

ons, and ideologies.[9] Scholars like Hillman are adamant that "what passed for evangelism during the past hundred years was in reality a dissemination of the western experiences and expressions of Christian faith."[10] That notwithstanding, the worldwide Christian resurgence is a proof that Christianity is a religion that transcends ethnic, national, and cultural boundaries.[11] The resurgence is also an acknowledgment that every culture has its own intrinsic merit and worthy of God's attention and special revelation in Jesus Christ.[12] Hence inculturation—incarnation of the gospel in particular cultural situation.

Inculturation is not an easy task. In chapters one and two we saw how metanarratives can be used as tools of domination. Missionary institutes, for all their good deeds and intentions, have sometimes been guilty of using theological narratives as tools of domination. We pointed out, for example, the way they have passed off their own particularly "culturally derived principles as biblical and universally mandatory."[13] Deciphering these culturally derived principles and isolating them from the gospel message is no mean task. It is well documented that some African leaders who have been thoroughly conditioned by the institutions introduced under colonialism work "even more zealously than their former colonial bosses, for the suppression of traditional African ways of being human and religious."[14] It speaks to the irony of the human situation that quite often it is those who need inculturation most that oppose it. One can get too accustomed and enthralled by one particular culturally derived principle that one begins to find other alternative expressions of the faith off-putting and anomalous. Christianity has felt so congenial in English, Italian, German, French, Spanish, Russian, and other Indo-European languages for long that we at times forget that the religion might feel equally congenial in other cultures like Amharic, Arabic, Korean, Chinese, Swahili, Shona, Twi, Igbo, Wolof, Yoruba, and Zulu.[15]

---

9. Hillman, *Toward an African Christianity*, 3.

10. Ibid.

11. Sanneh, *Whose Religion is Christianity?*, 7.

12. Ibid., 100.

13. See Burrow's "Culture, Inculturation, and Theologians," 46.

14. Hillman, *Toward an African Christianity*, 10.

15. *Whose Religion is Christianity?*, 105.

Inculturation is an important and yet a delicate task.[16] Without inculturation the Church is unrecognizable and unsustainable. Many in Africa still live a liminal existence. They are thrust in the ambiguity of two seemingly disparate worlds: the world of their traditional African life and the world of the highly Westernized Christian life. At key moments in their life when they have to mark the birth, marriage or death of a loved one, Africans celebrate in two separate and disparate ways: one traditional (according to their local customs and values) and the other Christian (according to Christian rites). There is little integration between the two. Marriage is celebrated at home in the traditional manner and an added Christian matrimonial rite is celebrated in the church later.[17] The lack of integration between church ceremonies and traditional rites often lead to "gross injustices and patent absurdities,"[18] feeding the perception that Christianity is still very much alien and alienating for the African. Take, for example, the practice of conferring foreign names on Africans at baptism, which is still common practice. For the most part, only officially recognized names of Church saints, who usually are Europeans, are permitted.[19] Although the situation has improved compared to, say fifty years ago, the use of African names at this significant ceremony is still very slow and tepid. Why is true inculturation difficult?

1. **Culture Is a Moving Viewpoint**

   Cultures are not static or fixed but complex and always in flux. In Africa, for example, not only do some ethnic groups and sub-cultures intertwine, they remain unintegrated.[20] Add to the mix is the other fact that in postcolonial Africa some speak of themselves in terms of Anglophone, Francophone, and Lusophone African cultures.[21] There are also other factors that further complicate the notion of culture: technological vs. traditional cultures, urban vs. rural mind-sets, youth values vs. values of

---

16. See Schineller, "Inculturation," 109–12.
17. Ibid., 109.
18. Hillman, *Toward an African Christianity*, 8.
19. Ibid., 12.
20. Schineller, "Inculturation," 109.
21. Oduyoye, "Christianity and African Culture," 79.

older generation and adults, etc.²² All these make inculturation difficult.

2. **Unrecoverable Lost Time**

    European missionaries who brought Christianity to Africa were not spared the problem of identity politics and parochial nationalism that bedeviled nineteenth/twentieth century Europe. The faith brought by the missionaries were in many instances Irish, Belgian, Italian, German or Spanish expressions of the Christian faith. Each of these European nationalities was intent on safeguarding its own national identity. Inculturation that should have taken place among ethnic groups in Africa had to be sacrificed if the national identity of the missionaries was to be safeguarded. "We are now engaged in catching up, and at times correcting the lack of inculturation in the past. This takes enormous amounts of time and energy."²³

3. **Overreliance on Past Successful Method**

    In the age of Rationalism and Enlightenment in Europe the faith benefited from some form of rationalism. Why rationalistic faith may have worked in Europe, when transported to Africa it becomes counterproductive, particularly if African thought-forms and expression of faith are not taken into consideration. There is also the other side of the coin, whereby theologians embracing ideas from African Traditional Religions (ATRs) incorporated them unfiltered into Christianity. This proved methodologically unhelpful and slowed the process of inculturation.²⁴ Today, due to lack of creativity, some are not making efforts to search for new and creative ways of making the Christian faith indigenous to the African. Rather they tend to rely too heavily on old ideas that while may have worked in the past do not meet the changing needs of the present time.

4. **Excessive Entanglement of Inculturation with Liturgy**

    In Roman Catholic circles, inculturation is often tied to the liturgy, particularly the Eucharist. This association makes it seem

---

22. Schineller, "Inculturation," 109.
23. Ibid.
24. See Ngong, "Theology as the Construction of Piety," 354.

like inculturation is limited only to the liturgy. And at times what passes for inculturation is mere liturgical adaptations (the use of drums, local music, dance, etc.). "A renewal of liturgical practice is not inculturation: whatever appears purely at the behavioral, performative level is acculturation, the effect of contact between Christianity (a 'culture') and a local community (a 'culture'), whether by imposition or exchange, proselytization or proclamation, translation or adaptation: it is a modification of culture, not necessarily faith."[25] True inculturation is broad, extensive, and all-encompassing, extending to all areas of the Church's life—theological, liturgical, catechetical, pastoral, juridical, political, economic, and familial.[26]

5. Resistance to Change

Albert Schweitzer's insightful idea regarding change is applicable to inculturation. He cautioned that whenever you come across a new idea that you should not expect people to clear the pebbles from your path, but you should expect them to throw stones and place boulders in your way. Since inculturation involves change, religious and cultural traditions have deep and conservative elements within them, which sometimes make them to be resistant to change.[27] There is also the related fact that inculturation is tied to issues of justice, marginalization, and power. Inculturation can make the ruling powers uncomfortable, especially when unjust social structures are questioned.[28]

6. The Problem of Syncretism

The Second Vatican Council encouraged "profound adaptation in the whole area of Christian life," while warning against "every appearance of syncretism and of false particularism" (Ad Gentes, section 22). The difficulty is that oftentimes what constitutes syncretism is not easy to identify. More recently some theologians have been attempting a rehabilitation of the concept of syncretism to make the concept acceptable, at least, for the process of acculturation (if not inculturation) to take place. But some of

25. Gittins, "Beyond Liturgical Inculturation," 49.
26. Schineller, "Inculturation," 109.
27. Ibid., 111.
28. Ibid.

these theologians approach the matter from an anthropological (not theological) perspective. In spite of this rehabilitation, the word "syncretism" still carries contrasting meanings, many of which are pejorative.[29] Peter Schineller, who has attempted to distinguish legitimate inculturation from syncretism, has suggested seven helpful criteria:

(i) The Acceptance of Risk—it is clear from the Council of Jerusalem and from the writings of St. Thomas (who used Aristotelian philosophy) that the Church must be willing to accept risk.

(ii) Attitude of Freedom—the ancient hymn to the Holy Spirit: *flecte quod est rigidum* shows that what is rigid is dead and what is flexible is open to growth and development.

(iii) A Sense of the Reign of God—to truly witness to the reign of God the Church cannot be too narrowly focused and unable to expand.

(iv) Patience—inculturation is a "slow journey" and a difficult process that requires patience.

(v) A Sense of God at Work in the World—Tradition is a resource, not an end in itself.

(vi) A Sense of the People of God—the authenticity of inculturation is to be sought in *sensum fidelium*, i.e., in the concrete living out of the gospel by a community of people in a given cultural context.

(vii) Listening—an attitude of speaking and listening is required to uncover the truth of the spirit present in all cultures.[30]

As helpful as these criteria are, they are still not easy to decipher in concrete cultural situations.

7. Cultural Identity and the Complexity of Nation-State

Christian practice of forming local Christian communities on the basis of numbers of individuals within a prescribed

---

29. Schineller, "Inculturation and Syncretism," 50.
30. Ibid., 53.

geographical zone comes with its own problems.[31] For example, about two hundred nation states in sub-Saharan Africa alone live on both sides of the state boundaries drawn by the colonial rulers for administrative convenience. It is easy, for example, to find Massai, Kikuyu, Yoruba, Hausa, Igbo, Luo, Efik, and Nuer living in more than one state boundary.[32] If a nation state is a people that self-consciously identify as a distinct people with the global family of humankind and are also recognized as such by their neighbors who distinguish themselves ethnically and culturally from them, then African nation states are no different from, say the European Basques, Irish, Welsh, Croats, Serbs, Russian, Scots and Flemings, and also no different from North American Quebecois, Lakota, and Inuit.[33] The response of postcolonial African states to their artificial geographical entities has varied from prudent acceptance to active resistance,[34] and herein lies the dilemma, as least as far as inculturation is concerned. "In a nation-state enclosed by arbitrary colonial boundaries drawn without respect for the pluralistic ethno-cultural composition of the population, is the church supposed to take on the cultural flesh of the numerically or politically dominant nation, and just let other peoples adapt themselves to the cultural ways of this one nation or cognate groups of nations?"[35] Or assuming most of the "Christians happen to be identified ethnically and/ or culturally with one of the less numerous peoples, is their limited cultural system and ephemeral world-view to be given priority in the process of inculturation?"[36]

8. Problem of Cultural Romanticism

One of the problems of inculturation is the temptation of cultural romanticism. "Reminiscent of Enlightenment concepts of the natural person, this cultural romanticism will tend to see only good in a culture and to believe that the ideal state of the

---

31. Hillman, "Good News for Every Nation Via Inculturation," 346.
32. Ibid., 338–39.
33. Ibid., 389.
34. Ibid., 340.
35. Ibid., 346.
36. Ibid.

culture would be reached if it were left untouched by the outside world."[37] An interaction between gospel, church, and culture that is authentic and dynamic will certainly change aspects of cultural practices. "The Christian message, after all," as Schreiter correctly points out, "is about change: repentance, salvation, and an eschatological reality to be realized. To think that Christianity will not change a situation is to rob the Christian message of its most important part."[38]

9. Conversion Is a Complex Phenomenon

The Christian faith has always done well with people on the margins of society. In some societies the poor, orphan, women, and widows find succor in the church because church gives them protection, dignity, and self-worth that society has denied them. What would inculturation mean for this people in their thought but a return to servile life style?[39] Inculturation demands a shift in horizon and a radical shift in perspective. The newly converted has to act "as if one's eyes were opened and one's former world faded and fell away,"[40] for conversion to be morally, intellectually, and religiously effective. It is only then that "something new that fructifies in inter-locking, cumulative sequences of developments on all levels" of society can actually take place.[41]

Ten Semiotic Habits

Generally speaking, inculturation is a complex phenomenon and never a finished project. As an on-going project, inculturation is always a search and an exploration into an otherwise neglected region of human and ecclesial life. The complexity of inculturation, at least for Africa, can be sorted out semiotically. Semiotics (the kind deriving from Peirce-Lonergan) is not content with things as they are and always aims for improvement and development. This semiotics seeks to know anything that can be known, discover anything that can be discovered, and affirm anything that can

---

37. Schreiter, *Constructing Local Theologies*, 29.
38. Ibid.
39. Ibid. 28.
40. Lonergan, *Method in Theology*, 130.
41. Ibid.

be affirmed in human and ecclesial life. A semiotic approach to African theology of inculturation is akin to constructing a ship. In constructing a ship one has to go the whole way. "An effort that is in principle incomplete is equivalent to a failure."[42] Half measures hardly do any good. "Only a comprehensive strategy can be successful. To go half measure is to leave open "a base from which a counteroffensive promptly will be launched."[43] Real inculturation, therefore, cannot be content with half measures, like the liturgical adaptations that are common place in Africa. What about real inculturation in areas like liturgical rite, liturgical calendar, church ministries, lay ministries, church leadership and authority, appointment of bishops, and structure of the diocese? The world church needs what Lonergan calls a second Enlightenment—one that will be culturally significant and have a social mission. If the second enlightenment is to offer hope to people alienated by "large establishments under bureaucratic management,"[44] then it must take seriously a semiotic approach to the theology of inculturation.

The ten *habits* outlined below are precepts that embody the attentiveness, intelligence, reasonableness, and responsibility needed in a semiotic approach to African theology of inculturation. They are *imperatives* inherent in the notion of Catholicity. They remind us that Catholicity is not identified with uniformity, but with reconciled diversity and that Catholicity also demands different forms in different times, places, and cultural settings.[45] Thus, these *habits* or *imperatives* work better in concert, not in isolation. They are, therefore, to be taken as whole.

1. **Habit One: Avoid Classicism**

    Now a classicist would feel it was perfectly legitimate for him to impose his culture on others. For he conceives culture normatively, and he conceives his own to the norm. Accordingly, for him to preach both the gospel and his own culture, is for

---

42. Lonergan, *Insight*, 7.

43. Ibid.

44. See Lonergan, "Prolegomena to the Study of the Emerging Religious Consciousness of Our Time," 63 and 65. The Second Enlightenment, as Lonergan describes it, "is a profound transformation in mathematics and natural science. It is paralleled by a transformation in philosophy. It is complemented by the vast development in human studies stemming from the initiatives of the German Historical School. It has found allies in sociological and psychological tendencies away from the reductionist postulate of positivist philosophy" (65).

45. See Dulles, *The Catholicity of the Church*, 26–29.

> him to confer the double benefit of both the true religion and the true culture.
>
> —Bernard Lonergan, *Method in Theology*

The Swiss theologian Hans Urs von Balthasar (1904–86) has suggested that unless we recover the transcendental beauty that has been lost in mainstream theology ours will continue to be a world characterized by widespread skepticism, moral and aesthetic relativism, fragmentation of knowledge, and conflicting religious worldviews.[46] Classicism and the traditions it birthed are largely responsible for the splintering of knowledge and conflicting worldviews that Africa has been part of since the introduction of Christianity in the continent. Classicism promoted and thrived on the assumption that the unity of faith can be built on everyone subscribing to one culture and by so doing disparaged everything else that does not fit its way of viewing the world. Take the instance of the tradition of conferring names in Christian liturgy. Much has been made of the fact (and rightly so) that the beauty of African names was never been fully explored and integrated into Christian naming ceremonies. In the missionary era, for example, names given to African babies at baptism were often indicative of the worldviews of the particular missionaries in that territory. For example, in territories were the missionaries were Irish African babies were given names like Patrick and Maureen (anglicized form of Mairin, Mary). In territories where the missionaries were Italians, African babies were baptized with such names as Pasquale, Teresa, and Franka, and in territories where the missionaries were Germans African babies were baptized as Adolphus, Wolfgang, and Alice. Was the use of names with symbolism from the home country of the missionaries part of the larger game aimed at turning Africans into consumers of western produce, as critics have alleged?[47] Or could the insistence on the use of European names alone, notwithstanding that some of those names were names of canonically recognized saints, be much about planting European cultural values and diminishment of meaning for Africans?

46. See Dadosky, *The Eclipse and Recovery of Beauty*, 3.
47. Hillman, *Toward an African Christianity*, 12.

For Africans generally speaking, names carry a lot of symbolism. The Yoruba of south-west Nigeria, for example, have a class of names called *Oruko Amutorunwa* (literally= names a person brings from heaven) and *Oruko Abiso* (names that a child's parents give to the child on naming ceremony, usually eight day after birth). *Amuntorunwa* names are given immediately after birth and are non-negotiable. The names depict any special event or unusual circumstances surrounding the birth of the child. For example, a male child that is born with an umbilical cord tied around his neck is automatically called "Ojo." If the baby happens to be a female she is called "Aina." Or take the example of a baby that comes out of the womb with feet first, such a baby is called "Ige." Twins also have specially designated names: the first born of twins is called "Taiwo" and the second is called "Kehinde." The one born immediately after the twins is called "Idowu" and the one born after "Idowu" is called "Alaba." That these names are called *Amutorunwa* (names brought from heaven) is in itself an affirmation of the divine truth, unity, goodness, and beauty that Africans see in God's creation. Similarly, *Abiso* names reflect the oneness, goodness, truth, and divine beauty. These names are carefully chosen, again depending on the events and special circumstances surrounding the birth of the child. For example, a male child born to a family where the father is recently deceased is called "Babatunde" (meaning "father has made a comeback"). A girl born to a family where the mother has recently been deceased is called "Iyabode" (meaning "mother has made a comeback").

The system of conferring names in African traditions and cultures carries both religious and social significance. Apart from establishing the people's powerful and pervasive sense of belonging to one another in the unity of family, clan, ethnicity and culture, African names also convey mutual responsibilities between a person and his or her community.[48] In a nutshell, most traditional African names are explicitly theophoric (God-bearing names) in that they either have God as a prefix or suffix. Even those that do not explicitly have God as prefix or suffix often times imply it. That Africans are now striving to use traditional African names

---

48. Ibid., 13.

at baptism is indicative of the larger problem of classicism—the things that went wrong in the Church's prior situation.[49]

A semiotic approach to an African theology of inculturation must not only be mindful of the classicist mentality that dealt with individuals and cultures in abstraction and was intent on proving and demonstrating the true culture, but must also avoid these pitfalls. The old assumption that the unity of faith can be built on the classicist assumptions of one culture and that "within this set-up the unity of faith is a matter of everyone subscribing to the correct formulae" is, according to Lonergan, nothing more than "the shabby shell of Catholicism."[50] A church that approximates the classicist ideals is already a community at the dead end of its mission.[51] Thus, a semiotic approach to an African theology of inculturation must be mindful that people differ from one another not only in their mentalities, and their characters, but also in their ways of life.[52] A semiotic approach to an African theology of inculturation is also mindful that an entity like the Catholicism, which is a unity-identity-whole, endures and prospers in spite of change because it is constituted by conjugates interrelated in schemes of recurrence.[53]

2. Habit Two: Beware of the Dangers of One Single-Story Narratives

In *How to Do Things with Words*, the British philosopher of language John Langshaw Austin (1911–60) identified a set of speech acts that are like imperatives because they indicate that the issuing of an utterance is tantamount to the performance of the action. These speech acts Austin calls *performative utterances*.[54] There are, according to Austin, various kinds of performative utterances, like illocutionary act and percolutionary act. An illocutionary act is an utterance in which in saying something we are actually doing something. For example, if a judge says "I

---

49. See Lonergan, "The Transition from a Classicist World-View to Historical Mindedness," 1–9.

50. Lonergan, *Method in Theology*, 327.

51. Ormerod, "A Response to O'Malley and Schloesser," 846.

52. Lonergan, *Method in Theology*, 302.

53. See Rixon, "Derida and Lonergan on Human Development," 231. See also Lonergan, *Insight*, 280–83.

54. See Austin, *How to Do Things with Words*, 6.

sentence you to five years of hard labor," the judge is not stating an intention to do something, nor is she describing what she is doing. The judge is simply producing an effect by her action. What illocutionary speech acts do then is produce effects. According to Austin, illocutionary acts are supported by linguistic and social conventions.[55] Percolutionary act, on the other hand, is an utterance that initiates a set of consequences—saying something produces certain consequences. "The consequential effects of percolutions are really consequences, which do not include such conventional effects as, for example, the speaker's being committed by his promise (which comes into the illocutionary act)."[56] We see from Austin's distinction that illocutionary acts proceed by way of convention and illocutionary acts proceed by way of consequences.[57] Implied in this distinction "is the notion that illocutionary speech acts produce effects without any lapse of time, that the saying is itself the doing, and that they [are implied in] one another simultaneously."[58] Judith Butler has built on Austin's helpful distinction to suggest that language is a powerful force because we are constituted within its terms. Butler cautions that we be mindful about the way we frame narratives of the other because not only can narratives be injurious, they also can bring about oppressive situations, regardless of whether or not one intends it.

The Rwanda genocide (1994), a mass slaughter of ethnic (minority) Tutsis and moderate Hutus by a well-organized and potent extreme Hutu majority, is a good example of how a badly framed speech can constitute a person in a subordinate position. In this genocide that led to the death of close to a million people, a conscious decision was made by some members of the ruling elite to frame a narrative promoting hatred of Hutus for Tutsis and Tutsis for Hutus. Hate speech produced by extremists on both sides of the conflict are, in J. L. Austin's terms, the illocutionary acts that precipitated the genocide. But easy to forget is the percolutionary act, i.e., the act initiating the set of consequences that

---

55. Butler, *Excitable Speech*, 17.
56. Austin, *How to Do Things with Words*, 102.
57. Butler, *Excitable Speech*, 17.
58. Ibid.

produced a favorable climate for the genocide. The percolutionary acts in the Rwandan case go back to the historical foundation of the Rwanda nation-state. Following the 1884 Berlin Conference, the nation that was conveniently put together as Rwanda was given to the Germans. In order to strengthen their control and grip of the region, the Germans used a system of strict racial classification that divided the people into three groups: Hutu (85 percent), Tutsi (14 percent), and Twa (1 percent). Compared to Hutu and Twa, the Tutsi were a little light skinned. The German rulers essentialized this racial difference and offered more privileges to the Tutsi whom they (Germans) thought their "light skin" made them "superior" to the Hutu and Twa, even though the Hutu far outnumber the Tutsi. The racial privilege accorded the Tutsi continued under Belgian rule (1914–62). The Belgians continued the German racist policy and created a system of education that was less favorable to the Hutu majority. As the racial divide widened in post-colonial Rwanda, Hutu resentment against minority Tutsi continued to grow. Needless to say it was this resentment and counter-resentment that morphed into ideologies that set the stage for the 1994 massacre. The genocide took place irrespective of the fact that the two parties involved in the conflict were predominantly Catholics.

The point here is that one cannot approach the Rwandan genocide without attention to the ideologies or what J. L. Austin calls illocutionary and percolutionary acts that made the carnage possible. Speech acts can and do produce effects, which at times can and do constitute social sin. In the Rwandan example alone we can isolate four variants of social sin: (i) inbuilt injustices and dehumanizing trends that are built into social, political, economic, and religious institutions of Rwandan society (ii) light skin as cultural symbols, which make legitimate patterns of injustice and inhumane practices possible (iii) false consciousness created by colonial structures, which became ideologies through which the people involve themselves collectively in destructive action and (iv) shared or "collective decisions, generated by distorted consciousness, which increases the injustices in society and intensifies the power of dehumanizing trends."[59]

---

59. These are the four variants of social sin identified by Gregory Baum. See Hinze,

The same speech acts that produced the Rwandan violence can be found, albeit in different forms, in many of the nation-states of Africa where the violence can be traced to the single-story narratives used to frame these nations. A semiotic approach to an African theology of inculturation must do away with single story narratives in so far as single-story narratives are antithetical to the self-affirmation of the knower. Single-story narrative leads to reductionism—an attempt to explain complex wholes, in matters of being, truth, and value, in terms of their simpler parts. Single-story narratives, like reductionism, is a "seductive ideology" and a pervasive intellectual vice.[60] It "inevitably results in an unwarranted exclusion of relevant data (such as intentionality and finality) when investigating the ontological constitution of persons, historical processes, and the world as 'mediated by meaning.'"[61] Reductionist mentality comes in different forms, scientism—the view that only those beliefs and practices that can be subjected to well accredited scientific methods are objectively true and anthropological reductionism—the attempt "to explain persons exclusively and exhaustively by appeal to non-personal processes, events, and mechanism."[62] Since single-story narratives and the reductionism they engender undermine a person's capacity for truth or authentic understanding, a semiotic approach to an African theology of inculturation acts as a counter force to reductionism by taking seriously a holistic account of the human subject as knower, doer, believer, and lover.[63]

A semiotic approach to an African theology of inculturation must not only address the collective blindness or bias of single-story narratives, but must also take steps towards healing the historical memories that have constituted the ethnic and religious other in subordinate position. It acknowledges the "wrongs done

---

"Ecclesial Repentance and the Demands of Dialogue," 230, quoting Baum, *Religion and Alienation*, 71–75.

60. Aiken, "Bernard Lonergan's Critique of Reductionism," 233 and 234.
61. Ibid., 234.
62. Ibid., 235.
63. Ibid., 241.

by those who have borne or bear the name of Christian."[64] This acknowledgement is essential if the purification of memory is not become what Arthur Noble facetiously called a "euphemism for the whitewashing of history."[65] The Hutu-Tutsi carnage, a violence perpetrated by Catholic Christians against fellow Catholic Christians, belong in the annals of the "Church and the Faults of the Past" and can be purged only by a genuine act of reconciliation. The outrageous acts of individual Hutu on Tutsi wounds not only the Hutu-Tutsi fraternity/sorority, but the entire body of Christ. More importantly, the egregious act of individual Christian wounds the confraternity of African Christianity.

3. Habit Three: Broaden Your Horizon

> The Christian message is to be communicated to all nations. Such communication presupposes that preachers and teachers enlarge their horizons to include an accurate understanding of the culture and the language of the people they address. They must grasp the virtual resources of that culture and that language, and they must use those virtual resources creatively so that the Christian message becomes, not disruptive of the culture, not an alien path superimposed upon it, but a line of development within the culture.
>
> —Bernard Lonergan, *Method in Theology*

The old juridical way of conceiving the Church's relations to peoples of other cultures assumed that one and only one set of meaning and values was valid for all places and all times.[66] This cannot be true, at least as far as Africa is concerned, since Africa

---

64. See International Theological Commission, "Memory and Reconciliation." Speaking at an event hosted by the Symposium of Episcopal Conferences of African and Madagascar (SECAM) in Rome in 20014 as part of the event celebrating the canonization of John XXIII and John Paul II, the head of the Pontifical Council for Culture, Cardinal Gianfranco Ravasi, took a bold step towards this acknowledgment by noting European complicity in the suffering of Africans and stating that the "first characteristic" of the African church is suffering. Admitting that Europeans cannot escape culpability in the suffering of Africans, Cardinal Ravasi stated that the suffering of Africans "has often been brought by the continent I represent." See McElwee, "Cardinal Laments 'Fatigue' of Christian Europe."

65. See Noble, "'Purification of Memory.'"

66. Lonergan, "Dialectic of Authority," 7.

is home to myriads of cultures and religions. The continent is home to African Traditional Religions (ATRs), a religion that is inextricably tied to all of African cultures. Africa is also home to Islam. Although Islam is not indigenous to Africa in the same way that ATRs are, Islam is traditional to Africa in other ways. Africanization of Islam began in 615 AD when the first Muslims left the Arabian Peninsula for refuge in Abyssinia (Ethiopia). It culminated in Islam becoming a central force in the emergence and development of African kingdoms and city-states, like the old Mali, Ghana, Songhai, Kanen-Bornu, and Sokoto empires, ever before the first Europeans set foot on African soil. That these kingdoms and city-states indigenized Islam is evident by the influence of Islam on African names, cities, food, art, sculptor, architecture, etc. Today there is hardly any part of Africa that is not touched by the presence of Islam. About half of the population of the continent is estimated to be Muslim.

A semiotic approach to an African theology of inculturation must shy away from a limited to a broad vision. Lonergan's distinction between the realms of meaning (commonsense, theory, interiority, and transcendence) become significant. Because the realm of commonsense understands things only as they relate to us, the old style theology, which thought there was only one set of meanings and values for all places and all times, saw ATRs and Islam only as these religions relate to us, not as they are related to one another. Old style theology thought the forms of meanings of ATRs, Islam, and Christianity were opposed to each other. But on the contrary, these set of meanings inform one another. Because it takes seriously the various realms of meaning, a semiotic approach to an African theology of inculturation pays attention to the influence of ATRs and Islam on African psyche and ways of life, sees commonsense meaning and theory as complementary, and therefore moves towards an integration. ATRs, Islam and Christianity all represent a horizon that delimits the vision, scope of knowledge, and range of interests of Africans that encounter them. "As fields of vision vary with one's standpoint, so too the scope of one's knowledge and the range of one's interests vary with the period in which one lives, one's social background and milieu, one's education and personal development."[67]

4. Habit Four: Seek Higher Viewpoint

> All understanding has its universal aspect, for similars are similarly understood. But it is one thing to exploit this universal aspect in a professional manner; it is another to exploit the intelligibility, which is by itself universal, by adding further intelligibilities until one comes to grips with concrete situations. The latter line of development we have named common sense, so that by definition common sense deals with the particular.
>
> —Bernard Lonergan, *Insight*

When the shortcomings of a previous position is recognized seek a higher viewpoint. An African theology of inculturation cannot be done without attention to human rights, particularly the rights of women. Globalization has changed the world as we know it. The female underside of globalization, which has long been neglected, must be front and center of an African theology of inculturation. Thanks to globalization, global economy is interconnected. Millions of women from poor countries of the global south, Africa included, migrate to Europe and America in search of better life. These migrating women cut across all ages: young girls, mothers, and grandmothers. This pattern of female migration, a reflection of a worldwide gender revolution, has been dubbed the new "feminization of migration."[68] It is quite different from what obtained in the 1950s and the 1970s when men dominated the labor migration to northern Europe. Today women far outnumber men in immigration patterns. In fact, over half of world's 120 million legal and illegal migrants are now believed to be women.[69] "Most women, like men, migrate from the south to the north and from poor countries to rich ones. Typically, migrants go to the nearest comparatively rich country, preferably one whose language they speak or whose religion and

---

67. Lonergan, *Method in Theology*, 236.
68. See Ehrenreich and Hochschild, *Global Woman*, 3 and 5.
69. Ibid., 5.

culture they share."[70] As migration patterns increase so does the cross-fertilization of ideas and with which comes a new trend towards global re-division of women's traditional work and roles. "The globalization of women's traditional role poses important challenges to anyone concerned about gender and economic inequity."[71] Although reliable statistics is hard to come by regarding the number of African migrant women to the north, millions of African women are part of this worldwide feminization of globalization. Globalization and efforts of women's rights advocates, like Senegal's Marie Angelique Savane, have brought to our awareness "that being a woman can mean other things than simply having children, taking care of the house."[72]

Granted that globalization has brought new opportunities and in some instances improved means of livelihood for women in developing countries, it has also introduced painful new emotional realities, like exploitation of women workers, abuse, sex slaves, etc., for women from developing countries.[73] These painful emotional realities show that "we need to develop a global sense of ethics to match emerging global economic realities."[74] As we have pointed out time and time again, the elephant in the room is classicism. Classicism is not just an ideology but also a mindset, a mentality—a way of seeing the world that pays little or no attention to the contribution of women. This parochial way of seeing the world has colluded with globalization to further the exploitation of women. As Lonergan pointed out that if a remedy has to be at the level of the disease and the disease is a succession of lower viewpoints, then the remedy must be the attainment of higher viewpoints.[75] A semiotic approach to an African theology of inculturation sees a need for a higher viewpoint. "The needed higher viewpoint is the discovery, the logical expansion, and the recognition of the principle that intelligence contains its own immanent norms and that these norms are equipped with

70. Ibid., 6.
71. Ibid., 13.
72. Ehrenreich, "Maid to Order," 93.
73. Hochschild, "Love and Gold," 28.
74. Ibid.
75. Lonergan, *Insight*, 259.

sanctions which man does not have to invent or impose."⁷⁶ This higher viewpoint takes seriously both the plight and contributions of African women to African socio-political and ecclesial life. It is apt to recall a story told by Clifford Geertz about his experiences in Bali to buttress this point about the plight of women in developing countries and the need for a higher viewpoint. It is a rather long story about a holiday the Balinese celebrate, in Geertz's own words, with "an odor of sanctity." The story is about the Rajah of a neighboring state who died on the 20th of December, 1847, whose his body was burned with great pomp with three of his concubines sacrificing themselves in flames. The summary of this long story is that the Balinese celebrate this day with pomp.⁷⁷ Geertz remarks that while it is false to say that we can never genuinely apprehend in some fashion another's people history like we do our own, the truth of the matter is "that we can never apprehend another people's or another period's imagination neatly, as though it were our own. . . . We can apprehend it well enough, at least as well as we apprehend anything else not properly ours; but we do so not by looking behind the interfering glosses that connect us to it bur through them."⁷⁸

The Balinese story and the human rights implications of the celebration suggests all the more the need for distinction between "standpoints" and "viewpoints."⁷⁹ Standpoints can be inherently subjective, and static, fixed, and unchangeable. "Human value judgments are the most obvious examples of standpoints, since, while claiming to be objective, they nevertheless bear the marks of the unique subjectivity, the individual life-experience, of the one making the value judgment."⁸⁰ All standpoints affirm some truth but never the whole truth.⁸¹ Women in developing countries, Africa in particular, have been victims of fixed standpoints that fail to recognize changing realities of modern society. A semiotic approach to an African theology of inculturation must

76. Ibid.
77. Geertz, *Local Knowledge*, 37.
78. Ibid., 44.
79. See Scharlemann, *The Being of God*, 31–38.
80. Bracken, "Authentic Subjectivity and Genuine Objectivity," 291.
81. Ibid., 303.

move beyond standpoint to viewpoints. Viewpoints are fluid and amenable to change. "In principle viewpoints are cumulative, so that by progressively walking around an object and looking at it from different viewpoints one should be able to acquire a comprehensive or universal viewpoint which takes in all dimensions of the object in question."[82]

5. **Habit Five: Always Differentiate (Consciousness)**

> Here the basic distinction is between preaching the gospel and, on the other hand, preaching the gospel as it has been developed within one's own culture. In so far as one preaches the gospel as it has been developed within one's own culture, one is preaching not only the gospel but also one's own culture. In so far as one is preaching one's own culture, one is asking others not only to accept the gospel but also renounce their own culture and accept one's own.
>
> —Bernard Lonergan, *Method in Theology*

Africa is a complex society and this complexity plays out in myriads of ways. Take the example of the republic of South Sudan, a landlocked country in the northeastern Africa that gained independence from Sudan on July 9, 2011. Republic of South Sudan emerged as an independent country from the ashes of parent country, the Sudan, after more than a decade civil war. The war was between the north and the south and more than a million people were killed and million others paralyzed and displaced. South Sudan became independent following self-determination referendum in which the citizens overwhelmingly voted for total autonomy from the then Sudan. Independence from the north has not fully solved the South's problem. The republic of South Sudan remains today one of the poorest countries in the world. The country is still plagued by all kinds of economic hardships: one in seven women die in childbirth, eighty-four percent of women are illiterate, half of the population has no access to drinking water, one in nine children will not live to see their fifth birthday, and only one-third of its people have formal education.[83] Barely

---

82. Ibid., 291.

83. "Humanitarian Crisis in South Sudan," Care.org, http://www.care.org/emergencies/south-sudan-humanitarian-crisis?autologin=true&s_src=SouthSudan&s_subsrc

two years after independence (December 2013), conflict erupted between forces loyal to President Salva Kiir and those loyal to his deputy at the time, Riek Machar. What was thought to be a mere political conflict degenerated into an all-out ethnic conflict between the Dinka (President Kiir's tribe) and the Nuer (vice-president Machar's tribe). The New York Times reported that the fighting in South Sudan "produced a replay of its recent bloody history. Thousands have died, and more than one million people have been displaced. Famine is threatening, and cholera has broken out in some places. Sexual violence is on the rise. And the United Nations and other observers said another ghost of wars past is again rearing its head: the recruitment of child soldiers."[84] As many as four million people in South Sudan (nearly one third of the population) still face food insecurity.

The problem of South Sudan is symptomatic of the problem of Africa where political disputes quickly morph into ethnic and religious conflicts. The failure to distinguish what is properly a political conflict from ethnic and even religious problem often leads to wars with dire consequences. To conflate political impasse with ethnic or identity politics is to be caught in the world of immediacy, i.e., the world of sense objects. "In the world of immediacy the only objects are objects of immediate experience, where 'experience' is understood in the narrow sense and denotes either the outer experience of our senses or the inner experience of our consciousness."[85] Like common sense, the world of immediacy does not define, it does not syllogize, and it does not enounce universal principles. It revels rather in using analogies of ethnicity that foment violence.[86] A semiotic approach to an African theology of inculturation operates, not on the world of immediacy, but in a world mediated by meaning and motivated by values. The world mediated by meaning is mediated by intelligent inquiry—experiencing, understanding,

---

=redcpcg_SouthSudan&cr=crisis_3M&gclid=CNmQndmu8r4CFew-MgodqksAnA (accessed Feb. 16, 2015).

84. Isma'il Kushkush, "In South Sudan, A Ghost of Wars Past: Child Soldiers," *New York Times*, June 7, 2014, http://www.nytimes.com/2014/06/08/world/africa/in-south-sudan-a-ghost-of-wars-past-child-soldiers.html?_r=0 (accessed Feb. 16, 2015).

85. Lonergan, "Unity and Plurality," 240.

86. Ibid., 241.

Ten Habits of Highly Effective Work

judging, and deciding. In the world mediated by meaning "terms are defined, systematic relationships are sought, and procedures are governed by logic and methods."[87] Take the example of the German art historian who observed that in spite of the fact that Balinese language had no word for artist that the life of the Balinese people "overflows with a blossoming richness of festivals, temples, images, jewels, and decorations, gifts that are witness to an extravagant enjoyment in form-making and play."[88] It is only through the application of the compound process of experiencing, understanding, judging, and deciding that one may catch on to the critical fact that it is naive to dismiss the Balinese as devoid of artistic expression but that the Balinese are actually "a nation of artists" since for them art is not a word but a way of life.[89] To return to the conflation of political impasse with identity politics in Africa, Lonergan was right in his cryptic remark that "constants disappear when you differentiate."[90] The "constants" here that will disappear when you differentiate is ethnicity and religion, two volatile matters that evoke much passion and emotion in Africa.

6. Habit Six: Foster Spiritual and Cultural Development

> Further, the church is a structured process. As does human society, it trains personnel. It distinguishes roles and assigns to them tasks. It has developed already understood and accepted modes of cooperation. It promotes a good of order in which Christian needs are met regularly, sufficiently, efficiently. It facilitates the spiritual and cultural development of its members. It invites them to transform by Christian charity their personal and group relations. It rejoices in the terminal values that flow from their lives.
>
> —Bernard Lonergan, Method in Theology

According to the United Nations Industrial Development Organization, Africa only commands a meagre 1.5 percent share of the world's total manufacturing output. Why is it not common to

---

87. Ibid.

88. Geertz, *Local Knowledge*, 52.

89. Ibid.

90. Ormerod, "A Response to O'Malley and Schloesser," 837, quoting Lonergan's unpublished "File 713—History."

find manufacturing goods with, say "made in Guinea" or "made in Gabon" label? Why is it common to find "made in China" or "made in Taiwan" labels on everything ranging from, say, T-shirts and shoes to watches and televisions? Is it theologically inappropriate to investigate why there are rarely labels that point to origins in Africa, like "Made in Nigeria" or "Made in Chad," for example?[91] Why does Africa continue to lag behind in manufacturing goods, in spite of the much-vaunted recent economic growth in the continent? Is the goal of Christian theology only the construction of piety with no attention to economic development? Is authentic Christian theology antithetical to economic growth? If authentic Christian theology is not opposed to scientific imagination and technological progress then how might a theology of inculturation help Christians relate to the natural and supernatural order in a wholesome way?[92]

Industrialized nations with highly sustained economic growth, in addition to their rising productivity in agricultural sector and development of a skilled workforce, are often characterized by their expansion of the manufacturing sector, their spread of technologies, and economic or structural diversification.[93] The reason why Africa has yet to make any appreciable growth in these regards is because it has only succeeded in making "little structural transformation."[94] There is also the problematic of the highly spiritualized African cosmology that can at times stand in fierce opposition to modern scientific imagination. For example, views that see diseases, such as HIV as due to witchcraft; that HIV can be cured through sexual intercourse with a female virgin; and that human physical illness are divine in origin and do not derive from physical causes are ridiculous. Such views are antithetical to modern scientific imagination. A semiotic approach to an African theology of inculturation cannot accept uncritically any kind of cosmology, even if that

---

91. See a recent BBC investigation on the subject: Alexis Akwagyiram, "Made in Africa: Is Manufacturing Taking off on the Continent," BBC News Africa, May 28, 2014, http://www.bbc.com/news/world-africa-27329594 (accessed Feb. 16, 2015).

92. Ngong, "Theology as the Construction of Piety," 347.

93 See Africa Progress Panel report: http://africaprogresspanel.org/wp-content/uploads/2014/05/APP_AR2014_LR.pdf (accessed June 30, 2014).

94. Ibid.

cosmology has already been used to promote the spread of the Christian faith by those who have uncritically appropriated it. "Uncritically embracing the spiritualized cosmology of African traditional societies in salvific discourses promotes a form of piety that is ill equipped to overcome marginalization of the continent in the modern world."[95]

In order to foster spiritual and cultural development, a semiotic approach to an African theology of inculturation must pay attention to the structural transformation of African society and promote only those things needed to bring African society up to speed with modern scientific imagination. The structure of the human good is, after all said and done, a universal phenomenon that is realized in a variety of stages: technological, economic, political, religious, and cultural development.[96] We saw an example of the kind of role African Christian theology can play in public life in chapter one when we highlighted the role of the Churches in dismantling of apartheid. A semiotics approach to an African theology of inculturation must be an active force in dismantling of all unjust structures and unhelpful cosmologies (worldviews) in the continent.

Classicism and the traditions that emerged out of it have conspired to promote what is now known in political and economic circles as "methodological individualism"—the position that all policies, actions, and behaviors are explicable only in terms of their relationships to individuals, not society. Methodological individual assumes "that all social interactions are after all interactions among individuals. The individual in the economy or in the society is like the atom in chemistry; whatever happens can ultimately be described exhaustively in terms of the individuals involved."[97] Thus, the theory assumes that socially oriented actions do not yield any result; that only individualistic concepts lead to quick, expedient, and beneficially acceptable results.[98] Could this be an instance of the loop-holes in social arrangement that Lonergan warns that egoists could exploit "to

95. Ngong, "Theology as the Construction of Piety," 361.
96. Lonergan *Method in Theology*, 359–60.
97 Arrow, "Methodological Individualism and Social Knowledge," 3.
98. For more, see Mises, *Human Action*.

enlarge their own share and diminish the share of others in current instances of the particular good?"[99] The Christian doctrine of incarnation (our analogue for inculturation), the story of God who "dwells among us" must provide a different vision of economic and political power than the one based on exploitation and domination.[100]

Methodological individualism is opposed to the self-sacrificing love that is at the heart of self-transcendence. It promotes an ideology that corrupts the social good and turns societal progress into cumulative decline. It is an instance of the disregard for the transcendental precepts: be attentive, intelligent, be reasonable, and be responsible that leads to alienation.[101] Attentiveness, intelligence, reasonableness, and responsibility are requisite demand of a semiotic approach to the theology of inculturation. Our semiotic approach does not admit of "stratification of individuals into classes of higher and lower competence."[102] A semiotic approach to an African theology of inculturation must emphasize that which is at the core of Catholic and Christian social teaching, "the intrinsic dignity of all human beings, the solidarity of all human beings, and the primacy of the common good over individual interest and advantage."[103] Such a theology that is grounded in the story of the incarnation and the good news that comes with it must scour through all nooks and corners and villages and towns, redeeming and making them sacred.[104] This is the "politics of the incarnation," i.e., "the story of God who 'dwells among us' and who invests local existence with an eternal significance."[105]

7. Habit Seven: Celebrate Pluralism

> The pluralist acknowledges a multiplicity of cultural traditions. In any tradition he envisages the possibility of diverse

---

99. Lonergan, *Method in Theology*, 360.
100. Katongole, *The Sacrifice of Africa*, 131.
101. Lonergan, *Method in Theology*, 55.
102. Ibid., 357.
103. Brown, "Aiming Excessively High and Far," 24.
104. Katongole, *The Sacrifice of Africa*, 144.
105. Ibid.

differentiations of consciousness. But he does not consider it his task either to promote the differentiation of consciousness or to ask people to renounce their own culture. Rather he would proceed from within their culture and he would seek ways and means for making it into a vehicle for communicating the Christian message.

—Bernard Lonergan, *Method in Theology*

Until the recent outbreak of civil strife in Central African Republic (CAR) in 2013, many have hardly heard of this tiny landlocked country in Central Africa. Decades of bad governance and economic mismanagement conspired to bring this tiny country to its knees. Rebels who took up arms in 2013 supposedly fought along ethno-religious lines. When the crisis first erupted into a full blown war, the United Nations (UN) raised the specter of the country becoming a failed state. There was also, according to the UN, the risk of genocide against ethnic Muslims in CAR. Typical of wars fought along ethno-religious lines, many of the innocent people who took up arms to defend perceived threat to their ethnic and religious identity did so without being aware of the ideologies driving the conflict. The truth is that CAR has been unstable since its independence from France in 1960 and the root cause of the 2013 uprising cannot be divorced from the colonial policy of the French and the manner in which the French transitioned and left the country. What was billed as a religious conflict in the end had not much to do with religion. Rather, the problem goes back to the historical foundation of the country. Politicians are very adept at playing up ethnic differences and conflating them with religion to fan up embers.

To understand the cause of conflict that is endemic to Africa one would have to move beyond common sense explanations of things and be ready to make differentiations. Common sense, after all, is not common to all peoples per se but to a particular group of people.[106] Because common sense is not uniform there are many brands of common sense as there are different ethnicities and tribes. A semiotic approach to an African theology of inculturation understands the problematic of undifferen-

---

106. Lonergan, *Method in Theology*, 272–73.

tiated consciousness—that political differences that can easily be resolved appear difficult and twisted when consciousness is undifferentiated. Because undifferentiated consciousness uses indiscriminately the procedures of common sense, its explanations and insights into situations become rudimentary and jejune, and the other that ought to be a friend and collaborator is now perceived as strange, weird, and expendable. Thus, a semiotic approach to the theology of inculturation must pay attention to the different brands of common sense and go beyond the limitations of common sense.

Differentiations foster pluralism. Christianity has always benefitted from pluralism of expression. The apostles who preached the first kerygma addressed the Jews and the Greeks alike in their thought-forms and their language and idioms.[107] "When Scholastic theology recast Christian belief into mold derived from Aristotle, it was deserting neither divine revelation nor scripture nor the councils. And if modern theologians were to transpose medieval theory into the categories derived from contemporary interiority and its real correlatives, they would be doing for our own age what the greater Scholastics did for theirs."[108] Thus, the pluralism that must take place is pluralism, not of doctrine, but of expressions and communications, using the available narratives, parables, metaphors, modes of praise and blame, etc. of the people.[109] Among all the world religions Christianity is the most culturally translatable and therefore the most truly universal religion in that it is able to be at home in every cultural context without damaging its essential character.[110] Our semiotic approach, therefore, encourages drawing from the resources of people to whom the gospel is preached and creatively using their languages and thought-forms, without however being confined to their limitations. The church will benefit from such pluralism in many ways.

8. Habit Eight: Promote Christian Fellowship

---

107. Ibid., 327.
108. Ibid., 327–28.
109. Lonergan, "Unity and Plurality," 243.
110. Bediako, *Jesus and the Gospel in Africa*, 32.

Ten Habits of Highly Effective Work

> Through communication there is constituted community and conversely, community constitutes and perfects itself through communication. Accordingly, the Christian church is a process of self-constitution, a *Selbstvollung*. While there still is in use the medieval meaning of the term, society, so that the church may be named a society, still the modern meaning, generated by empirical social studies, leads one to speak of the church as a process of self-constitution occurring within worldwide human society. The substance of that process is the Christian message conjoined with the inner gift of God's love and resulting in Christian witness, Christian fellowship, and Christian service to mankind.
>
> —Bernard Lonergan, *Method in Theology*

A 1968 document titled "Catholicity and Apostolicity" by an eighteen-member Joint Theological Commission (nine members each from the World Council of Churches and the Roman Catholic Church) spoke of "catholicity" as a sine qua non condition for ecumenism and Christian solidarity. The document clarified the meaning of "catholicity" and identified four aberrations that blurs the meaning of the concept. These aberrations are (i) restriction of Christian communion to certain races, nations, or classes (ii) formation of sects or parties within the Church (iii) pride in one's own faith confession to the detriment of another's and (iv) misuse of the term "catholic" to support ideas or practices destructive of Christian identity.[111] Our semiotic approach to an African theology of inculturation shares the Commission's position that Christian unity "is hindered whenever Catholicism is identified with something less than itself and whenever the definition of it is based upon what is really local, temporary, [and] partial." [112]

9. Habit Nine: Be Creative

> For if the gospel is to be preached to all nations (Mt.28:19), still it is not to be preached in the same manner to all. If one is to communicate with persons of another culture, one must use the resources of their culture. To use simply the resources of one's

---

111. See Joint Theological Commission of WWC, "Catholicity and Apostolicity," 452–83, cited in Dulles, *The Catholicity of the Church*, 25.

112. Ramsey, *The Gospel and the Catholic Church*, 148.

own culture is not to communicate with the other but to remain locked up in one's own. At the same time, it is not enough simply to employ the resources of the other culture. One must do so creatively. One has to discover the manner in which the Christian message can be expressed effectively and accurately in the other culture.

—Bernard Lonergan, *Method in Theology*

How is the good news of Jesus Christ to be proclaimed in an environment where a vast majority of the people are beset by poverty, malnutrition, famine, and war? Does Jesus offer aby hope to a people ravaged by deadly diseases, such as Ebola and HIV? Does the good news of Jesus Christ bring relief to a people whose life seem but an eternal meaninglessness? How can theology be made relevant to their situation? Africa is a complex society. A one size fit all theology cannot adequately address the African situation. The gospel must be proclaimed in a manner that accords with the assimilative powers of the culture to which the gospel is preached.[113] A semiotic approach to an African theology of inculturation must speak to the specificity of the people, as well as the place, and time. The outbreak of the deadly Ebola virus in some parts of West Africa like Guinea, Sierra-Leone, Liberia, and Nigeria in July 2014 will willy-nilly change the theological landscapes of those countries. Some churches are beginning to revise liturgical guidelines and adopt new measures for the celebration of liturgy. The Catholic Archdiocese of Abuja (Nigeria), for example, announced new procedures for worshippers at their Masses to check the likely spread of the Ebola virus. The new procedures include the administration of the Holy Communion on the palm of the faithful, as against the normal practice of placing communion on the tongue of the recipient. The diocese also put a temporary halt to handshake by worshippers done during consecration of the Holy Communion as sign of peace.[114] While these precautionary measures taken to curb the spread of the Ebola virus are laudable, the irony cannot be missed. Many African episcopal conferences have long resisted the urge to make the administration of Holy Communion in the

---

113. Bediako, *Jesus and the Gospel in Africa*, 328.

114. See "Ebola: Catholic Church Adopts New Measures," *Vanguard*, August 11, 2014, http://odili.net/news/source/2014/aug/11/338.html (accessed Feb. 16, 2015).

palm of the faithful the norm, even when sanitary and theological reasons dictated otherwise. It took the spread of the Ebola virus to do, even if temporary, what is expedient. More creativity is needed.

10. Habit Ten: Relish in Self Correcting Process of Learning

> The satisfaction of mistaken understanding, provided one does not know it as mistaken, can equal the satisfaction of correct understanding. Yet the pure desire scorns the former and prizes the latter; it prizes it, then, as dissimilar to the former; it prizes it not because it yields satisfaction but because its content is correct
>
> —Bernard Lonergan, *Insight*

The "Principle of the Empty Head" in hermeneutics encourages one not to "read into" a text what is not there. It suggests that one should rather allow the text to speak for itself. "If one is not to 'read into' the text what is not there, if one is not to settle in a priori fashion what the text must mean no matter what it says, if one is not to drag in one's own notions and opinions, then one must drop all preconceptions of every kind, attend simply to the text, see all that is there and nothing that is not there."[115] The principle is commendable in so far as it insists that we resist the temptation of imputing into the text what the author does not express. The problem, however, is that the principle takes for granted "that all an interpreter has to do is to look at a text and see what is there."[116] The principle, like the old style (colonial) theology, rests on a naive intuitionism because it suggests that the interpreter forgets his or her own views and let the author interpret himself or herself. What is "out there" that needs to be interpreted, as Lonergan correctly points out, is nothing but "a series of signs" that need to be mediated by the experience, intelligence, and judgment of the interpreter.[117] "The less that experience, the less cultivated that intelligence, the less formed that judgment, the greater the likelihood that the interpreter will impute on the author an opinion that the author never entertained. On the other hand, the wider the interpreter's experience, the deeper and fuller the development

---

115. Lonergan, *Method in Theology*, 157.
116. Ibid.
117. Ibid.

of his understanding, the better balanced his judgment, the greater the likelihood that he will discover just what the author meant."[118]

Unlike the Principle of Empty Head, a semiotic approach to an African theology of inculturation sees culture as series of signs and symbols to be mediated by experience, intelligence, and judgment. Cultural system, it must be emphasized, is to be treated "as significative systems expositive questions."[119] Doing inculturation, like the act of interpretation, is not just a matter of looking at signs. As Lonergan points out, the matter of looking at signs is already assumed and is already imperative.[120] "But it is no less imperative that, guided by the signs, one proceed from one's habitual general knowledge to actual and more particular knowledge; and the greater the habitual knowledge one possesses, the greater the likelihood that one will be guided by the signs themselves and not by personal preferences and by guess-work."[121] The point here is that in a semiotic approach to the theology of inculturation there is a mutual dialogue by which the gospel is informed by culture and culture is informed by gospel—a synergy of unity-identity whole. We grasp the unity-whole (gospel + culture) only through the parts (signs and symbols informing the culture), which are at the same time determined in their meanings by the whole which each part partially reveals.[122] Just like the meaning of a word stands in relationship to the sentence as a whole and the meaning of the sentence stands in relationship to the paragraph and the meaning of paragraphs stand in relationship to chapters and meaning of chapters stand in relationship to books,[123] the meaning of the gospel text comes to fuller fruition on the basis of its cultural understanding. This network of reciprocal dependence of gospel and culture is not mastered by any conceptual set of procedures, but by "the self-correcting process of learning, in which preconceptual insights accumulate to complement, qualify, [and] correct one another."[124]

118. Ibid.
119. Geertz, *Local Knowledge*, 3.
120. Lonergan, *Method in Theology*, 157.
121. Ibid., 157–58.
122. Ibid., 159
123. Ibid., 208–9.
124. Ibid., 209.

Bibliography

Adichie, Chimamnda Ngozi. "The Danger of a Single Story." Ted, July 2009, https://www.ted.com/talks/chimamanda_adichie_the_danger_of_a_single_story (accessed August 10, 2013).
Aiken, David W. "Bernard Lonergan's Critique of Reductionism: A Call to Intellectual Conversion." *Christian Scholar's Review* 61 (2012) 233–51.
Anderson, Allan. *African Reformation: African Initiated Christianity in the 20th Century.* Trenton, NJ: Africa World, 2001.
Arbuckle, Gerald A. *Culture. Inculturation, and Theologians: A Postmodern Critique.* Collegeville, MN: Liturgical, 2010.
Arrow, Kenneth J. "Methodological Individualism and Social Knowledge." *American Economic Review* 84 (1994) 1–9.
Arrupe, Pedro. "Letter to the Whole Society on Inculturation." In *Studies in the International Apostolate of Jesuits*, 1–9. Washington, DC: Jesuit Missions, 1978.
Asad, Talal. *Genealogies of Religion: Disciplines and Reasons of Power in Christianity and Islam.* Baltimore: Johns Hopkins University Press, 1993.
Austin, J. L. *How to Do Things with Words.* Edited by J. O. Urmson. Cambridge, MA: Harvard University Press, 1962.
Bakhtin, Mikhail. *The Dialogic Imagination: Four Essays.* Edited by Michael Holquist. Austin: University of Texas Press, 1985.
———. *Problems of Dostoevsky's Poetics.* Edited and translated by Caryl Emerson. Minneapolis: University of Minnesota Press, 1984.
Barrett, D. B. *Schism and Renewal in Africa.* Nairobi: Oxford University Press, 1968.
Baskouda, Jean B. *Baba Simon, le Pere des Kirdis.* Paris: Cerf, 1988.
Baum, Gregory. *Religion and Alienation: A Theological Reading of Sociology.* New York: Paulist, 1975.
Bediako, Kwame. *Jesus and the Gospel in Africa: History and Experience.* Maryknoll, NY: Orbis, 2004.
Bell, Vikki. "New Scenes of Vulnerability, Agency and Plurality: An Interview with Judith Butler." *Theory, Culture, & Society* 27 (2010) 130–52.
Benedict, Ruth. "Edward Sapir." *American Anthropologist* 41 (1939) 465–77.
Benveniste, Émile. *Problems in General Linguistics.* Translated by Mary Elizabeth Meek. Coral Gables, FL: University of Miami Press, 1971.
Bevans, Stephen B. *Models of Contextual Theology.* Maryknoll, NY: Orbis, 1992.
Biko, Steve. *I Write What I Like.* San Francisco: Harper & Row, 1978.
Blomjous, Joseph. "Development in Mission Thinking and Practice, 1959–1980: Inculturation and Interculturation." *African Ecclesial Review* 22 (1980) 393–98.
Bloomfield, L. *Language.* New York: Holt, Rinehart, and Winston, 1933.

Bibliography

Boas, Franz. "Edward Sapir." *International Journal of American Linguistics* 10 (1939) 58–63.

Bosch, David J. *Transforming Mission: Paradigm Shifts in the Theology of Mission*. Maryknoll, NY: Orbis, 1991.

Boskovic, Aleksandar. "Clifford Geertz: Writing and Interpretation." *Sociologija* 44 (2002) 41–55.

Botha, Nico. "If Everything is Contextualization, Nothing is Contextualization: Historical, Methodological, and Epistemological Perspectives." *Missionalia* 38 (2010) 181–96.

Bowie, Fiona. "The Inculturation Debate in Africa." *Studies in World Christianity* 5 (1999) 67–92.

Bracken, Joseph. "Authentic Subjectivity and Genuine Objectivity." *Horizons* 11 (1984) 290–303.

Brown, Patrick. "Aiming Excessively High and Far: The Early Lonergan and the Challenge of Theory in Catholic Social Thought." *Theological Studies* 72 (2011) 620–44.

———. "Classicism: A Prelude." Paper presented at the 28th Annual Fallon Memorial Lonergan Symposium, Loyola Marymount University, Los Angeles, CA, April 4–6, 2013.

Bujo, Bénézet. *African Theology in Its Social Context*. Translated by John O'Donohue. Maryknoll, NY: Orbis, 1992.

———. *African Theology in the Twenty-First Century*. Edited by Juvenál Ilung Muya. Translated by Silvano Borruso. Nairobi: Pauline Publications Africa, 2003.

Burrow, William R. "Culture, Inculturation, and Theologians: A Postmodern Critique." *International Bulletin of Missionary Research* 36 (2012) 46.

Butler, Judith. *Excitable Speech: A Politics of the Performative*. New York: Routledge, 1997.

———. "Explanation and Exoneration, or What Can We Hear." *Social Text* 20 (2002) 177–88.

Byrne, Patrick. "The Fabric of Lonergan's Thought." In *Lonergan Workshop*, edited by Fred Lawrence, 6:1–84. Chico, CA: Scholars, 1986.

———. "Ressentiment and the Preferential Option for the Poor." *Theological Studies* 54 (1993) 213–41.

Caton, Steven C. "Contributions of Roman Jakobson." *Annual Review of Anthropology* 16 (1987) 223–60.

———. *"Peaks of Yemen I Summon": Poetry as Cultural Practice in a North Yemeni Tribe*. Berkeley: University of California Press, 1990.

———. "What Is an 'Authorizing Discourse'?" In *Powers of the Secular Modern: Talal Asad and His Interlocutors*, edited by David Scott and Charles Hirschkind, 31–56. Stanford, CA: Stanford University Press, 2006.

Chomsky, Noam. *Language and Mind*. Enlarged ed. New York: Harcourt Brace Jovanovich, 1972.

Chung, Paul S. "Inculturation and Recognition of the Other." *Studies in Interreligious Dialogue* 20 (2010) 79–97.

Clifford, James, and George Marcus, eds. *Writing Culture: The Poetics and Politics of Ethnography*. Berkeley: University of California Press, 1986.

Collins, Paul M. "The Praxis of Inculturation for Mission: Roberto de Nobili's Example and Legacy." *Ecclesiology* 3 (2007) 323–42.

Comby, Jean. *How to Understand the History of Christian Mission*. London: SCM, 1996.

Cone, James H. *A Black Theology of Liberation*. 20th anniv. ed. Maryknoll, NY: Orbis, 2006.

Bibliography

Craig, K. *The Nature of Explanation*. Cambridge: Cambridge University Press, 1952.
Crumbley, Deidre Helen. *Spirit, Structure, and Flesh: Gendered Experiences in African Instituted Churches among the Yoruba of Nigeria*. Madison: University of Wisconsin Press, 2008.
Crollius, Roest. "What Is So New About Inculturation? A Concept and Its Implications." *Gregorianum* 59 (1979) 721–37.
Crowe, Frederick E. *Method in Theology: An Organon for Our Time*. Milwaukee: Marquette University Press, 1980.
Dadosky, John. *The Eclipse and Recovery of Beauty: A Lonergan Approach*. Toronto: University of Toronto Press, 2014.
———. "Towards a Fundamental Theological Re-interpretation of Vatican II." *Heythrop* 49 (2008) 742–63.
Dhavamony, Mariasusai. *Christian Theology of Inculturation*. Rome: Editrice Pontificia Universita Gregoriana, 1997.
De Gruchy, John W. *Christianity and Democracy*. London: Cambridge University Press, 1995.
De Lubac, Henry. *Catholicism: Christ and the Common Destiny of Man*. Translated by Lancelot C. Sheppard and Elizabeth Englund. San Francisco: Ignatius, 1988.
De Mul, Sarah. "The Holocaust as a Paradigm for the Congo Atrocities: Adam Hochschild's *King Leopold's Ghost*." *Criticism* 53 (2011) 587–606.
Derrida, Jacques. *Limited Inc*. Evanston, IL: Northwestern University Press, 1990.
Dilthey, Wilhelm. *Selected Writings*. Edited by H. P. Rickman. London: Cambridge University Press, 1976.
Doran, Robert. "Foreword: Common Ground." In *Communication and Lonergan: Common Ground for Forging the New Age*, edited by Thomas J. Farrell and Paul A. Soukup, ix–xvi. Kansas City: Sheed and Ward, 1993.
———. "Lonergan and Balthasar: Methodological Considerations." *Theological Studies* 58 (1997) 61–84.
Douglas, Mary. *Natural Symbols: Explorations in Cosmology*. New York: Pantheon, 1970.
Doyle, Dennis M. "The Concept of Inculturation in Roman Catholicism: A Theological Consideration." *U.S. Catholic Historian* 30 (2012) 1–13.
Duffey, Michael K. "Guatemalan Catholics and Mayas: The Future of Dialogue." *International Bulletin of Missionary Research* 34 (2010) 87–92.
Dulles, Avery. *The Catholicity of the Church*. Oxford: Clarendon, 1985.
Ehrenreich, Barbara. "Maid to Order." In *Global Woman: Nannies, Maids, and Sex Workers in the New Economy*, edited by Barbara Ehrenreich and Arlie Russell Hochschild, 85–103. New York: Holt, 2002.
Ela, Jean-Marc. *African Cry*. Translated by Robert R. Barr. 1986. Reprint, Eugene, OR: Wipf and Stock, 2005.
———. "Ancestors and African Faith: An African Problem." In *Liturgy and Cultural Religious Traditions*, edited by Hermand Schmidt and David Power, 39–49. New York: Crossroad, 1977.
———. "Christianity and Liberation in Africa." In *Paths of African Theology*, edited by Rosino Gibellini, 136–53. Maryknoll, NY: Orbis, 1994.
———. "The Church—Sacrament of Liberation." In *African Synod: Documents, Reflections, Perspectives*, edited by Maura Browne, 131–38. Maryknoll, NY: Orbis, 1996.

Bibliography

―――. "The Memory of the African People and the Cross of Christ." In *The Scandal of a Crucified World: Perspectives on the Cross and Suffering*, edited by Yacob Tesfai, 17–35. Maryknoll, NY: Orbis, 1994.

―――. *My Faith as an African*. Translated by John P. Brown and Susan Perry. Maryknoll, NY: Orbis, 1988.

Ela, Jean-Marc, and Stuart E. Brown. "First Colloquium of African and European Theologians, Yaoundé, Cameroon, 4–11 April, 1984—General Report." *Mission Studies* 1 (1984) 57–59.

Englund, Harri. "Rethinking African Christianities." In *Christianity and Public Culture*, edited by Harri Englund, 1–24. Athens: Ohio University Press, 2011.

Erskine, Noel. *Decolonizing Theology: A Caribbean Perspective*. Maryknoll, NY: Orbis, 1981.

Forest, Michael. "Lonergan and the Classical American Tradition." *Method: Journal of Lonergan Studies* 23 (2005) 17–44.

Foucault, Michel. *Discipline and Punish: The Birth of the Prison*. Translated by Alan Sheridan. Harmondsworth, UK: Penguin, 1979.

―――. *The History of Sexuality: An Introduction*. London: Penguin, 1979.

―――. *Power/Knowledge*. New York: Pantheon, 1980.

Gade, Christian. "The Historical Development of the Written Discourses on *Ubuntu*." *South African Journal of Philosophy* 30 (2011) 303–29.

―――. "Restorative Justice and the South African Truth and Reconciliation Process." *South African Journal of Philosophy* 32 (2013) 10–35.

―――. "What Is *Ubuntu*? Different Interpretations among South Africans of African Descent." *South African Journal of Philosophy* 31 (2012) 484–503.

Gallagher, Michael P. *Clashing Symbols: An Introduction to Faith and Culture*. London: Darton, Longman and Todd, 1997.

Geertz, Clifford. *Available Light: Anthropological Reflections on Philosophical Topics*. Princeton: Princeton University Press, 2000.

―――. *The Interpretation of Cultures: Selected Essays*. New York: Basic, 1973.

―――. *Islam Observed: Religious Development in Morocco and Indonesia*. Chicago: University of Chicago Press, 1970.

―――. *Local Knowledge: Further Essays in Interpretive Anthropology*. New York: Basic, 1983.

―――. *Negara: The Theatre State in Nineteenth-Century Bali*. Princeton: Princeton University Press, 1980.

―――. "Religion as a Cultural System." In *Anthropological Approaches to the Study of Religion*, edited by Michael Banton, 1–46. London: University of Cambridge, 1966.

―――. "Religion as a Cultural System." In *Language, Truth, and Religious Belief: Studies in Twentieth-Century Theory and Method in Religion*, edited by Nancy K. Frankenberry and Hans H. Penner, 176–217. Atlanta: Scholars, 1999.

―――. "What Is a State if It Is Not a Sovereign? Reflections on Politics in Complicated Places." *Current Anthropology* 45 (2004) 577–93.

Geertz, Clifford, et al. *Meaning and Order in Moroccan Society: Three Essays in Cultural Analysis*. Cambridge: Cambridge University Press, 1979.

Gifford, Paul. *African Christianity: Its Public Role*. Bloomington: Indiana University Press, 1998.

―――. "Democratization and the Churches." In *The Christian Churches and the Democratization of Africa*, edited by Paul Gifford, 1–13. Leiden: Brill, 1995.

Bibliography

Gilliland, Dean S. "How 'Christian' Are African Independent Churches?" *Missiology* 14 (1986) 259–72.

Gittins, A. J. "Beyond Liturgical Inculturation: Transforming the Deep Structures of Faith." *Irish Theological Quarterly* 69 (2004) 47–72.

Greenblatt, Stephen. "The Touch of the Real." In *The Fate of "Culture": Geertz and Beyond*, edited by Sherry Ortner, 14–29. Berkeley: University of California Press, 1999.

Greenham, Thomas G. *The Unknown God: Religious and Theological Inculturation*. Bern: Lang, 2005.

Guarino, Thomas. "Postmodernity and Five Fundamental Theological Issues." *Theological Studies* 57 (1996) 654–89.

Haleblian, Krikor. "The Problem of Contextualization." *Missiology* 11 (1983) 95–111.

Hastings, Adrian. "Christianity in Africa." In *Turning Points in Religious Studies*, edited by Ursula King, 201–10. Edinburgh: T. and T. Clark, 1990.

———. *A History of African Christianity, 1950–1975*. London: Cambridge University Press, 1979.

Healey, Joseph G. Review of *African Cry*, by Jean-Marc Ela. *International Bulletin of Missionary Research* 12 (1988) 36.

Herskovits, Melville J. *Man and His Works: The Science of Cultural Anthropology*. New York: Knopf, 1952.

Hetjke, Jan. "Baba Simon of Cameroon, Mentor of Jean-Marc Ela." *Exchange* 29 (2000) 147–55.

———."Thinking in the Scene of Disaster: Theology of Jean-Marc Ela from Cameroon." *Exchange* 29 (2000) 61–68.

Hillman, Eugene. "Good News for Every Nation via Inculturation." *Louvain Studies* 25 (2000) 336–47.

———. *Toward an African Christianity: Inculturation Applied*. New York: Paulist, 1993.

Hinze, Bradford. "Ecclesial Repentance and the Demands of Dialogue." *Theological Studies* 61 (2000) 207–38.

Hochschild, Adam. *King Leopold's Ghost: A Story of Greed, Terror, and Heroism in Colonial Africa*. Boston: Houghton Mifflin, 1998.

Hochschild, Arlie Russell. "Love and Gold." In *Global Woman: Nannies, Maids, and Sex Workers in the New Economy*, edited by Barbara Ehrenreich and Arlie Russell Hochschild, 15–38. New York: Holt, 2002.

Hoekema, David A. "Faith and Freedom in Post-colonial African Politics." In *Jesus and Ubuntu: Exploring the Social Impact of Christianity in Africa*, edited by Mwenda Ntarangwi, 25–46. Nairobi: Africa World, 2011.

Holquist, Michael. *Dialogism: Bakhtin and His World*. London: Routledge, 1990.

Idowu, Bolaji. *Towards an Indigenous Church*. London: Oxford University Press, 1965.

Innis, Robert E. *Susan Langer in Focus: The Symbolic Mind*. Bloomington: Indiana University Press, 2009.

Inoue, Miyako. *Vicarious Language: Gender and Linguistic Modernity in Japan*. Berkeley: University of California Press, 2006.

International Theological Commission. "Memory and Reconciliation: The Church and the Faults of the Past," Vatican, December 1999, http://www.vatican.va/roman_curia/congregations/cfaith/cti_documents/rc_con_cfaith_doc_20000307_memory-reconc-itc_en.html (accessed June 30, 2014).

Jakobson, Roman. "Closing Statement: Linguistics and Poetics." In *Style in Language*, edited by Thomas A. Sebeok, 350–77. Cambridge, MA: MIT Press, 1960.

Bibliography

Jenkins, Philip. *The Next Christendom: The Coming of Global Christianity.* New York: Oxford University Press 2007.

———. *The New Faces of Christianity.* Oxford: Oxford University Press, 2006.

Joint Theological Commission of the World Council of Churches. "Catholicity and Apostolicity." *One in Christ* 6 (1970) 452–83.

Kasper, Walter. *Jesus the Christ.* New York: Paulist, 1977.

Katongole, Emmanuel. *The Sacrifice of Africa: A Political Theology for Africa.* Grand Rapids: Eerdmans, 2011.

Kaunda, Kenneth. *A Humanist in Africa.* Nashville: Abingdon, 1966.

Kavunkal, Jacob. "Inculturation and Future Scanning." *Missiological Studies* 7 (1990) 94–97.

Kealotswe, Obed. "The Rise of the African Independent Churches and Their Present Life in Botswana. Who Are the African Independent Churches (AICs)? Historical Background." *Studies in World Christianity* 10 (2004) 205–22.

Kroeber, A. L., and Clyde Kluckhorn. *Culture: A Critical Review of Concepts and Definitions.* New York: Vintage, 1963.

Kruss, G. "A Critical Review of the Study of Independent Churches in South Africa." In *Religion Alive: Studies in the New Movements and Indigenous Churches in Southern Africa*, edited by G. C. Oosthuizen, 21–32. Johannesburg: Hodder and Stoughton, 1986.

Lakoff, George. "Whorf and Relativism." In *Women, Fire and Dangerous Things*, 304–37. Chicago: University of Chicago Press, 1987.

Lang, Alfred. "Thinking Rich as Well as Simple: Boesch's Cultural Psychology in Semiotic Perspective." *Culture and Psychology* 3 (1997) 383–94.

Langer, Susanne K. *Philosophical Sketches.* Baltimore: Johns Hopkins University Press, 1962.

———. *Philosophy in a New Key.* New York: New American Library, 1949.

Lawrence, Frederick. "The Fragility of Consciousness: Lonergan and the Postmodern Concern for the Other." *Theological Studies* 54 (1993) 55–80.

———. "Lonergan as Political Theologian." In *Religion in Context: Recent Studies in Lonergan*, edited by Timothy P. Fallon and Philip Boo Riley, 1–21. Lanham, MD: University Press of America, 1988.

Levi-Strauss, Claude. *The Raw and the Cooked.* New York: Harper & Row, 1969.

———. *Structural Anthropology.* Translated by Claire Jacobson and Brooke G. Schoepf. New York: Basic, 1963.

Lonergan, Bernard. "The Absence of God in Modern Culture." In *A Second Collection: Papers*, edited by William Ryan and Bernard Tyrell, 101–16. London: Darton, Longman and Todd, 1974.

———. "Belief: Today's Issue." In *A Second Collection: Papers*, edited by William Ryan and Bernard Tyrell, 87–99. London: Darton, Longman and Todd, 1974.

———. "Dialectic of Authority." In *A Third Collection: Papers*, edited by Frederick E. Crowe, 5–22. Mahwah, NJ: Paulist, 1985.

———. "Dimensions of Meaning." In *Collection*, edited by Frederick E. Crowe, 252–67. London: Darton, Longman and Todd, 1967.

———. *Doctrinal Pluralism.* Milwaukee: Marquette University Press, 1971.

———. "Foreword to David Tracy, *The Achievement of Bernard Lonergan*." In *Shorter Papers*, edited by Robert C. Croken et al., 287–88. Collected Works of Bernard Lonergan 20. Toronto: University of Toronto, 2007.

Bibliography

———. "The Future of Thomism." In *A Second Collection: Papers*, edited by William Ryan and Bernard Tyrell, 43–53. London: Darton, Longman and Todd, 1974.

———. *Insight: A Study of Human Understanding*. Edited by Frederick E. Crowe and Robert M. Doran. Collected Works of Bernard Lonergan 3. Toronto: University of Toronto Press, 1992.

———. *Method in Theology*. Toronto: University of Toronto Press, 1990.

———. "Prolegomena to the Study of the Emerging Religious Consciousness of Our Time." In *A Third Collection: Papers*, edited by Frederick E. Crowe, 55–73. Mahwah, NJ: Paulist, 1985.

———. "The Response of the Jesuit as Priest and Apostle in the Modern World." in *A Second Collection: Papers*, edited by William Ryan and Bernard Tyrell, 163–87. London: Darton, Longman and Todd, 1974.

———. "Theology and Praxis." In *A Third Collection: Papers*, edited by Frederick E. Crowe, 184–201. Mahwah, NJ: Paulist, 1985.

———. "The Transition from a Classicist World-View to Historical Mindedness." In *A Second Collection: Papers*, edited by William F. Ryan and Bernard Tyrell, 1–9. Toronto: University of Toronto Press, 1996.

———. "Theology in Its New Context." in *A Second Collection: Papers*, edited by William Ryan and Bernard Tyrell, 55–67. London: Darton, Longman and Todd, 1974.

———. *Verbum: Word and Idea in Aquinas*. Edited by D. B. Burrell. Notre Dame: University of Notre Dame Press, 1967.

Longman, Timothy. *Christianity and Genocide in Rwanda*. Cambridge: Cambridge University Press, 2009.

Maboea, S. I. "Causes for the Proliferation of the African Independent Churches." In *Afro-Christianity at the Grassroots: Its Dynamics and Strategies*, edited by G. C. Oosthuizen et al., 121–36. Leiden: Brill, 1994.

Magesa, Laurenti. *Anatomy of Inculturation: Transforming the Church in Africa*. Maryknoll, NY: Orbis, 2004.

———. Review of *African Cry*, by Jean-Marc Ela. *African Ecclesial Review* 29 (1987) 255–56.

Mall, R. A. *Intercultural Philosophy*. Lanham, MD: Rowman and Littlefield, 2000.

Mandelbaum, David. "Edward Sapir." *Jewish Social Studies* 3 (1941) 131–40.

Mamdani, Mahmood. "Reconciliation without Justice." *Southern African Review of Books* 46 (1996). http://web.uct.ac.za/depts/sarb/X0045_Mamdani.html (accessed October 6, 2013).

Martin, Marie-Louise. *Kimbangu: An African Prophet and His Church*. Translated by D. M. Moore. Oxford: Blackwell, 1975.

Mbiti, John. "Ascents in African Theology." *International Review of Mission* 79 (1990) 105–8.

McElwee, Joshua. "Cardinal Laments 'Fatigue' of Christian Europe, Celebrates African Example." *National Catholic Reporter*, April 24, 2014. http://ncronline.org/news/global/cardinal-laments-fatigue-christian-europe-celebrates-african-example (accessed July 8, 2014).

Mendieta, Eduardo. "Identities: Postcolonial and Global." In *Identities: Race, Class, Gender, and Nationality*, edited by Linda Martin Alcoff and Eduardo Mendieta, 407–16. Oxford: Blackwell, 2003.

Meynell, Hugo A. *The Theology of Bernard Lonergan*. Atlanta: Scholars, 1986.

Bibliography

Micheelseen, Arun. "'I Don't Do Systems': An Interview with Clifford Geertz." *Method and Theory in the Study of Religion* 14 (2002) 2–20.

Mises, Ludwig von. *Human Action*. 4th rev. ed. Irvington-on-Hudson, NY: Foundation for Economic Education, 1996.

Mladenov, Ivan. "Unlimited Semiosis and Heteroglosia (C. S. Peirce and M. M. Bakhtin)." *Sign System Studies* 29 (2001) 441–61.

Moore, Jerry D. *Visions of Culture: An Introduction to Anthropological Theories and Theorists*. 2nd ed. Walnut Creek, CA: AltaMira, 2004.

Montaigne, M. *Les essais de Michel de Montaigne*. Edited by P. Villery. Paris: Universitaires de France, 1978.

Mueller, J. J. "The Role of Theological Symbols in Mediating Cultural Change." In *Communication and Lonergan: Common Ground for Forging the New Age*, edited by Thomas J. Farrell and Paul A. Soukup, 294–311. Kansas City: Sheed and Ward, 1993.

Mukerji, Chandra, and Michael Schudson. "Rethinking Popular Culture." In *Rethinking Popular Culture: Contemporary Perspectives in Cultural Studies*, edited by Chandra Mukerji and Michael Schudson, 1–61. Berkeley: University of California Press, 1991.

Murphy, Charles M. "The Church and Culture since Vatican II: On the Analogy of Faith and Art." *Theological Studies* 48 (1987) 317–31.

Mveng, Engelbert. "Impoverishment and Liberation: A Theological Approach for Africa and the Third World." In *Paths of African Theology*, edited by Rosini Gibellini, 154–63. Maryknoll, NY: Orbis, 1994.

Ngong, David T. "The Theologian as Missionary: The Legacy of Jean-Marc Ela." *Journal of Theology for Southern Africa* 136 (2010) 4–19.

———. "Theology as the Construction of Piety: A Critique of the Theology of Inculturation and the Pentecostalization of African Christianity." *Journal of Pentecostal Theology* 21 (2012) 344–62.

Niebuhr, Richard H. *Christ and Culture*. New York: Harper & Row, 1951.

———. *Christ and Culture*. New York: HarperCollins, 1975.

Nietzsche, Friedrich. *On the Genealogy of Morals. The Basic Writings of Nietzsche*. Translated by Walter Kaufmann. New York: Modern Library, 1968.

Nkrumah, Kwame. *Consciencism: Philosophy and Ideology*. New York: Monthly Review, 1970.

Noble, Arthur. "'Purification of Memory': A Vatican Euphemism for the Whitewashing of History." European Institute of Protestant Studies, April 17, 2000, http://www.ianpaisley.org/article.asp?ArtKey=purification (accessed February 19, 2015).

Ntarangwi, Mwenda. "African Christianity, Politics, and Socioeconomic Realities." In *Jesus and Ubuntu: Exploring the Social Impact of Christianity in Africa*, edited by Mwenda Ntarangwi, 1–23. Nairobi: Africa World, 2011.

Nyerere, Julius K. *Freedom and Socialism*. New York: Oxford University Press, 1968.

O'Brien, David. *Public Catholicism*. Maryknoll, NY: Orbis, 1996.

Oduyoye, Mercy Amba. "Christianity and African Culture." *International Review of Mission* 84 (1995) 77–90.

Okoye, James C. "Inculturation and Theology in Africa." *Mission Studies* 14 (1997) 64–83.

Okure, Theresa, et al., eds. *32 Articles Evaluating Inculturation of Christianity in Africa*. Eldoret, Kenya: AMECEA Gaba, 1990.

Olkovich, Nick. "Conceptualism, Classicism and Bernard Lonergan's Retrieval of Aquinas." *Pacifica: Australasian Theological Studies* 26 (2012) 37–58.

Bibliography

Omenyo, Cephas N. "Man of God Prophesy unto Me: The Prophetic Phenomenon in African Christianity." *Studies in World Christianity* 17 (2011) 30–49.

Oosthuizen, G. C., et al., eds. *Afro-Christianity at the Grassroots: Its Dynamics and Strategies*. Leiden: Brill, 1994.

Ormerod, Neil. "The Structure of a Systematic Ecclesiology." *Theological Studies* 66 (2002) 3–30.

———. "System, History, and a Theology of Ministry." *Theological Studies* 61 (2000) 432–46.

———. "The Times They Are A-Changin': A Response to O'Malley and Schloesser." *Theological Studies* 67 (2006) 834–55.

Ortner, Sherry. "Thick Resistance: Death and the Cultural Construction of Agency in Hilmalayan Mountaineering." In *The Fate of "Culture": Geertz and Beyond*, edited by Sherry Ortner, 136–64. Berkeley: University of California Press, 1999.

Ortner, Sherry, ed. *The Fate of "Culture": Geertz and Beyond*. Berkeley: University of California Press, 1999.

Ositelu, Rufus. *African Instituted Churches: Diversities, Growth, Gifts, Spirituality and Ecumenical Understanding of African Initiated Churches*. Hamburg: LIT, 2002.

Palecek, Martin, and Mark Risjord. "Relativism and the Ontological Turn Within Anthropology." *Philosophy of the Social Sciences* 43 (2013) 3–23.

Pannenberg, Wolfhart. *The Historicity of Nature: Essays on Science and Theology*. Edited by Niels H. Gregersen. West Conshohocken, PA: Templeton Foundation, 2008.

Pato, Luke. "The African Independent Churches: A Socio-Cultural Approach." *Journal of Theology of Southern Africa* 72 (1990) 24–35.

Patterson, Amy. *The Church and Aids in Africa: The Politics of Ambiguity*. Boulder, CO: First Forum, 2011.

Paul VI. *Africae Terrarum*. Vatican, October 29, 1967, http://www.vatican.va/holy_father/paul_vi/apost_letters/documents/hf_p-vi_apl_19671029_africae-terrarum_it.html (accessed September 12, 2013).

Phan, Peter. "Cultures, Religions, and Power: Proclaiming Christ in the United States Today." *Theological Studies* 65 (2004) 714–40.

———. *In Our Own Tongues: Perspectives from Asia on Mission and Inculturation*. Maryknoll, NY: Orbis, 2003.

Peirce, C. S. *Collected Papers of Charles Sanders Peirce*. Edited by Charles Hartshorne and Paul Weiss. 8 vols. Cambridge, MA: Belknap, 1960–1966.

———. *The Essential Peirce: Selected Philosophical Writings*. Edited by Nathan Houser and Christian Kloesel. 2 vols. Bloomington: Indiana University Press, 1992–1998.

———. *Philosophical Writings of Pierce*. Selected and edited by Justus Buchler. New York: Dover, 1955.

———. *Semiotic and Significs: The Correspondence between Charles S. Peirce and Victoria Lady Welby*. Edited by Charles S. Hardwick. Bloomington: Indiana University Press, 1977.

Pius XII. "Allocution to the *Pontifical* Mission Aid Societies." *AAS* (1944) 210. http://www.vatican.va/holy_father/pius_xii/encyclicals/documents/hf_p-xii_enc_02061951_evangelii-praecones_en.html (accessed June 30, 2014).

———. *Evangelii Praeconis*. http://www.vatican.va/holy_father/pius_xii/encyclicals/documents/hf_p-xii_enc_02061951_evangelii-praecones_en.html (accessed June 30, 2014).

Bibliography

Pobee, John, and Gabriel Ositelu II. *African Initiatives in Christianity: The Growth, Gifts and Diversities of Indigenous African Churches—A Challenge to the Ecumenical Movement*. Geneva: WCC, 1998.

Potter, Vincent G. "Foundations: Lonergan and Peirce." In *Religion in Context: Recent Studies in Lonergan*, edited by Timothy P. Fallon and Philip Boo Riley, 181–91. Lanham, MD: University Press of America, 1988.

Rahner, Karl. "Towards a Fundamental Theological Interpretation of Vatican II." *Theological Studies* 40 (1979) 716–27.

Ramos, Alice M. *Dynamic Transcendentals: Truth, Goodness, and Beauty from a Thomistic Perspective*. Washington, DC: Catholic University of America Press, 2012.

Ramsey, Michael. *The Gospel and the Catholic Church: Recapturing a Biblical Understanding of the Church as the Body of Christ*. Peabody, MA: Hendrickson, 2009.

Ranger, Terrence. *Evangelical Christianity and Democracy in Africa*. Oxford: Oxford University Press, 2008.

Ratzinger, Joseph. "Christ, Faith and the Challenge of Cultures." Address given to the presidents of the Asian bishops' conferences and the chairmen of their doctrinal commissions, March 1993. http://www.ewtn.com/library/CURIA/RATZHONG.HTM (accessed June 15, 2014).

———. "Christ, Faith and the Challenge of Cultures." *Origins* (March 30, 1995), 681.

Rixon, Gordon. "Derida and Lonergan on Human Development." *American Catholic Philosophical Quarterly* 76 (2002) 221–36.

Rosaldo, Renato. "Geertz's Gifts." *Common Knowledge* 13 (2007) 206–10.

———. "A Note on Geertz as a Cultural Essayist." In *The Fate of "Culture": Geertz and Beyond*, edited by Sherry Ortner, 30–34. Berkeley: University of California Press, 1999.

Ryle, Gilbert. "Thinking and Reflecting" In *Collected Essays, 1929–1968*. London: Hutchinson, 1971.

———. "The Thinking of Thoughts: What is 'Le Penseur' Doing?" In *Collected Essays, 1929–1968*. London: Hutchinson, 1971.

Sanneh, Lamin. *Translating the Message: The Missionary Impact on Culture*. Maryknoll, NY: Orbis, 2009.

———. *Whose Religion Is Christianity? The Gospel beyond the West*. Grand Rapids: Eerdmans, 2003.

Sapir, Edward. "The Grammarian and His Language." In *Selected Writings of Edward Sapir*, edited by David G. Mandelbaum, 150–59. Berkeley: University of California Press, 1949.

———. "The Psychological Reality of Phonemes." In *Selected Writings of Edward Sapir*, edited by David G. Mandelbaum, 46–50. Berkeley: University of California Press, 1949.

———. "The Status of Linguistics as a Science." *Language* 5 (1929) 207–14.

Schall, James. "Belloc's Infamous Phrase." *Catholic Thing*, October 18, 2011. http://www.thecatholicthing.org/columns/2011/bellocs-infamous-phrase.html (accessed November 12, 2014).

Scharlemann, Robert P. *The Being of God*. New York: Seabury, 1981.

Schineller, Peter. "Inculturation: A Difficult and Delicate Task." *International Bulletin of Missionary Research* 20 (1996) 109–12.

———. "Inculturation and Syncretism: What Is the Real Issue?" *International Bulletin of Missionary Research* 16 (1992) 50–53.

Bibliography

Schreiter, Robert J. *Constructing Local Theologies.* Maryknoll, NY: Orbis, 2004.

———. "Inculturation of Faith or Identification with Culture." *Concilium* 2 (1994) 15–24.

Scherer, James A., and Stephen B. Bevans, eds. *New Directions on Mission and Evangelization 1: Basic Statements, 1974–1991.* Maryknoll, NY: Orbis, 1992.

Senghor, Leopold. *The Foundations of "Africanite."* Paris: Presence Africaine, 1971.

Shore, Megan. "Christianity and Justice in the South African Truth and Reconciliation Commission: A Case Study in Religious Conflict Resolution." *Political Theology* 9 (2008) 161–78.

Shorter, Aylward, *Toward a Theology of Inculturation.* 1989. Reprint, Eugene, OR: Wipf and Stock, 1999.

Shweder, Richard. Review of *Available Light*, by Clifford Geertz. *Science* 290 (2000) 1511–12.

———. "The Resolute Irresolution of Clifford Geertz." *Common Knowledge* 13 (2007) 191–205.

Silverstein, Michael. "Language Structure and Linguistic Ideology." In *The Elements*, edited by P. R. Clyne et al., 193–247. Chicago: Chicago Linguistic Society, 1979.

Society of Jesus. *Documents of the Thirty-First and Thirty-Second General Congregation of the Society of Jesus.* St. Louis: Institute of Jesuit Studies, 1977.

Stanley, Brian. "Inculturation: Historical Background, Theological Foundations and Contemporary Questions." *Transformations* 24 (2007) 21–27.

Starkloff, Carl. "Inculturation and Cultural Systems." *Theological Studies* 55 (1994) 66–81.

Suny, Ronald Grigor. "Back and Beyond: Reversing the Cultural Turn?" *American Historical Review* 107 (2002) 1476–99.

Swidler, Ann. "Geertz's Ambiguous Legacy." *Contemporary Sociology* 25 (1996) 299–302.

Tillich, Paul. *Systematic Theology.* 3 vols. Chicago: University of Chicago Press, 1951–63.

———. *A Theology of Culture.* New York: Oxford University Press, 1958.

Torres, Sergio, and Virginia Fabella, eds. *The Emergent Gospel: Theology from the Developing World.* Maryknoll, NY: Orbis, 1978.

Turner, Harold. *History of an African Independent Church.* Vol. 1, *The Church of the Lord (Aladura).* Oxford: Clarendon, 1967.

Turner, Victor. *From Ritual to Theatre: The Human Seriousness of Play.* New York: Performing Arts Journal, 1982.

———. *The Ritual Process: Structure and Anti-structure.* Ithaca: Cornell University Press, 1977.

Tutu, Desmond. "Black Theology and African Theology—Soul Mates or Antagonists?" In *A Reader in African Christian Theology*, edited by John Parratt, 46–57. London: SPCK, 1987.

———. "Foreword." In *Afro-Christianity at the Grassroots: Its Dynamics and Strategies*, edited by G. C. Oosthuizen et al., vii–viii. Leiden: Brill, 1994.

Volf, Miroslav. *Exclusion and Embrace: A Theological Exploration of Identity, Otherness, and Reconciliation.* Nashville: Abingdon, 1996.

Volisinov, V. N. *Marxism and the Philosophy of Language.* Translated by Ladislav Matejka and I. R. Titunik. Cambridge, MA: Harvard University Press, 1929.

Wa Thiong'o, Nguigi. *Decolonizing the Mind.* Portsmouth, NH: Heinemann, 1986.

Whorf, Benjamin Lee. *Language, Thought, and Reality.* Edited by John B. Carroll. Cambridge, MA: MIT Press, 1997.

Bibliography

Wielzen, Duncan R. "Popular Religiosity and Roman Liturgy: Toward a Contemporary Theology of Liturgical Inculturation in the Caribbean." PhD diss., Katholieke Universiteit Leuven, 2009.

Wijsen, Frans. "Global Christianity: A European Perspective." *Exchange* 38 (2009) 147–60.

Wilson, Richard. *The Politics of Truth and Reconciliation in South Africa: Legitimatizing the Post-apartheid State*. Cambridge: Cambridge University Press, 2001.

———. "Reconciliation and Revenge in Post-apartheid South Africa: Rethinking Legal Pluralism and Human Rights." *Current Anthropology* 41 (2000) 75–98.

Wrong, Michela. *In the Footsteps of Mr. Kurtz*. New York: HarperCollins, 2001.

Yamamoto, E. K. "Race Apologies." *Journal of Gender, Race and Justice* 1 (1997) 47–88.

Index

Abstract, 19, 30, 33, 71–78, 93, 115, 149
Abstraction, 31, 117, 178
Accommodation, xvi, 3, 64, 146–47, 149–51
Acculturation, xvi, 29, 92, 150, 158–60, 171
Adaptation, xvi, 3–4, 19, 26, 142–43, 147, 149–51, 164, 171
Adaptations, 12, 20, 62, 127, 150, 171, 175
Addressee, 33, 45
Addressor, 33
Ad Gentes, 171
Adichie, Chimamanda Ngozi, 39n10, 40–46
Africa, xiii-xv, 1, 3–7, 9–12, 14, 16–22, 25, 30–31, 37–39, 41–42, 47; partition of Africa, 50; scramble for Africa, 50, 52–54, 57–59, 63, 65–68, 107, 124, 140, 150, 153, 155–57, 162–63, 166–170, 173–74, 176, 181–82, 186–90, 193–95
Africae Terrarum, 3
African bishops, 2, 3, 23
African Christianity, 3–4, 25, 54, 58, 63, 182
African story, xv, 41, 49
African synod, 7, 34, 143, 151
African theologians, 3, 11, 14n63, 25, 64n142
African theology/African theology of inculturation, xiv, 1, 7–8, 25, 30, 36–38, 56, 68, 99–100, 166–67, 175, 178, 181, 183–84, 186, 188, 190–92, 195–96, 198
African Independent/Instituted Churches (AICs), xv, 29, 37, 54–68
Africanization, 3, 13, 26, 29, 57, Africanization of Islam 183

African names, 176–177, 183
African socio-political life, 1, 26, 186
African Traditional Religions (ATRs), 3, 63, 166, 170, 183
Allport, Gordon, 106
Analogy, 132, 135, 145, 149, 152
Ancestors, 62, 64–65, 142
Anthropology, xiii-xv, 29, 70–73, 75, 82, 85, 90–91, 93, 97, 105–107, 110–12, 115, 120, 122–23, 125, 130
Apartheid, 1, 26, 28, 58n113, 191
Aquinas, Thomas, 47, 127, 141
Arrupe, Pedro, 102–103, 164–165
Artistic, 31; voices artistically organized, 32, 84; meaning communicated artistically, 133, 189
Asia, xiii, 39, 58, 108, 124, 126, 140–41, 143, 150, 152–53, 155, 165
Asian Bishops, 143, 152, 165
Association of Third World Theologians (ETWOT), 38–39
Augustine, 93
Austin, J.L., 82n66, 97, 178–180
Authentic, 2, 3, 13, 25, 27, 35, 41, 62, 174, 181, 189
Authenticity, 16, 24, 101, 172
Authorial, 32, 34
Authority, 35, 175

Baba Simon Mpecke. 5–6
Bahktin, Mikhail, xiv, 38, 41, 94
Bali, 106–7, 116, 120, 122–23, 145–46, 186, 189
Bantu, 6, 29
Baptism, 169, 176, 178
Bathes, Roland, 104
Bediako, Kwame, 35
Behavior, 78, 82, 114

Index

Belgium/Belgian, 49, 51, 178
Benveniste, Emil, 81
Bevans, Stephen, 154
Bible, 8, 26, 62, 74, 76, 155,162,
Binary, 75n36, 87
Black, blackness, Black theology 1, 4, 15n70, 18, 22, 26, 58–60, 154, 163
Blomjous, Joseph, 151
Berlin Conference, 40, 180
Bourdieu, Pierre, 104
Burke, Kenneth, 33, 119
Burlesque, 114
Butler, Judith, xv, 31, 44–47, 179

Cameroon, 4–7, 149
Canada, 7, 72
Capitalism, 110
Capitalist, 11, 14–15
Caribbean, 127–8, 140
Catechesis, 143
Catechesi Trandendae, 142
Catholic, xiii–xiv, 3–6, 11–12, 54, 129, 135, 137, 150, 153, 182
Catholicism/Roman Catholic Church, 2, 14n63, 19, 27, 39, 54, 58, 99, 138–43, 146–47, 149, 164–65, 170, 178, 180, 192, 196
Catholicity, xvii, 149, 175
Caton, Steven, xi, 78n53, 86n95, 89, 92, 95, 105, 119–20
Change [theological and cultural change], 6, 15, 39, 51, 54, 56, 65, 73, 78n53, 93, 96, 100, 110, 126–27, 138, 158, 166, 171
China, 146, 150, 190
Chomsky, Noam, 72, 77–79, 83
Christendom, 55, 137–39, 141, 156–57
Christianity, xiv–xv, 1, 3–6, 10–11, 14, 18, 20, 22, 24, 25, 39, 53–61, 63, 65–68, 129, 134, 137–40, 144, 146, 150, 152, 154, 160, 166–70, 174, 176, 182–83, 194
Church, Catholic. *See* Catholicism/Roman Catholic Church
Church, Protestant, 2, 14n63, 67, 129, 143
Christology, 10, 24, 98
Christological metaphors/slogan, 10, 99

Class/class conflict, 32, 39, 93, 98, 121, 192, class of names, 176
Classical culture, xiii, 97, 126–7, 131–32, 135–36, 137, 165; classical control of meaning, 132; classical self-understanding, 98; classical works of Confucianism, 146
Classicism/classicist, xiii, xvi, 99, 103, 127–29, 132, 134, 136, 139, 147–48, 152, 161, 175–76, 178, 185
Clergy, 7–8, 13, 143
Cockfight, 106, 108, 116, 123
Colonial, colonial rule, colonial state, colonial powers 2–4, 13–14, 16, 18, 27, 40, 43, 48–50, 52, 57, 120–21, 140–41, 158–59, 167–68, 173, 180, 193; colonial ideology, 159; colonial imagination, 22, 50
Colonialism, 2–3, 8, 43, 48, 50, 54, 139, 168
Commonsense, 30, 46, 123, 126, 133–35, 137, 165, 183–84, 188, 193–94
Communication/communications, xiii, 33–35, 59, 68–70, 77–78, 83–86n95, 89–90, 94, 97, 115, 134, 163, 182, 194–95
Community, xiii, 6, 22, 29, 35, 42, 62, 77, 84, 96, 142, 161, 167, 171–72, 177–78, 195
Cone, James, 154
Congo, 28, 49–55, 59
Constantine, 10
Consciencism, 15
Contextualization, xvi, 59, 65, 100, 154–55
Conversion, 139, 174,
Copts, 57n104
Corrupt, 128, 192
Counterposition, xvi, 134
Crisis, 37, 187n83, 193
Culture [empirical notion], 126. *See also* classical culture, classicism, and cultural turn
Culture, Pontifical Council, 182n64
Cultural Turn, 103, 112, 130
Customs, 122, 142, 145, 150, 169 [African customs] 31,
Cybernetics, 71

Index

Decolonization, 7
De Nobili, Robert, 150–51
Description, 8, 44, 56, 78n53, 97, 99, 108, 121, [thick description], xvi, 96, 105n15, 107, 110n38, 113, 123, 132 [thin description] 114
Derrida, Jacques, 35, 100, 104
Development/developments, 4, 14, 16, 30, 46, 56, 58n113, 60, 71, 73, 78n53, 82, 84, 96, 110, 127–28, 132, 136, 138, 153, 162, 164, 167, 172, 175n44, 183–84, 189–91, 197,
Dialectic, 35, 167; dialectically interconnected, 91; dialectical relationships, xvi, 95–96
Dialogue, xiv, 6, 32–33, 36, 95, 134–35, 140, 153, 163–64, 198
Dialogical, 35, 38, 131, 147
Dialogicality, xv, 38, 95
Dilthey, Wilhelm, 90, 130
Diversity, xvii, 2, 31–32, 122, 175
Division, 72
Divination, 62–63
Dogma, 10, 72, 162–63
Dogmatic Constitution on the Church (*Lumen Gentium*), 102
Domination, 1, 10, 14–15, 21, 25, 57, 168, 192
Dostoevsky, Fyodor, 31
Doyle, Dennis, 129. *See also* Foreword
Dutch Reformed Church, 26
Dyadic, 33

Economic, 1, 6, 14–15, 17, 20–21, 26, 30, 48, 52, 65, 97, 105, 171, 185, 187, 190
Economy, 49, 184
Ecumenical Association of African Theologians (EAAT), 14
Ela, Jean-Marc, xiv, 4–27, 29–31, 33–35, 37–38, 99, 149, 156, 163
Ethiopia, 57n104
Ethnic (group), 32, 167, 169–70, 173, 179, 181, 189, 193, ethnic tension, 37, 188
Ethnicity, 4, 177
Emotion, 33, 116, emotional, 55, 86, 185
Enculturation, 157
Enlightenment, 40, 68–69, 170, 173, 175

Eschatological hope, 24, eschatological reality, 174
Ethnography, 107, 109, 123
Ethnographical work, 92, 108, 132
Exploitation, 11, 16–18, 26, 185, 192
Eucharist, 20–23, 170
Europe, 2, 5, 14n63, 22
European, 2, 8, 16, 20, 38, 48–51, 54, 57–58, 67–69, 104, 121–22, 128, 150, 153, 158–59, 167, 169–70, 173, 176; European cultural norms, 17, 23, 137–41, 148, 176; European theology, 33–34, 37–39, 182n64, 183–84; European thought systems, 19
Evangelii Nuntiandi, 102, 142
Evangelization, 2, 18, 38, 53, 142–43, 156, 162
Evangelize, 53, 142
Exorcize, 64

Faith, 2, 4, 7, 11, 12–13, 19–21, 23–24, 27, 31, 35, 55, 60, 67–68, 84, 102, 109, 121, 126, 129, 135, 137–38, 141, 144, 147, 151, 157, 163–64, 168, 170–71, 174, 176, 178, 191, 195
Famine, 9, 26, 41, 188, 196
Foucault, Michel, 42–43
Frames we use, xv, 44–46, 82n66, 107, 135, 149, 179, 181, frame an ideology, 38, 43, 50, 124
Framework, 33, 166
France, 56, 14n63, 48, 193
French Revolution, 70
Freud, Sigmund, 69, 97, 122–23
Functionalist, 122
Functional specialty, xiii, xvi, 35, 162

Gadamer, Hans-Georg, 108
Gaudium et Spes, 103
Geertz, Clifford, xiv, xvi, xvii, 71, 88, 93, 96–97, 103, 104–25, 128–34, 145, 148–49, 161, 186
Genocide, 179–80, 193
Gesture, 86, 90
Gifford, Paul, 48
Gilbert, Ryle, 113
Ghost of Leopold, 49

213

Index

God, 9–10, 12–13, 19, 24, 27, 30, 39, 55n92, 62, 64–65, 126–28, 139, 141, 154, 161–62, 165, 168, 172, 177, 192, 195; god of capitalism, 15; god of socialism; 15, belief in gods, 116

Gospel, xiii, xvi, 2–3, 5, 8, 18–19, 36, 59–62, 65–68, 96, 129, 138, 142–43, 150–51, 153–54, 156–61, 163–64, 165–68, 172, 174–75, 187, 194–96, 198

Grammar, 45, 82–83, 90, 92–93

Grandee idea, 112

Grass root, 34, 36

Great Britain, 5, 15, 58n112

Gruchy, John de, 37

Gutierrez, Gustav, 11

Habits, xvii, 77, 139, 166, 174–75

Harmony, 32, 55, 58n113, 141

Harvard, xi, xv, 106

Hastings, Adrian, 1

Healing, 30, 60, 62–63, 181

Heaven, 64, 177

Hermeneutic (cultural), xvi, 69, 103–105, 108, 197; hermeneutic of communication, 68; hermeneutical key, 9; hermeneutic of recovery, 68, 167; critical hermeneutic, 167

Heteroglossia, 32–34, 38, 41

Heterogeneity, 48, 111, 121

Heteroglot, 94

Heteromorphous, 97

Higher viewpoint, 184–86

Hillman, Eugene, 168

Hochschild, Adam, 49–50, 52–53

Holquist, Michael, 33

Holy Spirit, 55n91, 172

Horizon, 97, 132, 174, 182–83

Humanism (African), 15

Hunger, 84, hungry masses, 15n70

Icon, 89

Identity, xv, 4, 18, 31, 40, 50, 69, 96, 126–28, 140–42, 152, 169–70, 172, 188–89, 193, 195

Ideology, 32, 58n113, 90–92, 94–95, 159, 181, 185, 192

Igbo, 168, 173

Imperial agenda, 18; imperial Roman 137–138

Imperialism, 18

Inaestimable Donum, 23

Incarnate, 20

Incarnation, 12, 163, 164, 192

Inculturation, xiii–xvii, 2–4, 11–36, 54, 57, 59, 61–62, 66, 68–69, 86, 90, 96, 99, 100, 102–3, 119, 121, 133, 138–47, 151, 153, 156–75, 178, 181, 183–97

Inculturate, 3, 14; inculturated, 4, 38–39, 163–164

Independence, 3, 14, 16, 18, 48, 51, 54, 71, 126, 187–88, 193

Independent Churches. *See* AICs

Index, 89, 161

India/Indian 72, 75, 150, 152

Indigenization, xvi, 59, 67, 155–56

Indigenized Christianity, 59; indigenized liturgy, 65, indigenized Islam, 183

Indonesia, 106, 121

Injury, 44–45

Injurious (speech), 40, 44–46, 179

Injustice, 9, 15n70, 180

Innovation, 62, 69, 98

Intelligibility, 132

Interculturation, 151–52

Islam, 120, 182–83

Jacobson, Roman, 86n95

Jamaica, 127

Japan, 146

Jesus (Christ), 9, 21, 23–24, 55n89, n91, n92, 166, 196

Jesuits, 102, 164–65

Jews, 194

John Paul II, 142, 152, 182n64

Justice, 7, 26, 29, 171; Justice Commission, 28

Kampala Address, 3

Kaspers, Walter, 10

Katongole, Emmanuel, 8, 11–12, 49–54

Kaunda, Kenneth, 15

Kenya, 27, 43, 55n91, 59

Kirdi people, 5–6, 8, 22

Kimbanguist church, 55n91

Index

Kingdom of God, 39, 139
Kluckhorn, Clyde, 106, 115
Knowledge, 27, 47, 79, 97–98, 100, 108, 115, 132, 134, 136, 161–62, 176, 183, 198
Kroeber, Alfred, 106, 115
Kuhn, Thomas, 104

Lakoff, George, xv, 75n38, 76, 81
Langer, Sussane, 70, 8–86, 97, 109, 112n49, 115–18
Language, xv, 11, 19–20, 32, 34, 38, 40–41, 43, 48, 53, 68, 100–101, 109, 117, 121, 138, 142, 154–55, 167–68, 182, 184, 189, 194; African language, 34, 163; subjectivity of language, 31; language of exclusion 43–47; metapragmatics use of language, 69–87; language and ideology, 89–97, 179
Latin America, xiii, 39, 58, 126, 140–41
Levi-Strauss, Claude, 86, 91–92
Liberation, 1, 4, 6, 11–14, 20, 28, 30–31, 35, 37, 48, 128, 156
Liberation theology, 4, 11–12, 37
Lineamenta, 34
Linguistics, 70–71, 73–78, 82, 93, 97, 136
Liturgy, 13, 20, 22–23, 55, 65, 128, 170–171, 176, 196
Local, 2, 5, 63, 96, 121, 146, 150, 155–56, 160–61, 164, 169, 171–72, 192, 195; local church, 11, 98, 129, 144
Localization, 4, 143–45
Lonergan, Bernard, xiii, xiv, xvi–xvii, 30, 35, 46, 83–84, 91, 99–101, 141, 148; Lonergan and Geertz's influence, 125–33; antidote to counterposition 134; Lonergan and Peirce 135–37; semiotic understanding of culture 161–67, 174–98
Lumen Gentium, 102

Mali, 183
Malinowski Bronislaw, 123
Mandela, Nelson, 26n141, 28
Marriage, 169
Marx, Karl, 69, 97, 99, 12123
Marxist/marxism, 11, 14, 93–95, 120
Mary, 163, 176

Massai, 173
Materialist, 120
Mbiti, John, 19, 25
Meal, 21–22, 118
Meaning-making, xv, 82, 97
Medvedev, Pavel, 94
Metaphors, xv, 12, 44, 50, 75n38, 82, 84, 90, 99, 112n49, 116, 161, 194
Metapragmatics, xv, 69–70, 96, 100
Methodist, 74
Metz, Johann Baptist, 11, 37
Millet, 8, 21–23
Missionary, 1, 3, 8, 14n63, 18–19, 25, 36, 38, 53–54, 66–67, 102, 139, 146, 150–51, 156, 159, 163–64, 168, 176
Moltmann, Jurgen, 11, 37
Monoculturalism, 137–38
Monoglossia, xiv, 38
Monologue, 33
Morphological, 32–33
Morocco, 108
Mosteller, Frederick, 106
Montaigne, Michel de, 122
Murray, Henry, 106
Mveng, Engelbert, 7
Mystic, 74
Myth, 15, 39–40, 69, 87, 131, 135, 162

Narrative, xv, 27, 37–44, 46–47, 49, 52, 54, 61, 66, 128–29, 168, 178–79, 181, 194
Nation-state, 2, 4, 52, 121, 124, 166, 172–73, 180–81
Naude, Beyers, 26
New Testament, 10, 55n89
Neocolonial, 13–14, 17, 19, 22, 110
Negritude, 15, 23–24
Ngugi wa Thiong'o, 43
Niebuhr, Richard, 2, 143
Nietzsche, Frederick, 27, 69, 97, 99
Nigeria, 27, 40–42, 55n91, 58n112, 59, 177, 190, 196
Nkrumah Kwame, 15
Nobili, Roberto de, 150–51
North Africa, 108
Novel/novelist/ novelistic discourse, 31–32, 34, 40, 42, 44, 104
Nyerere, Julius, 15, 17, 29

215

Index

Oppression, 9, 17, 19, 25, 27, 65
Oral expression/theology, 34–36, 61
Orthodox, 14n63, 55n89
Orthodoxy, 72

Pastoral Constitution on the Church in the Modern World (*Gaudium et Spes*), 103
Paul VI, 3, 102, 142
Paradigm/paradigmatic, 9n39, 25, 51, 61, 86n95, 97, 107, 116, 121, 142
Paradox, 20, 23, 66, 116, 143
Peirce, C. S, xiv, xvi–xvii, 85, 88–90, 94, 97, 115, 117–18, 134–36, 161–62, 165, 174
Pentecostal, 9n39, 27, 56, 61, 65, 67–68
Persuasive, 33–35, 90, 120
Phenomenon, 32–33, 48, 56, 58, 63–64, 67, 72, 94, 114, 118, 159–60, 174
Philippines, 153
Phonological, 33
Pius XII, 138
Pluralism, xiii, 10, 22, 30, 121, 149, 153, 192, 194
Poem, 33, 40, 42, 44
Polygamy, 53
Polyphony, xiv, 31–33
Poly-vocal, xv, 95
Poor, 9n39, 11, 14, 27, 31, 41, 126, 154, 161, 166, 174, 184
Postcolonial, 14, 16, 37, 48, 52, 124, 166, 169, 173
Postmodernism/postmodernity, 69, 97, 110
Positivist, 71, 110–11, 114, 120, 175n44
Poverty, 9, 14, 16–17, 25–26, 41–42, 65, 77n49, 196
Power/powerful, xv, 5, 7,9n39, 15–16, 21, 26–27, 34, 42–45, 48, 53–54, 56, 63–66, 79, 85, 87, 89, 95–96, 114, 116, 120, 123, 127, 133, 159, 171, 177, 180, 192, 196; colonial powers, 2, 158; powerful speech, 3, 5, 38
Pragmatics, 83, 100
Praxis, xiv, 30, 67, 167
Prayer, 21, 149
Preaching, 65, 187

Priest/priesthood, 5, 19–21, 138
Privilege, 34–35, 118, 154, 180
Protestant, 2, 14n63, 67, 129, 143

Race, 40, 65, 85, 195
Racism/racist, 110, 180
Rahner, Karl, 39, 138
Redemption, 23, 30, 101
Reductionism, 134, 181
Religion, xvi, 3, 10, 27, 39, 54, 59, 63, 68–70, 74, 84, 87, 98, 101, 137–40, 146, 151, 155, 166–68, 170, 183–84, 189, 193–94; religion as a cultural system, 104–16, 109, 111, 119–20, 123, 125 (see African Traditional Religions)
Ressentiment, 27
Resurgence, 13, 168
Ricoeur, Paul, 108–9
Rite, 19, 22, 149, 169, 175; rites controversy 147
Ricci, Matteo, 146–47, 150
Roman Catholicism. *See* Catholicism/Roman Catholic Church
Romanticize, romanticization, 23, 61, 173; cultural romanticism, 156; romantic nostalgia, 69
Rome, 14n63, 34, 39, 127, 139, 164, 182n64
Rorty, Richard, 104
Rousseau, Jean Jacques, 69
Rwanda, 4n15, 179–81
Ryle, Gilbert, 109, 113–14

Sahara (south of), xiv, 2, 14, 20, 26, 57, 59, 64, 173
Sahlins, Marshall, 104
Salvation, 17, 23–25, 39, 65, 139, 149–50, 174
Sapir, Edward, xv, 71–78, 80, 82–83, 85, 97
Saussure, Ferdinand de, 86, 118
Scholasticism, 127, 136
Scramble (for Africa), 47–48, 50
Schreiter, Robert, 96, 98, 174
Scriptures, 1, 61, 194
Semantics, 74, 83, 117, 124
Semiotics/semiotician, xiv–xvii, 4, 25, 30–31, 36, 38, 43, 68–69, 81, 85–86, 90, 93–94, 99–100, 104, 109, 161;

Index

semiotics and inculturation, 119, 123, 125, 128, 130, 134–36, semiotic approach/ understanding 113, 115, 152, 161–62, 65; ten semiotic habits, 174–98 (*see also* Bakhtin, Mikhail; Benveniste, Emil; Peirce, Charles Sander; Geertz, Clifford)
Senghor, Leopold, 15
Shade-tree, xiv, 7–9, 11, 29, 33–35, 37
Shorter, Aylward, 137, 151, 164
Signs. *See* symbols, semiotics
Single-Story, 42–44, 46, 49, 54, 178, 181
Slave/slavery, 7, 27, 127, 185
Socialism, 15
Sociology, 7, 98–99, 106, 109
South Africa, 1, 4, 15n71, 26–29, 57–60, 154
South African Council of Churches (SACC), 26
Spirituality, 27, 67, 140
Straus, Claude Levi, 86–87, 91–92
Stouffer, Samuel, 106
Structuralism, 86
Sudan, 187–88
Symbols, 15, 21, 27, 62–63, 70, 83, 85, 88–90, 92–93, 96, 104, 111, 115–20, 123–24, 134, 140–41, 145, 148, 163, 180, 198
Syncretism, 171–72
Syntactic, 32, 83
Systematics, xvi, 30, 32, 35, 62, 124, 155, 162, 167, 189; systematic exigence, 133, 137; systematic totalization, 128

Talcott, Parsons, 106, 109
Tanzania, 12, 15, 17, 29, 38
Thick description, xvi, 96, 105n15, 107, 110n38, 113, 123, 132
Thin description, 114
Translation (models), 29, 34, 41, 74, 149, 155, 171

Tribe, 32, 166–67, 188, 193
Truth and Reconciliation Commission, 26, 29n153
Turner, Viktor, 89–90
Tutu, Desmond, 26, 28, 60, 62

Ubuntu, 15n71, 29
Ujamma, 15
United States, 14, 58, 72, 78n53, 153–54

Values, xvi, 3, 6, 15n70, 27n143, 49, 66, 68, 75n38, 96, 111, 124–26, 131, 134, 139–141, 146, 148, 152, 160; cultural values, 29, 176; gospel values, 164–54, 169, 182–183, 188–89
Vatican Council II, 3, 39, 102–3, 126, 129, 135, 138–39, 142–43, 149, 164, 171
Voice, xiv, 4–5, 24–25, 31–35, 38, 40, 86, 95, 101, 135
Volosinov, Nikolaevich Valentin xv, 94–95, 101
Vygostky, Semyonovich, Lev, 94

Whorf, Benjamin Lee, xv, 72–97
Weber, Marx, 109, 123, 130
West Africa, 5, 58
Williams, Raymond, 104
Wink, 113–14
Wittgenstein, Ludwig, 108–9, 125
World Council of Churches (WCC), 26n141, 143, 154, 195

Xavier, Francis, 146
Xhosa, 29

Yoruba, 168, 173, 177

Zaire, 28, 49, 51, 55n91
Zambia, 15, 89
Zulu, 29, 168

www.ingramcontent.com/pod-product-compliance
Lightning Source LLC
Chambersburg PA
CBHW051642230426
43669CB00013B/2400